CW01262315

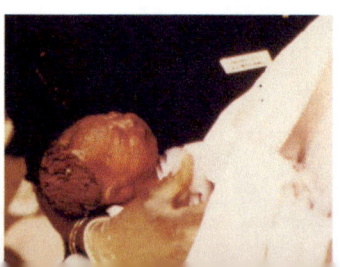

Tell Me Something
I Don't Know!

ALLYSON INGRID WILLIAMS MBE

Dear Fatima,
   Greetings & thanks. I hope you enjoy my life's journey.

   Allyson Williams
   March '25

Tell Me Something I Don't Know
Authored by Allyson Ingrid Williams MBE

© Allyson Williams MBE 2023

Cover design Marcia M Publishing House

Edited by Lee Dickinson, Marcia M Publishing House editorial team.

All rights reserved 2023 Allyson Williams MBE.

Allyson Williams MBE asserts the moral right to be identified as the author of this work. The opinions expressed in this published work are those of the author and do not reflect the opinions of Marcia M Publishing House or its editorial team.

Published by Marcia M Spence via Marcia M Publishing House, author services, LONDON UNITED KINGDOM, on behalf of Allyson Williams MBE. Email: info@marciampublishing.com

This book is sold subject to the conditions it is not, by way of trade or otherwise, lent, hired out or otherwise circulated in any form of binding or cover other than that in which it is published. No part of this publication may be reproduced, stored in a retrieval system or transmitted in any form or by any means (electronic, mechanical, photocopying, recording or otherwise) without prior written permission from the Author.

Allyson Williams MBE has written this memoir from his memories of situations, locations and conversations., all names and identifying characteristics have been changed, to protect the privacy and anonymity of individuals. The author has indemnified Marcia M Publishing House Ltd and its team against any action, legal or otherwise in relation to this publication.

A copy of this publication is legally deposited in The British Library.

ISBN: 978-1-913905-79-8

Dedication

This book is lovingly dedicated to my late husband, Vernon Roderick "Fellows" Williams, still affectionately known as "the Head Nigger" by his peers in the community, who benefited from his love, knowledge, support and generosity.

He was a pillar in the community, who was held in high esteem and who will never be forgotten. He was a gentle father who advocated that the only discipline a child needed was a lot of love. He shared these qualities with me and our children and we enjoyed a loving and wonderful family life together.

He was a passionate and committed advocate of the Notting Hill Carnival of which he was a founder member. He consistently taught and supported prospective band leaders, while managing our family costume band called Genesis.

Acknowledgements

To all the people who supported and encouraged me along this journey, a journey I started ten years ago when the idea was first suggested to me:

To my parents, Conrad and Eldica Layne who cared for me and my siblings Arthur, Patricia, Penelope and Phillip and the rest of my many cousins, uncles and aunts.

Thanks to all my school friends here and abroad, and especially to those who have remained lifelong friends, for their friendship and love.

Very special thanks go to Evadne who was the first friend I met on my first day in London and who has remained a treasured friend to this day.

To all the midwives who I have worked with and admired, I thank you for your passion and pride in our profession. We have shared fond memories and had been great advocates for the women and their families in our care.

My heartfelt thanks go to my mentor Anne Rider who recognised my potential and allowed me to shine. She was truly visionary and inspirational and I admired her greatly.

To my precious gifts, my children, Symone and Kevin. They have given me such joy and pleasure and zest for life. I thank them for being so strong, courageous, loving and respectful, despite the many challenges they face in life.

To Michelle, Gerard and Natasha for their unfailing love and support

Last but not least, to my beautiful grandchildren, Layne and Kayden. They are simply adorable and lovable and very millennial. I pray they will understand and appreciate the unconditional love and legacy left to them through this book.

Chapters

Chapter One: In The Beginning 1

Chapter Two: Childhood Escapades 7

Chapter Three: Forty-seven Eleven (4711) 13

Chapter Four: Trini Family Values 18

Chapter Five: We Don't Speak "Trinidadianese" In Here! 29

Chapter Six: Sweet Innocence 36

Chapter Seven: New Beginnings 40

Chapter Eight: Moving Into The Big League 47

Chapter Nine: Answering The Call 53

Chapter Ten: Getting The Key To The Door 64

Chapter Eleven: "Leave Them To God" 71

Chapter Twelve: Finding My Feet In The "Motherland" 79

Chapter Thirteen: Cause and Effect 89

Chapter Fourteen: "And What Did You Say Your Name Was?" 98

Chapter Fifteen: Life, Love and Laughter 107

Chapter Sixteen: Bringing New Life Into The World 116

Chapter Seventeen: The Ups And Downs Of Family Life 119

Chapter Eighteen: Buying Our Own Home 124

Chapter Nineteen: The Birth of Genesis 129

Chapter Twenty: The Pursuit of Financial Freedom 132

Chapter Twenty-One: My Life Changing Situation 141

Chapter Twenty-Two: Learning About My Son's Hyperactivity....148

Chapter Twenty-Three: Life Begins At 40! 154

Chapter Twenty-Four: The Developing Community Midwifery Service 169

Chapter Twenty-Five: Condolences But A Celebration of Life 177

Chapter Twenty-Six: My Personal and Professional Development183

Chapter Twenty-Seven: Yet More New Beginnings 193

Chapter Twenty-Eight: Challenging The Status Quo 201

Chapter Twenty-Nine: On-Going Changes At Home and At The Office 211

Chapter Thirty: The Beginning of The End.............................219

Chapter Thirty-One: Retirement....A Time To Start Working At Living... 228

Chapter Thirty-Two: New Blessings In My World 236

Chapter Thirty-Three: Being Bitten By The Travel Bug 240

Chapter Thirty-Four: "Don't Judge Me Until You Walk In My Shoes"255

Chapter Thirty-Five: Dealing With The Body Blows Coming Thick And Fast 265

Chapter Thirty-Six: Redefining All Aspects of Life 272

Chapter Thirty-Seven: My Continuing Journey 286

Chapter Thirty-Eight: Consequences of The Pandemic............. 290

Chapter Thirty-Nine: The Joyful Experience of Re-Imagining Carnival 295

Conclusion (What Do You Think About It So Far??)................. 302

Tell Me Something
I Don't Know!

CHAPTER ONE:
In The Beginning

Don't get me wrong, my life has by no means been perfect, but it has been a fascinating journey, nonetheless. I enjoyed many highs and some lows throughout this journey. Although I thought that my mother controlled my life at all times and I seemed to have little freedom, I wouldn't have had it any other way. In fact, I felt as free as you possibly could, as my mother and I were on the same page.

I think my earliest memories of myself are from three to four years old. I remember my home in Trinidad was a warm and sunny place with my mum and dad and my brother. Mummy was a nurse in the hospital and Daddy was a carpenter. The sunshine was there all day, except when it rained, but it was still warm. I remember the sky had lots of stars at night that were very bright and seemed so close that you could count them. There were lots of trees, full of fruit sometimes and flowers, although our yard (garden) seemed to be a bit barren, with a broken-down fence at the front.

Our house was interesting too. It was wooden with lots of windows and shutters. It also had two addresses we could use. The front house in the big yard belonged to the owner and it had its own address. She lived alone and her yard was full of flowers. She would call us in when we passed by and we would sit on the veranda and chat with her. Our house was behind this one, but the front of our house was on another street, so we had another address.

My mum had a lot of friends, most of them working with her in the hospital. We also had a family of aunts and uncles and cousins, but I didn't know them very well at this point. Daddy would take us to meet Mummy sometimes after work and we would go into this huge, ugly building that looked grey and was noisy all the time. There were lots of people, some looking sick, some crying and screaming in pain, some in uniforms of different colours. I soon realised my mum's best friend was Auntie Jenny, who was also a nurse there.

Auntie Jenny was very tall and pretty. She was friendly and very generous about giving us gifts. Even at my age, she used to apologise to me all the time because she said she was asked to be my godmother but couldn't be. She was Catholic and we were Anglicans. She said she has always been devastated by this because my mother was her best friend, but she just couldn't go against her religion. I used to wonder about this and ask myself how she became my mum's friend in the first place with such strong beliefs. Of course, I was too scared to ask her, so I never found out.

Our house was quite big and consisted of two large rooms. The front room was the living room, dining room and had some cupboards of stuff and shelves full of knick-knacks, lots of pictures on the wall and a large chest of drawers that had Mummy's special things. I was always curious and wanted to examine everything in the drawers, but I was always warned not to touch any of it. This chest of drawers would be my undoing in later life.

The second room was the bedroom where we all slept, with screens separating the beds. We had bunk beds and wardrobes that my father built, and Mum and Dad had a large bed for themselves.

Our kitchen and bathroom were separate rooms in the yard. We could get to the kitchen straight from the bedroom, as it had a covered walkway, but we had to go out in the open air, up a few stairs to the toilet and bathroom. The toilet and shower room were clean and primitive by today's standards, but that was all we knew and we were happy there. I remember having birthday parties at home with cake and biscuits and sweets and soft drinks, with my cousins mostly and friends from school.

My first memory of school was going to Teacher Dolly's Nursery School at age 3 to 4. I remember Dolly was quite a large woman and lovely, and she smiled a lot. She was very friendly but would get serious when it was time to work.

The school was in part of her house and was close to my home, so Mummy would take me to the entrance of the house and watch me run down to the school door. The whole area where we lived was quite hilly, and every home and garden seemed to slope.

I remember always being asked about my clothes. Mummy used to make everything we wore, down to our socks, which she crocheted. I loved school and I was chatty and playful. We were very busy and we learnt to read and do sums (which was what we called arithmetic) and spelling and she would read stories to us. We also played lots of games like jacks, hopscotch and hula hoop.

I remember two clear incidents during my time there. The first was about my spelling. We would often have spelling tests, and it seemed to get harder and harder as we got older and nearer the time when we would be leaving school. At one test, I was unable to spell the word 'between'. I had never seen or heard the word before, so I couldn't imagine how to spell it. I remember teacher Dolly was so annoyed with me that I got 'licks' (a smacking). She kept saying, "You are not trying hard enough." Of course, she reported back to Mummy, who gave me a tongue-lashing. Thankfully, I didn't get any more licks. I certainly never forgot how to spell it. I remember I used to think about this a lot, and was amazed teacher Dolly thought I could spell this word easily. I used to say that she must have thought I was so smart.

The next time I got in trouble was because of my hair. I had lots of hair and I remember Mummy always used to tell me not to interfere with my hair when I was at school. It was such a problem to comb as it was thick and natural and I hated how it was pulled about when she combed it. This particular day, a few of us started comparing and complaining about our hair, but still showing off about who had the most hair. One of my friends said she could plait and she could do a nice style for me. I was so excited that I didn't think of the consequences. So, in my wisdom, I opened up my plaits for my friend to redo them. I think my friend was shocked at the job she was expected to do and she panicked, said no and went home.

I was devastated and scared. I just didn't know what to do, because I knew Mummy would be furious, and I couldn't plait at all, at 4 years old. Worst of all, teacher Dolly just stood there and said, "Please be sure that you are ready to go home when your Mummy comes." I was crying hysterically and asking her to help. She said, "You had no business doing what you did."

When Mummy came to collect me, I refused to go home. After a while she had to come and get me. Well, the rest is history! Mummy was angry and I got so many 'licks'. She said, "You defied my instructions," and said it was so disrespectful and embarrassing for her. I certainly never did that again. I had to apologise to Dolly for my behaviour at school. To say the least, that girl was never my friend again.

My granny, I have fond and amazing memories of her. Her name was Albertina Piggott, but we all called her Granny Piggott. She lived on her own, but she was nearby and I loved her cooking and the way she dressed. She always looked so elegant and stylish. She wore lovely hats to church with a matching handbag always. She never wore loud colours but liked dresses in floral prints. She would come to meet us from her home and we would all go to church with our neighbour, Uncle Neville, who was a taxi driver. After church, I would go home, as it was usually still quite early in the morning. Later, I would spend the afternoon with her and enjoy her tasty Sunday dinner. She had a lovely home that I enjoyed.

Her bed was so big and high. Granny had a stool you had to stand on to get up on the bed. I loved how firm it was and used to jump on it a lot. She also had this beautiful item of furniture that she called her wash stand. The top was covered in beautiful tiles in blue and white, and the same tiles surrounded the mirror. In the middle there was a white bowl and jug and a tiled soap dish, and there were a few drawers on each side and shelves in the middle. It was such a pretty piece of furniture that looked very expensive, but she used it daily and looked after it well.

CHAPTER TWO:
Childhood Escapades

Uncle Neville was a close friend of Mum and Dad. He used to take us to church and other places. Sometimes he would invite us all over, as he lived opposite us. One day my brother and I went to visit him and his daughter at home. I remember I couldn't believe my eyes when I saw he had a tin of chocolate half open on the table. I built up the courage to ask him for some and, to my shock, he said no and put the tin in the drawer. I was so upset that my begging fell on deaf ears. As we played and listened to the radio, I had this urge and determination to take some of the chocolate. I sneaked away from the others and took two pieces of chocolate from the tin and was convinced that Uncle Neville would not notice the missing pieces. All was well until a few hours after we returned home. I started feeling unwell and started having diarrhoea and vomiting with stomach pain. Mummy was so worried that she went over to Uncle Neville to ask him about what I had eaten because I was so ill. My brother was fine and well, so it was even more puzzling to her. After some chat, he had a thought and went to the chocolate tin. He realised I had stolen a few pieces, as he kept a check on it. We discovered that it was not chocolate but a laxative called Brooklax made to look like chocolate bars. I was so ashamed to have been caught. I had to confess what I had done and, guess what – I got punished again, irrespective of how sick I was feeling. Mum said she was ashamed of me. She said I was rude for stealing from our friend, and that I had embarrassed the family.

I had to apologise to Uncle Neville for stealing from him. He calmly asked me, "Do you understand now why I said no to you?" It was a traumatic and painful experience. I remember saying sorry to Mummy so many times as well, because I was so worried that she would not love me anymore. She said, "I am so annoyed with you, because you are the eldest and should be setting a good example. You should learn to listen and not sneak around and steal anything that does not belong to you."

Everyone in the family heard about my escapade. Auntie Jenny was not pleased with me either, and neither was Daddy.

Despite this trauma, I continued to enjoy activities like going to fun fairs and to the beach. I had family all around, so I would visit my auntie up the hill, and Granny a few streets away, and school friends around me. My life as a youngster was exciting and fun and very simple and normal. I really didn't have a problem that I could think of, except for my baby sister when I was older. It was always warm and sunny and breezy. There were lots of insects flying around, birds chirping, lizards, mosquitos that ate you alive at night, heavy rain in the rainy season that was warm and dried quickly if you got wet. I remember lots of banged up and noisy cars on the road. My cousin had a car and, when you got in and looked down, you could see the road passing by from the hole in the flooring.

My home was such a beautiful place that I often wondered if everybody was as lucky to live in such warmth day and night, with loads of flowers and green plants. Even the wooden houses and broken fences and lots of dogs and cats roaming the streets seemed normal. You could take a bus or taxi to the seaside to have a dip in the sea after school or after work when we got older. I had to be cautious by the sea, but I loved it all the same.

During school, I was insanely jealous of one of my friends, because she lived near the sea and would run down there to swim every morning before school. She always pleaded with me that she would teach me to swim, but I couldn't take the chance. This was because I was born with a hole at the top of each ear. This caused fear and trepidation in me from the older family and friends we knew, because I was constantly told this meant that I would die by drowning, so I had to be careful by the sea. This really made me scared of water.

Some of my parents' friends were not very nice to me sometimes. They would blatantly say I was an odd child anyway, because I had a few odd things about me which made me different. I was also the only person in all my family who was left-handed and I was also born on Friday the 13th of July. Imagine growing up thinking you were odd and different from everyone else. My mother would get very angry with her friends and family and defend me vigorously. She asked them, "Please leave Allyson alone and stop forcing her to write with her right hand. I am a nurse and I know what I am talking about. Being a left-hander means that the right side of her brain is more developed and trying to change that is interfering with nature."

Over time, I was left alone with my oddities, to get on with life, but I have grown up with a real fear of the sea and of learning to swim. My mum was so gracious and caring that she would say I was the luckiest person born on the 13th that she knew. She always said I was different in the best possible way. I used to feel so special and I wanted to be the best daughter a mother could have. I loved her so much and wanted to be like her in every possible way.

Our landlady was building a new fence at the front of our house to replace a broken one. My younger brother and I used to watch the men at work, as they broke rocks into small pieces and mixed them with cement. One day I challenged my brother to jump from the balcony. He refused and warned me I would get in trouble and hurt myself if I did. I did it anyway and, as I jumped, I heard my neighbour screaming my name. I was told that I landed on one of the rocks and cut my eye very badly. My mother ran to the front of the house and fainted when she saw me. I was taken to the hospital and was cleaned up because my eye was bleeding profusely. I had to be given a huge number of stitches. The doctors told Mummy I was lucky not to have damaged my eye permanently. I remember feeling the thrill of the adventure, without any concept of the stupidity of it or the danger it spelt out. I don't remember what my mother said, but she was so happy that I had not died or broken all the bones in my body or lost one of my eyes. I was so sorry about what I had done and I have a permanent scar over my eye to remind me of my stupidity for the rest of my life.

My mother loved sewing and sewed almost everything I wore, which continued with my other sisters well into teenage life. We wore the most gorgeous clothes, and she was known for the animals and toys she crocheted or embroidered into our clothes. Looking back, I would say she was the ultimate fashionista of her time. She would also often make similar outfits for our teachers and their children. All my life until about 13, I wore crocheted socks made by her. She also made all our vests and panties. I tried to be studious and help as much as I could, but that left hand got in the way all the time. I could not understand her instructions when she tried teaching me to knit and crochet. To this day, I have never learnt. It was very frustrating at the time as there were no guides to follow or left-handed tools to use in those days. This also happened when my brother tried to teach me to play the guitar. He just thought I was stupid because I didn't understand. I used to remember my mother saying how lucky I was, but it didn't seem so at times like these.

My mother's style was everywhere. She designed and sewed clothes relentlessly for herself and friends and family. I always came back to talking about this bottom drawer that was in her special chest of drawers. Although I was warned about it, Mummy did explain that it contained special bits and pieces for special occasions. On probing, she would say, "I may need to go to hospital or stay with a client for work or a friend or even for a holiday. It is not always nice to take your everyday clothes, especially your underwear and night clothes with you as they would look worn and old." She would say you must always look your best in public.

One day I finally managed to inspect this bottom drawer myself. I was breathless with excitement. It contained so many beautiful things I had never seen before. She had night dresses, dressing gowns, soaps and jars of cream, toothbrushes and toothpaste, new bedroom slippers, a shawl, new panties and bras and perfume. Everything was so soft and comforting to touch.

I was intrigued by the bottle of perfume, which was called 4711. It was a beautiful glass bottle with green and gold labels. The name 4711 was written in black and gold lettering. The cover of the bottle was gold with a red top and red band around it, with the name 4711 in gold and red. In the early 50s, that was the most gorgeous thing I had ever seen. It seemed in its right place among the other lovely items in the drawer. Sadly, it was my undoing, because I opened a bottle and I was captivated by the smell. Needless to say, I had to sample it.

There I go again, following this innate desire to follow the thrill of the challenge with no fear of the consequences. I had no idea about the etiquette of putting on perfume, so you could smell me a mile away down the road from the splash I had given myself. Even I was choking from the smell. I knew I would be in trouble and I was terrified. I was so happy that none of the perfume fell on Mummy's beautiful clothes. Needless to say, I was punished for disobeying her orders, but from that time, I have been bowled over by this smell to this day.

CHAPTER THREE:
Forty-seven Eleven (4711)

I felt we were a special and lucky family. I remember thinking that my mother was so beautiful inside and out and was so stylish with such good taste. There was even more excitement at home around my mother's purchase of a huge amount of beautiful dishes and plates and cups just before Christmas one year. I later found out the dishes were called a Royal Doulton dinner service. I remember Mummy arriving at home with two of my aunties in a taxi surrounded by boxes and boxes of these dishes packed in tons of straw. I had never heard of this, nor seen anything so beautiful and delicate. I was told they were not simply dishes but special china from England. There were so many plates and bowls of different sizes and shapes and teacups and saucers.

As life went along, I found out my mother had many important and famous clients through her life as a nurse and midwife. They were her private patients and she worked in their homes. One client was the owner of a jewellery company and another owned a company that produced handmade mahogany furniture of all kinds. She was clearly well loved and respected by her clients. They introduced her to another world of luxury and she embraced it well. They were very generous about her needs, and she surrounded us with lovely things as we grew up. My father built a beautiful piece of furniture that we called a buffet cabinet and the china lived in its pride of place there. Any guests we had at home were treated, as it was used for 'best'.

I suppose, on reflection, it would seem my mother had delusions of grandeur, but I called it exquisite taste. I knew it was Mum trying to make life comfortable and meaningful for us. I think she was a dreamer who was born before her time. I say that because I think she would have excelled at the education she wanted and would have had more choices in her life; maybe she would have had a completely different life. On the other hand, I think she did that anyway, because she brought magic and purpose to my life.

My mother was my idol and my rock. I always thought she was so beautiful and knowledgeable and full of fun and very easy to talk to. She was so hilarious and said some outlandish things.

My mother was born in 1920. She had one sister and two brothers. She was a nurse in the general hospital in the city. It was there that I met many of her nursing colleagues and got a chance to wander the corridors of the hospital. She also looked after her mother, Granny Piggott, whom I loved dearly.

We were all loving towards each other and we hugged and kissed each other a lot. Even when we were punished and we were annoyed, or "vexed" as we called it, we still had to go through the ritual. If we didn't want to, Mummy would say, "Oh, you are more vexed than me; come here and say goodnight properly!" So we had to give the hugs and kisses as usual.

No matter what happened, I always knew that Mummy loved me by her actions and her interest in my life. She also said it, but her actions were so much greater than her words. I had four brothers and sisters with a variety of ages. My brother Arthur and I were born in 1947 and 1948, then my sister Pat was born in 1953. Then, eleven years after having me, my baby sister was born in 1958 and my baby brother in 1959. I remember being horrified when Mummy was having my sister Penelope. I was so angry with her. I kept telling her she was too old to be having more babies. She would only laugh at me as if unable to give a response.

My best friend through all of this was my brother, Arthur. He was very much like our Dad – very quiet and reserved. We were always close, but it became more inevitable when our baby sister Pat was born five years after me and during her growing up. She was so beautiful and looked like a real-life doll with a round face and saucer-shaped eyes. Everyone loved her and she became very spoilt very quickly. She soon learnt that throwing a tantrum would get her places. Mum and Dad took her everywhere and, when we complained, they would say she was only a baby and Arthur and I could keep each other's company. I really resented her for this, but Arthur and I still managed to have fun with each other. Whenever she was with us, we did manage to have fun too, but the jealousy about her was always there. Unfortunately, the relationship between me and my sister remained somewhat strained throughout our later life as well.

Mummy was strong and warm and seemed to have a solution for everything. She was outgoing, friendly and chatty. Dad was much quieter and more serious in his demeanour. It was clear to me from an early age that she was always in charge and had a clear plan about how we should live. I remember around the time that she bought that beautiful china service, she talked at length about us moving out of the city, to a home of our own with space for us to run around and play without the fear of running into cars or bikes. I remember her always working extra days and nights and saying she was saving towards getting us this home. I remember these times as low points, as we begged her to stay at home with us. To her greatest credit, she always managed to be involved in all aspects of our lives. She would attend all important events in school that we were involved in, like concerts and sports day and my netball tournaments and parents' evenings, and the school bazaar. I felt very special and important when I saw my mother get involved in all these events.

All along the way, her discipline was ever present and high on her agenda. On reflection, I have realised that we had powerful lessons in life skills all along the way. She never let up in ensuring we did and said the right thing. She used to say that she knew half the island of Trinidad and the other half knew her, so she would always know what we got up to, no matter how long it took. I can confirm that I have lived to see that statement come to life over and over, for example, going to my friend's home near the beach without her permission, and going to swim in the sea. Maybe she would never have found out if the heavens hadn't opened and all our clothes got soaked with rain. We had to dress in wet clothes to return to my friend's house and put her mother through the trauma of drying our school uniforms so we could travel home, which I didn't manage until about 9.30 p.m.

The problem was that my friends had told their parents that this was our plan B, so they were not at all worried. Of course, I hadn't told mine, because I knew there was no chance of my parents allowing me to go near the beach without adults. Thankfully, this scenario had a wonderful outcome. After I got a thrashing from my mother, she visited my friend's home to meet her mother and apologise for what we put her through. Over the years, these two mothers became firm friends. One thing I took with me through life was the way we had to address her friends. She would say, "My friends are mine and not yours, so show them respect and address them correctly, and not by their first names. The adult women should be called Auntie and the men Uncle. If you don't like that, then call them Mr or Mrs or Miss."

This became a family trend to this day, as I have said the same thing to my children. All my friends through school were in awe that I had such a large group of uncles and aunts in my life. They were equally stunned and impressed when I explained the rationale.

CHAPTER FOUR:
Trini Family Values

Mum also had a passion for towels and flannels and how best to use them. She would say that using a flannel was better to clean your skin than your hands. She explained that, after bathing, you rinse all the soap from the flannel and dry your skin with it. Then you dry your skin with the towel and you get a warm, fluffy feeling because your skin is not dripping wet.

That way, the towel lasts so much longer and you don't leave a smelly, soapy flannel lying around in the bathroom. I have been known to spread this philosophy to all my friends, who always said they had never heard anything so simple and logical in their lives. Interestingly, many of them tried and have persisted with this practice, including my children and their families.

She also had a thing about using the toilet. She would say, "Never use a toilet that is dirty, unless you are prepared to clean it before you come out again, because if you are caught, no one would believe it was not your mess if you leave it as you found it." She would say, "Always look back at the bowl when you are done to ensure you have not left any tracks behind." I always thought my mother was really smart and clever to think of these unusual but common sense, sensible rules of life, but I always wondered who taught her about some of these philosophies in her life. They were exceptional as far as I was concerned, but did she read them somewhere or make them up herself? Either way, they formed part of the solid foundation that informed my life forever. I think that everything was such basic good practice that everyone was aware of, but it always surprised me how many people had never thought of these ideas, let alone practised them.

I learnt early on that my parents had a strong sense of family. My mother was instrumental in keeping in touch with everyone. My mother had two brothers who had eight children each, her sister had one child, and she had five of us. My father had two sisters, one had three children and the other had eight. My parents also had a social circle of five family friends with a total of fifteen children. We saw each other all the time. My parents and their friends celebrated everyone's birthday and anniversary. My parents also liked socialising and they were always attending weddings and live concerts. We also spent a lot of time at each other's homes. We had parties in each other's gardens. We would picnic at the beach near or far away from home. It was especially exciting over the school holidays because we often rented a beach house on the other side of the island called Mayaro. We would travel there in a convoy of three or four cars and spend what seemed like weeks and weeks.

Primary school was quite an experience for me. I didn't enjoy it particularly, but I knew it was the place I had to shine to get into secondary school. In the beginning, I hated leaving my mother when she took me to school. One of those times, I remember myself busily working at my desk. I looked up and saw my mother and a teacher looking at me from the other side of the building. In a flash and with great excitement, I decided I had to get to her somehow. There were so many desks and chairs, I couldn't see my way around or through any of them. So I stood up from my chair, climbed on my desk and ran across the desk tops between the children until I got to my mother, in tears of joy. I had the teachers and children with mouths hanging open. I was so quick that no one had time to stop me.

My mother never forgot to keep telling me how lucky I was and I found this so positive and encouraging from a very early age. She believed it was important to capitalise on every opportunity I was given to educate myself and secure a happy, productive future for myself.

At this time we also had a devastating experience when one of my school friends, Marilyn died from a burst appendix. We were both about eight years old. It was so shocking because it was on a weekend that she was coming to stay at my home and I was bursting with excitement to see her. I waited and waited for her to come and she didn't, so I asked my mum to go get her. Mum came back and said she was in hospital as she had a severe tummy ache. I was worried and scared for her. Later that night her mum came to our house crying and screaming that Marilyn had died. We all bawled together from the shock of it all. Finally we then found out that her grandmother was complaining that she must have eaten some rubbish because my friend was complaining about a severe tummy ache. Gran said she needed to clear her bowel and gave Marilyn a dose of Epsom salts. This made her pain much worse and she began to vomit. She was rushed to hospital where the doctors tried to save her but she had a burst appendix, which is fatal for someone so little and so young. We continued crying together. When we visited the family, my friend's grandmother was in shock and devastated, blaming herself for the tragedy.

From then on, my mother would always tell us, "Never allow anyone to give you any medicine when you complain of a tummy ache." This is something I have lived by from that time on and, being a qualified nurse now, I understand the fatality of doing that.

The joy of primary school really started when I went upstairs in the school building to the more senior classes. In my last year we were taught by the head teacher herself, Miss Guy, and this was an amazing time. She treated us so well and taught us well beyond our years, I thought at the time.

I felt like the teacher's pet as she was always friendly towards me and, of course, my mother knew her well. I used to be allowed to go to her home early in the morning as she lived close to my home, a few streets away. I would carry her books or case as we talked and walked to school. That was such a special feeling. She was memorable and so intelligent.

In the classroom, we studied and explored other interesting subjects important to later life. She taught us biology, with a full explanation of the male and female genitalia and reproduction systems. This was fascinating stuff at age 10, but she was adamant we needed to prepare ourselves for teenage and adult life, based on facts and figures, not old wives' tales.

One of the highlights of my last year at primary school was preparing for the common entrance exams. The head teacher was kind and supportive and never seemed to put a lot of pressure on us. I remember getting tons of homework, especially in English vocabulary and grammar. I remember learning a lot of arithmetic, which we called 'sums' in those days. We would have breaks from working and learn to sing songs for school assembly. Our head did an IQ test on everyone in the final year. This was great fun and I distinctly remember successfully spelling the word "idiosyncrasy" during this test. This took me right back to the trauma I endured when I was unable to spell "between". I remember my score was about 120, and the head said that meant that I was clever. That was such a fun thing, but most of all I felt happy and reassured about forthcoming exams.

A free education system for children in primary school was established in 1901, and free secondary education was implemented in 1945, leading to the common entrance examinations which I took in 1960. My mother was so excited at the possibility of me going to the best school on the island – Bishop Anstey High School for Girls – and what that would mean. She talked about her dreams of going to the same school many, many years earlier, but this was out of reach for her parents, who were poor and couldn't afford it. At that time, secondary education was not free. So I buckled down with the same determination to achieve my goal of going to that school.

You could imagine the sheer joy and ecstasy when I found out I had passed the exams with flying colours and had been selected to attend the school of my choice – the best school in the country or even the Caribbean. The icing on the cake was that I placed thirteenth out of a field of 5,000 students who took the exam. There goes that oddity again – the number 13. I could not even contemplate how it was possible to tabulate these exam results, from one to 5,000, but I was so proud of me and my outstanding success. I felt I had the world at my feet. That was also the highlight of my life, because it was the first time my name was printed in the papers. My mother was so proud that she never stopped telling anyone who would listen. One of her favourite sayings was, "Aim for the sky, because you could fall on the top of the trees. If you aim for the top of the trees, you could fall flat on your face."

The only real disappointment I had with my mother was her refusal to allow me to learn to play the steel band as a young teenager. I was horrified and devastated at the time. I learnt there was a huge stigma attached to the steel pan, as only the "bad boys" from "behind the bridge" were involved in it. Behind the bridge related to a specific part of the city that was notorious for gangs and all sorts of criminal activities. I was warned when my mother said, "Decent young women don't talk about pan, so don't do that again in this house." So that was the end of that discussion. I thought this was so snobbish and degraded our world-famous instrument, but I had to trust in my mother's better judgement. She was right, of course, as the steel band groups were always embroiled in fights among themselves. This began to change when they all started to secure significant streams of funding from major corporations that allowed the bands to function more effectively, thus considerably improving their reputation in the community and the public eye as a whole. Unfortunately, this change was too late for me. The steel pan began to be taught in schools and became more and more an acceptable part of our culture. My baby sister in later life was a member of her school steel band orchestra. I think the steel pan is an extraordinary musical instrument and I am so proud of its creation in my home country. It is registered in the *Guinness Book of Records* as the only musical instrument discovered in the 20th century. Despite her opinion of the steel band, my mother was very interested in socialising and in cultural activities going on.

My relationship with my Dad was an interesting one, as I found him a bit distant and reserved with us as children compared with Mummy, who was the life and soul of our lives.

He was called Conrad Clyde Layne and was born in 1921. He didn't talk about his father and we never met him, but we knew his mother and stepfather very well. We called her Granny Layne and she was a practising, spiritual Baptist. I just loved visiting her, especially when there were special ceremonies going on. My favourite was the amazing food they cooked for each occasion. Her place of worship was attached to her home, so we felt safe and secure. When we got fed up of the chanting and shouting we could leave and go next door to her living room and listen to the radio.

Daddy was a qualified carpenter and we would often visit him at his workshop. As I mentioned, he was usually quiet, not very talkative or affectionate with me. He seemed to come alive with his friends, so it was lovely to see him laugh with them. Mum was our strong focal point and Dad was the strong, silent type. Mum also made him out to be the bad guy, as she would threaten us with punishment by saying, "Wait until your father comes home. He will deal with you." This was a terrifying prospect to us, because it meant he would take off his belt to punish us. I hated this so much, especially the waiting. Sometimes Mum was true to her word and we would be punished as she said. Sometimes the punishment never happened, but the waiting and wondering which way he would go was the worst torture.

There were many occasions when I would make arrangements with Mummy to do special things with my friends. She would ask if I had told my dad and she would threaten that I couldn't go if I didn't tell him. Then I would have to summon up the courage to tell /ask him for permission. Most times he would say, "You have already arranged your plans with your mother, so why are you asking me now?" Of course he was correct, and he knew this was just a formality.

The most amazing thing about my dad was that he was a superb baker. He developed this skill more and more when he changed his job. When we moved home, he trained as a fireman and started to work on the American naval base. He had an unusual work pattern as he was on duty for twenty-four hours with twenty-four hours off. We were so lucky at home because he baked all the time. His bread was wonderful and he made all kinds of scrumptious pastries and cakes. He was also a great lover of the carnival and got dressed in costume with his friends each season. As a family, we would go to the stands, which we called the bleachers. They were basic wooden structures with rows and rows of wooden seating. These were attached to each side of the grandstand, which was a permanent structure built in one end of the Savannah. All the costume bands would come in at one end of the Savannah, parading along the stage in front of the judges who were sitting in the grandstand and leave the Savannah at the other end, returning to the streets.

The highlight for us as children was looking out for my dad and his friends in costume as we sat in the bleachers. We would arrive as early as possible to get the best spot on the bleachers, which meant getting the best vantage point to watch the bands go by. Mum would prepare all the best treats for us to enjoy. For example, the food would be rice and peas, macaroni pie, chicken, coleslaw, potato salad, and local drinks such as sorrel and mauby.

Sorrel is made by boiling hibiscus leaves with cinnamon and cloves. The liquid is sweetened with sugar and essence, and angostura biters are added to taste. Mauby is made from a tree bark. It is also boiled with cinnamon and aniseed and sweetened.

Mum also took lots of local snacks such as sugar cakes, tamarind balls, and any fruits that were in season. We would get so excited when we saw Dad and his friends. Mum would have lots of food and snacks ready for them. We would touch and stroke the costumes, which were colourful and sparkling and full of layers.

After Dad's band had passed, I always calmed down and seemed to lose interest a bit. Many of us would sneak under the bleachers and play games, until Mummy called us to eat or drink or see a very special band going past.

When I was about 10, we finally moved home to what seemed like the countryside. It was outside the city and very quiet. It was full of hills and trees and our house was big with a huge yard full of all types of fruit trees, like plum, mango, avocado, pawpaw, guava, Chinese coconut and lime trees. The house was so spacious but it looked like the one we left in town. It was made of walls, called tapia, which is made from mud and straw compacted into a wooden frame. It was high off the ground and had a veranda across the front of the house and we could run around under the house. We had two bedrooms, a living room and a dining room, kitchen and bathroom, all under one roof.

Mummy told me she was very unhappy about the purchase. She gave Dad the responsibility to find us a new home, as she was working all the time. She was disappointed the house wasn't in better condition, but Daddy reassured her we would enjoy living there and eventually we could rebuild our own special home. I loved the idea that we had space to play and mountains and hills to explore. I admired Dad for thinking so strategically and recognising the potential in the place. He did say from the onset that it needed some work to be done, so we were sort of prepared. One thing that remained the same for a while was that we still had a toilet outside the house. I hated it, because I expected that from the move we would do better, but that was still to come.

As we enjoyed life at the new house, we discovered more and more about the place. We found a small, broken-down house at the back of the property. We speculated that it was probably where servants had lived, but there was no one to tell us the history of the place. My grandmother discovered that we had provisions in the ground that we could dig up and eat such as dasheens, sweet potato and yams. She even suggested that we could grow our own corn and pigeon peas when they came into season, which we did with great pride and enjoyment, and it became easier year after year. We were able to rear chickens in the back yard and built a large chicken coop for them. We even got a dog and he had a lovely dog house in the yard built by my dad. In the Caribbean, dogs did not come or stay in the house; they lived and were fed outside.

I felt so happy in this new place, although it seemed miles away from the people and places I had grown up with. We had to take a bus home after school.

Then, to my shock, my mother announced she was expecting a baby. She was happy and excited, but I couldn't believe my ears. I was so upset with her. I remembered saying to her, "Mum, we are all grown up. Aren't you too old to be having a baby?" I remember she laughed so hard and said she was not at all old. It wasn't until I was much older that I learnt she was only 36 at the time. My beautiful sister was born at one of the private nursing homes my mother worked at and they looked after her very well.

She was only home for about three or four months when she announced that she was expecting again. We were all flabbergasted. I remember her best friend, Auntie Jenny, was highly amused. She said, "Well I suppose you can call it an accident to get pregnant after so long, but to get pregnant for the second time in such quick succession was just being greedy." I was just happy that they were so gorgeous and I got stuck in and helped Mum as much as I could. I was pleased they could grow up surrounded by such green space and open air.

My baby brother was born exactly one month after my baby sister turned one, Mum certainly had her hands full, and I remember her being tired all the time.

CHAPTER FIVE:
We Don't Speak "Trinidadianese" In Here!

As a special treat for doing so well in my exams, Mum took me on holiday to Tobago with Auntie Sheila, whose family lived in the capital. Her husband, Uncle Tony, came with us too. Tobago is the sister isle to Trinidad and was considered the more popular tourist holiday destination. The crossing was long and rocky. In those days, the boat that travelled between the islands was old and very slow. We stayed in a cabin that had several beds, so we could relax.

We were all having drinks and food when Uncle came in and offered drinks to Mum and Auntie Sheila. Uncle was quite tipsy and kept insisting after they refused. Then he said, "You are going to have this drink if it kills you," and suddenly threw it all over Auntie. I was quite shocked and ran to get a towel for her. She was furious and started to relate a story to us. She was so funny despite her anger. She said, "My mother used to reject all the nice boyfriends that I had and would always find fault with them ... too tall, feet too big, ugly face, etc. So I had to choose and choose until I chose this piece of shit!" Uncle just turned and left the room. Then she said, "Allyson, always follow your mind and make your own choices. Don't listen to anyone." This was a profound piece of advice for a 12-year-old to hear. I was so gobsmacked, but I thought he deserved this insult because of his awful behaviour.

Despite this hiccup, we had a wonderful time. Auntie's family house was on a hill only feet away from the beach. We just had to run down the path and we were in the water, which was gentle and sheltered and very safe. I enjoyed my first trip away from home and felt very special. We had a wonderful day trip to the coral reef called Buccoo Reef that has made Tobago quite famous. I was in complete awe of the beautifully coloured fish in the water. The water is very shallow and warm and you can view the fish from the glass-bottomed boat that takes you out there or snorkel and swim with the fish. It was truly magical.

Secondary school at Bishop Anstey High School was an experience far beyond my expectation. I was truly in awe of being selected to attend that prestigious school and mixing with so many of the clever and friendly girls in my year. There was quite a range of girls from different social settings, many different shades of black, brown and white, and from the wealthy to the poor. It was a true representation of the very cosmopolitan nature of the country.

Trinidad and Tobago is reputed to be the most cosmopolitan country in the Caribbean, if not the world. We have a high number of East Indians and African Caribbean people, but we also have Caucasians who were born and bred there as second and third-generation children of the slave and plantation owners. We also have Syrians,

Lebanese, Chinese, Spanish and Indians. We all had one thing in common, though: we were all clever and deserving of this opportunity to receive the best education we could get.

Of course, my mother was unrelenting in giving her advice and encouragement in equal measure. She never stopped saying this was no time to relax. This result was only the beginning that gave me a glimpse into the future and the possibilities the future held.

I don't remember how easy or difficult it was to choose friends, but I soon became involved with a group of amazing girls, who were not as precious as some of the others I had met. We respected each other and all came from different parts of the island. My select group of friends were Esther, Carol and Vera . We were from similar types of families.

We all shared our stories of the discipline first and foremost from our parents. They had to have a full rundown of all details of where we were going out together or with whom. We enjoyed the same music and fun activities. My friend Vera was brought up by her father with an older brother. Her mother had passed away, so he was happy that she had friends who had both parents in their lives. Carol was beautiful and very light-skinned. Her family were very mixed, with Indian, Spanish and Caucasian. Her father was a huge man who was of pure African descent, and both of her brothers looked like their father, while Carol and her sister looked like their mother. She had a wonderful and very attractive characteristic in that she was very fair-skinned and her face was completely covered in freckles. Her Dad was very serious most of the time and spoke very little, so we never saw much of him when we visited the house. We had so much fun with her wonderful mother.

I also had a very special friend called Pat. She was very quiet but exceedingly intelligent. We became close friends and I was able to visit her often, as we lived close to each other, but her parents were very strict and she was not allowed to socialise, except when I was involved. I had to beg Pat's parents to allow her to go out with me. They were happy then, because they knew that my mum would collect us and take us home, so we were safe.

Esther was a great nature lover. She swam daily, even before coming to school each morning, as she lived about 500 yards from the beach. She would go fishing with her father and brothers. We each had other friends within our class, but we four tended to be with each other more. We spent a lot of time at each other's homes at the weekends and for special celebrations. We often arranged to meet up after the Sunday morning church service, as three of us were Anglicans. Esther and her family were Christians and attended a Church of God in the city. Whenever I stayed at her home, we always had to wake up early. We would sit in a circle and read passages from the Bible, after which we would pray. It was a wonderful experience for me, because even though I went to church every Sunday, I never had this close connection with reading and understanding the Bible with my family. I was in awe when Esther informed me they had read the Bible three or four times up to her secondary school days. I often wondered how long they managed to continue this family tradition as they all got older.

We would go to each other's homes for Sunday dinner with the rest of the family. In the Caribbean, Sunday dinner was the feast of all feasts. There would be all types of meats, fish, and vegetables, done Trinidad-style. My favourite Sunday dinner was baked chicken and stuffing, rice and peas, callaloo, stewed lentils, macaroni pie, potato salad, coleslaw, avocado, plantain and sweet potato.

Usually, dessert would be fresh fruit salad, cake of some kind and homemade ice cream or custard. Mum was an amazing cook and her Sunday dinners were really special.

Once we had rebuilt our home, Mum and Dad started a tradition of inviting all our family down to the house on New Year's Day. This was a wonderful day that we spent together, getting to know each other. Our guests included my mum's mother, her sister and daughter, her two brothers and their sixteen children and, on my dad's side, his two sisters, their husbands and eleven children. It was a huge crowd of people, but it was such fun as we shared memories and helped with the cooking and clearing up. As one of the kids, I would play games around the yard and had fun climbing trees and picking any fruit in season. As I grew older, I ended up in the kitchen doing some of the cooking or being responsible for setting the table for lunch.

My social life around school and my school friends was on going. There was always somewhere to go or something to celebrate, as my friends had similar ideas that it was important to celebrate and enjoy all occasions like birthdays and anniversaries. Our celebrations took various forms, from a simple beach picnic, with the icing on the cake being which beach we went to; some were much more upmarket than others. We also did barbecues in the back garden or parties in the house with lots of loud music.

One of my most wonderful memories of my mother has always been exploring her bottom drawer and discovering her special perfume, 4711. Despite being stubborn, hard-headed and determined, and the consequences of that, I will never forget the beautiful smell of the perfume. Every time I use it now, I remember the beauty of Trinidad, the fond memories of growing up. To this day, this cologne has become a lifelong and beautiful reminder of my mother. During this time of my life, she was never far from me, and was fully involved in my life.

She had an amazing habit of insisting on meeting the parents of my friends, every time I asked to go out with someone. She would say she had to be sure that I would be safe and that my friends' families had the same moral standing and values as we did. She never said that to them, thankfully. The first time she did it, I was so shocked and I worried about what my friends would say. I need not have worried, as my friends were all amused by her actions and their parents thought she was so charming. She never let up, either. If she could not physically visit, she would always talk to my friends' parents before the event. Over the years, my mother became close to several of my friends. I remember at the time that I was so irritated by this and thought Mum interfered in my life too much. On reflection, I now realise how important that attitude was in ensuring children have a sense of security and confidence that they are safe. It was a practice I carried out when I had my own children.

My mother was an amazing source of encouragement and support throughout my school days and encouraged me and my friends to participate fully in all activities. So I played netball and rounders and cricket and tennis. The only game I disliked was hockey. I belonged to Abercrombie House, so I represented them in challenges and tournaments. I was always tall for my age, so I was a master shoot in our netball games. Our house was always top of the leader board during my time in school.

I was also a Girl Guide for many years. It was a wonderful international organisation to belong to, as its focus was on supporting and empowering girls to grow up into confident women. There were other organisations like the boy Scouts, Cubs and Rangers, but the Girl Guides was primarily for girls. The badges they worked for were designed to develop skills in perseverance, patience, and communication. I particularly liked the many challenges that we took part in to secure the relevant badge that we could show off with and then wear proudly on our uniform. We had quite a cross section of different girls in the group, so we got the special opportunity to work together.

The teachers were amazing people as well, but especially our head teacher, who was a special character by herself. She was English, with a strong British accent, she spoke English impeccably. She was very tall and had an imposing presence. She had a way of always coming out of the woodwork when you least expected it. I had the misfortune once of getting on her bad side. After a confusing and garbled explanation about what I was up to on the school corridors;, she calmly said, "Now, just say all of that again in English. We don't speak *Trinidadianese* in here." That was certainly a wake-up call for me, as I think it was the start of my interest in the English language. I understood exactly what she meant, because we have our own local language that is full of slang, innuendo and patois, all of which is based on the English language and French. It is funny and sounds amazing and I love to speak it, but it sounds best in an informal setting with family and friends. I certainly never did that again in school or in front of a teacher.

CHAPTER SIX:
Sweet Innocence

I was also lucky enough to form friendships outside of school, when I met other teenagers who went to the same Anglican church in my local area. The church was quaint and quite small. It could probably have fitted about five or six times into the cathedral I was used to attending with my grandmother. There was a building next to it that was used as a meeting place for many different purposes, including the Anglican Young People's Association (AYPA). This was the first group outside school that I belonged to, and it was a special experience. We were a group of like-minded boys and girls who wanted to become strong Christians in the community. We had monthly meetings with chosen officers and members who led those meetings and we planned events such as Bible study, fundraising, debates and social events.

It was at this church that I met a special friend called Pearl. She was so friendly and made me feel welcome. I learnt soon after meeting her that my sister was going to the same secondary school as her. Our friendship grew and we socialised together as well. We both had huge teenage crushes on each other's brother. Her brother was like a god to me – tall and handsome and he rode this drop-dead gorgeous red motorbike. I realise now that I must have been very annoying, as I pestered him continually to take me for a ride on his bike. He consistently told me no, as he said that he was bound to have an accident with me as a pillion rider and he would get blamed. So, to this day, I have never felt the thrill of the ride on a motorbike.

However, thrills were yet to come in abundance around my 18th birthday. This was planned to be a low-key event with friends who were coming for Sunday dinner. I was staying with my beloved Auntie Sheila, the chef, to help her prepare food for a corporate event. This was going to be a treat for me on my birthday weekend, and I really looked forward to it. A few weeks earlier, I had taken a trip with my mother to her favourite dressmaker, whom she insisted should make me a dress for my birthday. My mother was a wonderful dressmaker herself, but she always used Jean's expertise when she wanted something special. She said this helped her to develop her own expertise. We were chatting and, as I looked around at the array of beautiful clothes around me, I spotted this dress that was simply exquisite. It was sleeveless and made of pink linen, but the showstopper was that the whole front of the dress was beaded with white pearls of different sizes in the design of a branch of a tree. I said to Jean that the dress was breathtaking and she agreed. Then she suddenly said to me, "Please can you do me a favour? The owner of the dress is unable to come for a fitting, and since you are the same size, could you try it on for me?" I thought I had died and gone to heaven. I felt like a princess in the dress, and I exclaimed that I wished I had one like it.

My mother said, "You can forget it, as I couldn't afford to have one made for you." After Jean had done her alterations on the dress and my own dress that she made for my birthday, we left and that was the end of that. I had no reason or expectation of anything else.

When I went to my aunt's house in the city, it was like going on a special journey. Aunt Sheila was pretty and very talented. Her husband was Uncle Tony and their children were Joanna and Andre. She talked at length about living and working in America, and I think a lot of this talk was influential to my parents later on. She trained as a chef so, over many years before and after having her family, she would travel back and forth. She had a green card, which I understood was a precious commodity that gave residential status to the individual, and safe passage to and from America, provided you did not stay away for more than two years. At first, I thought she was very luxurious to have weekend holidays to Puerto Rico or St Thomas or Miami, until I learnt the purpose was to renew her American residency. She was really nice to me and tried to satisfy my interest in food by asking me to help her. She made the most gorgeous pastries and exotic foods and fancy cakes and jellies for corporate events. I later learnt these were called canapés and hors d'oeuvres. I always enjoyed helping to make these, but the best part was that I got to dress up and accompany my aunt as her assistant, I suppose. I was always blown away by the luxury of the places we went to and the glamour of the ladies' clothes. This meant so much to me, because as a teenager, I was thrilled that I was considered mature enough and capable of helping in such a meaningful way. Actually, I felt really special.

So on the weekend of my birthday, I went to Auntie Sheila's and we cooked up a storm. I loved it when she made the Leaning Tower of

Pisa from potato salad. At the end, we got dressed and headed for the special venue. Along the way, Auntie said that the lemon meringue pie we made was for me and my friends at Sunday lunch, so she detoured to deliver it to my home. Along my street, I saw one of my friends, who waved to me. I was puzzled as to why she was there, but I decided that she must know other people on my street. We carried on, and to my surprise, I saw my best friend on the front patio as we drove into the driveway. She wasn't supposed to be there until the next day. When she saw me, she screamed and ran inside. I couldn't understand what was going on. I thought everyone had lost the plot.

Anyway, as we opened the front door, there was this almighty roar of "Surprise" and I saw my home full of friends and family. They all sang *Happy Birthday* and screamed and laughed. I couldn't believe what was happening. I just cried and cried. I felt so good. It was real proof that my mother was a full part of my life, as every friend I knew and loved was there. She used my close friends that she knew to invite the other friends that she didn't know herself. Then the icing on the cake was when she said that I should change into my birthday dress that I thought was the one she made for me. To my sheer delight and hysteria, she brought me the beaded dress that I had tried on. It was mine all along. I just bawled this time with joy and grateful thanks to my mother. She was a mother in a million and I praised her for her love and thoughtfulness. It was the party to beat all parties and a memory that has lived with me all my life.

CHAPTER SEVEN:
New Beginnings

A few years after we moved to the country, my parents decided it was time to rebuild and modernise the house. This was a bold and revolutionary event within our family circle, and we were considered leaders. It was a difficult, long process and we had to remain there and live through the dust and the dirt. Somehow we made a plan and were able to travel to school in the normal way. Mum would take us to school by car in the normal way, then my brother and I would make our way home on the bus. There was a special bus terminal for school children, so we were perfectly safe. If we ever needed help, Mum would take us to her brother's home. It was a complex building process, as my brilliant and stylish mother had designed the house we had to receive tons of soil that was used to pack the front part of the house to strengthen and support the foundation. At the front of the house was the patio, the living room, the dining room and kitchen and garage. Then there were four bedrooms and two bathrooms that made up the rest of the house. Under this part of the house was a wide-open space that was used for storage, washing and drying clothes on rainy days and playing games. It was so stylish and like nothing I had seen before. Mummy was blessed to have a brother who was a builder and clearly one of the best in the business.

She had great fun running around with him looking at his work and gaining ideas she could use in the house. I would occasionally go with Mum to pass by some of the lavish houses that her brother was building. It was a real eye-opener to how the other half lived. The houses were in areas that we always thought of as out of bounds. It was where the rich and the famous lived, not somewhere we mortals would visit. The houses often had huge swimming pools and perfectly manicured, colourful gardens. Not to mention, there were always two or three luxury cars in the driveways. My uncle was really kind and caring, because he chose two of his best workmen from his team and relocated them to our home to work on the renovation.

In our new-build, the kitchen was rehoused at the front of the house and the washroom was relocated to under the back of the house. Both rooms then became Mum and Dad's master bedroom with an en suite bathroom. It was truly gorgeous. The icing on the cake was that the bathroom was fully tiled from floor to ceiling in lovely, baby yellow tiles and it included a bidet. This was a far cry from the galvanised room we all used in our home in the city.

To me, it was luxury personified, as I had never seen this in any home I had visited. Mum was careful to explain exactly how and when to use it, although we were warned not to make a habit of it. I was even more impressed to learn that all the tiles used were left over from someone's swimming pool. The tiles could not be returned, so my mother was the lucky recipient.

Mum was truly blessed because some of her clients ran different types of businesses that she could patronise and benefit from. She was able to secure some really beautiful living room and bedroom furniture. Uncle Rod was kind and generous to his sister, my mum, and he helped ensure that Mum remained within her budget. This meant that she continued working day and night for such a long time so we could finally live comfortably in our new home. My mother was strong and determined to fulfil her dreams. I admired her courage and fortitude and her amazing skills of organisation. I always remembered listening to her and watching her make lists about how much she would be paid for extra work, then another list would show how she would spend this money. This flabbergasted me, but she always said that I must always make plans. Almost always, she managed to realise these plans and use the money she earned exactly as she planned.

I didn't know it at the time, but these life lessons registered with me and never went away. I was in awe of my mother, as I admired her strong, positive attitude about everything. She would always say, "Nothing in life is impossible, you just have to believe." She certainly showed us this philosophy time and time again. Her love and support always made things happen for us. Our friends noticed and commented on how lucky we were to have such a wonderful mother. They loved coming to my home and they were particularly interested that she could sew so well. It took very little to persuade her to sew something for them. She was also willing, no matter what was happening in her life.

When we moved home, Dad wanted to reconsider his job, as he felt travelling into town to work might not be cost-effective and he needed to earn a better income. The journey was negligible to my mind, but I could understand his reasons for wanting a new start. I also didn't know if there was any other reason for his decision, but I imagined that a new home and a growing family meant he had to contribute more. We were so happy when we heard that he had a new job on the American naval base, where he trained as a fireman. This was in the north-east corner of the island and was so beautiful because it was a fairly sheltered area. The beaches there, were full of clean white sand, but the area was off limits to the general public as it was a working naval base that was leased by the American government. It was not impossible to use the area, but Trinidadians had to get special passes to go beyond the security gates. The families of the locals who worked there were lucky, as access to the area was easier for them.

My father had an unusual work schedule, as he worked twenty-four hours on and twenty-four hours off. During his days at work, he was able to perfect his baking skills, as baking was a real passion of his. When he came home, he was full of lovely baked treats for us, like bread loaves, sweet breads, coconut tarts and scones. As a family we would visit Dad sometimes, but this didn't happen often, as he was on duty. It was really nice, though, to meet his work colleagues, who were both local Trinidadians and some Americans.

My school life continued at a pace, it seemed. We had teacher dramas, student dramas, girls getting pregnant and disappearing from school. I loved French and English and I really enjoyed geography and general knowledge, because I got this amazing insight into the rest of the world that seemed so exciting.

Our French teacher was a French woman. Her accent was to die for and she insisted that the class was conducted in French. At an early age, I had visions of working at the United Nations headquarters in New York as a French interpreter and travelling around the world. She made the language sound romantic and gentle. I tried to be a good student, but I found that I could become lazy.

I started to learn to play the piano, as I was so interested in music. I had a wonderful reputation among my mother's friends. When I was growing up, we didn't have a television, so we listened to the radio day and night. I also bought records and played music just as much. My younger brother played guitar and was in a band. I listened to every programme and all the music when I was at home. I became the font of knowledge about all types of music. I would easily recognise the singers and could say all the words of most songs. This included soul, R & B, country and western and calypso music. Even now, I am always singing along to songs that many of my friends don't even remember.

There was always a lot of pressure to perform and live up to the standards of the school, as I felt I was only average. There were many very, very clever girls who were excelling at their work. I remember Mum sitting up with me night after night while I did my homework and when I was studying for exams.

I also had interesting insight into my mother's work, as she would take me to the homes when she visited pregnant clients. I loved how they admired and respected her. I loved the inspiring way Mum talked about her work. She showed her skills and passion for her career. This started to instil thoughts in me that nursing and midwifery would be a rewarding and fulfilling career to undertake. Mum changed her job, like Dad, to be more flexible, and able to take us to and from school. She became an occupational health nurse working Monday to Friday during office hours. She had a wonderful assistant who became a long-standing family friend. She looked after the staff of the government railways, attending to their injuries and performing minor, general surgical procedures. The men were amazing people who respected my mother and her work. When she was unable to manage a difficult injury, she would refer them to the hospital, where they got preferential treatment, i.e. they would be attended to immediately, because of the nature of their work. They had the most wonderful habit of bringing her gifts for herself and her family. This gesture was so precious to us and we were always grateful because of the positive effect this had on the family. The gifts were always lots of local produce, like cases of orange and grapefruit juices, massive tins of biscuits and all types of fresh fruit that were in season.

I went to college to do my A levels because I didn't get the required grade in one subject to stay at school, despite getting distinctions in French and English. It was a huge disappointment, but I was pleased that I passed all my subjects. I must say that I am thankful for my good results to Mum's best friend, Auntie Jenny, who allowed me to stay at her home on the grounds of the hospital. It was such a beautiful flat, with brilliant white walls and wooden floors. The idea was that I could focus on studying and not be caught up with my younger siblings. As you can imagine, our home was a hectic, noisy place. I was well looked after there. Auntie Jenny was a matron at the time, so she was assigned a housekeeper, who cleaned the house and brought us three meals a day. It was like living in a hotel. Even our dirty clothes were taken away to be washed. My most meaningful experience living there was that I went to church each morning with Auntie Jenny. It was so comforting and uplifting to do this each day. By this time, she was much more flexible and chilled out about being Catholic and us being Anglicans. I was able to walk to school a short distance away to attend my exams. This arrangement was priceless, as it did help me to focus, but clearly I needed to focus much more.

CHAPTER EIGHT:
Moving Into The Big League

I was flustered and confused at the time because I had never considered going to college, so I didn't know much about them. It was one of my friends who told me about the college she was attending. I applied there and got a place. It was during those college days that I got the bug even more of heavy party-going and socialising. It was there that I also got the very confusing and scary advances of an older man at the college. I supposed my very sheltered life didn't prepare me for that. I was horrified to be invited on a date and told I was so tall and pretty. This was always my problem. I was always considered much older than I actually was because I was tall and very slender during my teenage years. I couldn't tell my mother, because I imagined with horror that she would bring the college to a halt! I relished the days when she picked me up so I didn't have to face this gentleman.

I managed to tell one of my very brave and streetwise friends and she had a word with him for me. He was equally horrified that I was not 21 years old, but only 18, as she informed him. He subsequently apologised both to her and me and we remained civilised friends throughout my time at the college. In today's climate his behaviour would be deemed sexual harassment, but back then, it was even worse to speak out and get a positive reaction or support from an adult.

The most interesting aspect of this was that my mother's teaching on sex education was awful and left a lot to be desired. My primary school headteacher did give us a very detailed teaching session on the biology of the reproductive organs and systems, including the menstrual cycle. However, this to me was a factual biology lesson in a classroom, and had no bearing on the physical and psychological trauma of being accosted by a male individual much older than yourself. My mother's take on sex was to say that I should never let a man touch me or I would be in trouble. There was no dialogue or discussion about it, so that statement put the fear of God into me. Imagine my torture at college, because I thought my life would be doomed if I even spoke about this man.

So I survived the fray by becoming fully engrossed in socialising with my new friends and old ones, some of whom stayed on at school and some who went to other colleges. My friend Esther went to nursing school after working for a while in a bank. Carol went to secretarial college as she wanted to become a secretary. Vera stayed on at school to do A levels as she wanted to go to university to study law. Many of my other friends did other options, college or A levels at school and trained in many amazing professions like banking, medicine, psychology, teaching, finance and law. I changed my mind and studied biology and chemistry, which was a far cry from the languages I loved. I think that, secretly, I was thinking those subjects would be more useful to me if I chose a career in nursing. At the time of A levels and even when I finished, I was still undecided about what I wanted to do for the rest of my life. It just seemed like a decision that needed a lot of thought. I couldn't even imagine being away from home without my friends and family.

In the meantime and with the help of a neighbour, I found a job as a clerical officer at the Ministry of Education. Our offices were located on the edge of the city and overlooked the playing fields of the most famous boys' secondary school. It was wonderful and relaxing watching boys of all ages exercise and play football and games. The area was green and sunny and always full of children, mainly boys. When we went for our lunchtime walks, we admired the huge, amazing homes we would pass. They were full of beautiful flowers and shrubs and sometimes fountains. This was an interesting environment and uplifting, but back at the ranch, we had to deal with a difficult and ineffective boss who threw his weight around.

One day we finally learnt that our complaints about him caught the attention of our new permanent secretary, who had just returned from study leave in London and Paris. He called a meeting in his office to discuss what was happening. He seemed to be biased that we were at fault and our boss was an experienced senior member of staff. I remember getting very upset that he didn't seem to believe us. I bravely stood up and rationalised the situation. I said, "If so many educated staff in our department are individually complaining about someone, then there must be something wrong with that person. You cannot dismiss us because he is the boss."

He agreed and promised to investigate further. After some time, our boss was removed and reposted to another ministry. The work was tedious and used tons of paper all the time. My job was dealing with teacher vacancies and finding replacements and cover for teachers on maternity leave and long-term absence. It was very satisfying and I was lucky to meet many headteachers who were anxious to help in providing the correct information to me. I met an amazing range of men and women at the office. There were single women, mothers with husbands and young children, young adults who were dating and a few young school leavers like myself.

At the end of my first three months at work, I was so delighted that I was able to use my own money to buy things and not go through the trauma of asking my mother. One day, she announced to me that she had given me some time to settle at work, but now I had to start paying her a monthly sum of money for rent, board and lodging, whatever I wanted to call it. I was so horrified that my mother wanted to now charge me for living at home. She quickly explained that I had to take responsibility for my life, because that's what working adults do. As the months went by, she never let up. On my payday, she would make sure she was paid the agreed amount of money. She also stressed that I was responsible for managing what was left, as I was not going to borrow from her. I had to find ways to budget or, as we would say, "stretch the money."

I was very lucky, though, because Mum sewed all my clothes, and she always came home with materials and remnants of materials that she would offer to me. I know she enjoyed sewing for me, because I would help her a lot when she was sewing for anybody. I would iron our patterns and cut materials once she pinned the patterns on. I could put in zips and make buttonholes as well. My young sister Pat, on the other hand, would get upset with Mum and accuse her of sewing too much for me. She never realised that most of the clothes were for other people as well. I also had this habit of wanting to wear something new to work each week on Monday morning. It would be either a shirt or blouse, or a skirt or a dress. I found it to be such fun, because by Thursday each week, we would start planning my outfit for the next Monday morning.

I was promoted twice in two years, I think because I had fresh eyes and I was in the right place at the right time. I made some amazing contacts and friends and I got involved in all the social activities that were arranged. I attended many weddings, birthday, engagement and wedding anniversary parties. We had picnics at the beach, both near and far away. My favourite was day-trip parties down the islands. "Down the islands" was a term used when trips were arranged for taking a boat to one of the islands off the west coast of Trinidad. There were five islands, called Monos, Chacachacare, Huevos, Gasparee and Gasparillo. Carreras Island was used as a prison. In fact, I learnt that there are twenty-one islands around the coasts of Trinidad and Tobago. They were available for use by the public except one, which was used as a leper colony. They were famous for their caves, dolphin sighting, homes for the rich and famous, snorkelling and scuba diving, fishing, a bird sanctuary and coral reefs. The beaches were unspoilt and the islands were clean and very green. We did the usual: the girls did the food and the guys brought the drink. It was always a lovely occasion, as the guys who were single were very protective towards us youngsters. We always had such fun.

Another one of the highlights of my time in the civil service was being able to host many parties at my home. Girlfriends admired my family home and started to ask if we could have parties because it was so big and welcoming and had a gorgeous front garden. We asked Mummy and she said, "Of course, you can have as many parties as you like. Just make sure you protect my parquet flooring. I don't want to see any holes from high-heeled shoes in my floor."

Well, we thought we were in heaven. A group of us then measured the size of the living room. We bought enough linoleum to cover the entire floor and we were away. At the end of each party, we would clean it and roll it up and store it at the back of the house.

At one point we had a party almost every weekend. Our rule was the girls provided the food and the guys dealt with the drink. My mother always caused a stir. She was very slim and well dressed and she blended into the crowd so easily. She never complained or said anything in anger to anyone, mainly because my friends were all so well behaved. They were always shocked when I pointed her out at the party. She was considered really cool and I loved that. Mum always said that she enjoyed being around them. The parties certainly helped to cement our friendships that developed into strong relationships and even marriage. It is truly uncanny, because this is the same way that my life progressed with my own children. I was well known and respected by their friends and I was part of all their lives.

CHAPTER NINE:
Answering The Call

During my life in the civil service, I joined a dance group which was an addition to one of the most famous groups in the country. This dance teacher came to the Ministry of Education looking for willing participants to help him form another branch of his dance school. I loved the idea and many of us were fresh out of school and interested. I loved music and dance anyway, as that was all we had. My favourite was Nancy Wilson, who sang a beautiful song called 'How glad I am'. I thought everything that was aired was so exceptional. The disc jockey would give a detailed history of the artist and the recent song they were singing. There were other singers, such as Chubby Checker singing 'The Twist'. We also had to learn the dance moves for the twist. We also heard Ike and Tina Turner, James Brown, Percy Sledge, Al Green and the Temptations. My mother would get me to sing any song that she and her friends had heard for the first time.

Of course, as Trinidadian born, you were expected to learn to wine to calypso music, which was our form of social commentary. It was a famous genre of our international carnival celebrations that we hold every year. This tradition has been in place for more than 200 years, during the years of slavery and since then, a celebration of the emancipation of slavery.

Trinidad and Tobago have a very interesting history. They are the most southerly of the Caribbean islands, with Venezuela off the west coast, Grenada to the north and the Atlantic Ocean on the east. It was inhabited by the Caribs and Arawaks who were native and indigenous to the Caribbean before the islands were discovered by Christopher Columbus on behalf of the Spanish. It changed hands over the centuries between the Spanish, French, Dutch and English. The British and Spanish established a roaring slave trade, with slaves from the continent of Africa, who brought all their cultures and traditions with them. During slavery, they would mock the traditions of their slave masters and these traditions have remained to this day as part of the annual carnival season. The emancipation of slavery continues to be celebrated as an appreciation of the legacy left by the forefathers.

The reputation in the civil service at the time was that no one left voluntarily, so it was seen as a place to have a job for life. I certainly loved the job and the exciting social life that surrounded it, but I couldn't do it for the rest of my life. Office work was not my dream job. If I was really honest, I was not particularly interested in boys or having a boyfriend. I think the scaremongering of my mother lived on in my head. Even though I was now a young adult, at 19 years old, I felt very childlike, with no romantic experience of dealing with male adults. My mother never let up and remained fully focused on our lives and comings and goings. I was also beginning to find out that some of my friends from school were getting boyfriends. We started to meet these men and get introduced to them.

My friend Esther met her partner in church and became engaged very quickly. Then I met Peter, who was the manager at a local pharmacy where I had gone to buy items for my mother. He was drop-dead gorgeous and six foot four, with lovely eyes and a slim, rocking body. I would laugh nervously when he tried to chat me up. He would tell me how beautiful I was and invite me out, but I resisted for some time. I had no sense of my own personality or beauty, so it was very difficult to respond to this charm offensive. I simply gave him my number and invited him home. Mummy said very little, but my brothers and sisters thought he was cool. Over time, I realised he was more about having fun than about being serious. I thought that this was not entirely unexpected, knowing that he was only slightly older than me. I was far too heavy and serious at the time! I took some time to tell him that I was planning to study abroad. It was still all in my head then, but I had no intention of changing my mind, so it didn't matter if he was serious or not. Mum was happy for him to come to our home and sit and chat with me, because I was banned from going to his home.

He would take me to the cinema and I would meet his friends and his brother and sister, who were lovely people. Peter was a beautiful soul who had a wild, adventurous streak about him. He was also very funny and told me a story about an incident with his mother. He was two years older than me and lived at home with his parents and brother and sister. He was the youngest, so he was heavily supervised, as I was. His mother would reprimand him about staying out late, and would tell him, "Don't come home late at night or you will be in big trouble." So, one night after a party, he went on with his friends to another party, and finally got home at 6 a.m. His mother was ranting as she thought something bad had happened to him. Before she could continue, he stopped her and said, "Mum, I wasn't disobeying you. You said I shouldn't come home late at night, so I came home first thing in the morning." He said she was so taken aback that they all just laughed and he apologised for worrying her all night.

Finally, that day of reckoning came. Mummy was clearly getting fed up with me and my socialising. She started to ask me about my plans for the future now that I had finished my studies. Anyone would think that I was a 30-something old maid! She kept saying, "You think that life is one big party. It's time that you get serious and make plans for your future."

She complained that I spent so much money on taking pictures and giving them all away to my friends. I also bought quite good cameras because I really loved photography.

Another complaint was that she was hardly at home a few minutes before I was off with her car and I never bothered to put petrol in it. We called it 'gas'. I remembered that I couldn't wait to turn 18. I started driving lessons on my birthday and passed my test within four months. I suddenly became the responsible adult, because some of my friends were not allowed out unless I was going as well.

Over time, I started to think seriously about training as a nurse. As I mentioned before, I was in awe of my mother and the obvious pleasure and passion she had for her work. I felt it was a rewarding and noble career. I started to talk to my many aunts at the hospital and they were thrilled about the idea. They all said that I had to train in London as it was the best place to train, and my qualifications would be accepted all over the world. I was advised to go to the Ministry of Health, who were recruiting for training jobs in England. I started to get excited at the prospect of travelling abroad and returning home with new qualifications and a career. My plans in my head were to travel throughout as much of Europe and Asia and Africa as I could before returning home.

Mum went with me to the Ministry. We were told that the British government was inviting male and female subjects from the colonies to train as nurses and midwives. This was in order to rebuild England after the country was ravaged by the Second World War. The newly formed NHS (National Health Service) was also suffering, as there was a huge shortage of nurses and midwives. The NHS was unique and forward-thinking about the health of the nation. The rationale was that all citizens should have free healthcare available to them at the time of need. This would improve the physical and mental health of the citizens. This was called creating a social welfare state.

As part of the process, I was interviewed by the officials at the ministry. They asked many questions about my reasons for wanting to train as a nurse and the usual questions about my abilities and future plans within the profession. I explained that my passion was to be like my mother, who loved her job as a nurse and midwife. I explained that I was encouraged to study in England by my mother and her peers, who were sisters and matrons at the hospital, because the training is of a high standard and recognised worldwide, so I could practise anywhere in the world. I would also take the opportunity to explore the world and learn how other communities lived, before returning home to join the health service.

A few days later, I was told that I was successful and was invited back to make arrangements for my training. I was given a full explanation of how the process would be conducted. I was shown lots of literature about many training hospitals across the country and was invited to choose one school. I was told that my nursing training would last for three years and my midwifery would last one year. Also, the hospital provided accommodation, and I would be expected to 'live in', as they called it, throughout my training. The training would consist of being taught in the classroom and practical, hands-on learning in the clinical ward areas. I immediately said that I would train in the city of London.

My secondary school education was entirely based on the British system, so I had a full working knowledge of the history of England. I had learnt so much about London and the beautiful historical buildings, so I believed London would be an exciting place to live. I also felt that I would have travelled 5,000 miles to get to London, which was certainly far enough. I couldn't imagine moving any further afield and living in the countryside. The official was very helpful and actually recommended a hospital in north London that had a good reputation for its training. It was also well known for having the highest numbers of black and ethnic minority staff from the Caribbean and Africa. He suggested that I might feel happiest there and more at home.

So, I was on my way, having answered the call. The officer at the ministry made all the arrangements with the British government and with the training school at the hospital. We also had to look at the schedule of training that the hospitals advertised, and we agreed a date for me to start my training, which was after the celebration of my twenty-first birthday.

At the same time, the whole of Trinidad received the life-changing news from the government that they intended to reclaim the American naval base called Chaguaramas on the north-west part of the island and return the area to the local community. This land was leased to the American government by the British before Trinidad and Tobago became an independent state. The lease was meant to last for ninety-nine years, but the prime minister at the time, Dr Eric Williams, was incensed about the arrangement and fought for its return. Once the country became independent, the British no longer had a say. There were mixed feelings about this massive change, as we had a wonderful relationship with the Americans. As part of these negotiations, the American government was very generous and offered all families of locals who worked for them permanent residence in America, including children who were younger than 21, should they wish to move to a place of their choice, anywhere in America. This was a mind-blowing gesture, giving immense opportunity to families that was beyond comprehension.

We had family meetings to discuss the opportunities and possibility of living abroad, as opposed to staying at home in the Caribbean. Because they were younger than me, they talked about going to school in America and the issues that would raise. My brothers and sisters were both excited and apprehensive about it. At the time, we had friends who were already living in America, so my parents got busy asking questions. While I was still at home and able to look after my young siblings, my parents travelled to New York for a holiday and fact-finding mission.

The idea of living in America had never been part of our life's plan until then. Mum and Dad thought it would be a wonderful way to live and have a fulfilling career. I was not considered as part of these plans because I was already approaching 21 years of age and the criteria excluded me because of my age. Also, I had already made plans to travel to London to start my nursing training. We talked about the possibility of me joining the family in America after I finished training in London. Secretly, life in America never appealed to me. I had no particular reason, but I resolved that when I finished my training I would take the opportunity to join the family.

My mother and I had a really interesting conversation during one of our discussions about the future. I pointed out: "I am astounded that you are so happy about me going to England on my own, because you are so focused on our lives and needed to keep tabs on our every move. How are you going to do that with me in London? I could do anything that I wanted once I got to London and you would be none the wiser."

She quietly and simply said: "No, no, no; you would not do anything you want. You were well brought up and you know the difference between right and wrong, so you will do what is right. I am confident about that."

That was such a strong and profound statement to make, and she was so right about it. I was called snooty and a snob because of my strong views about certain issues. I would never back down about my beliefs.

Although Peter was an important person in my life, I had no intention of involving him in my plans or decisions. He was lovely, but I did not imagine our relationship would last or develop into anything meaningful. He was a party animal like me, but he was not particularly interested in furthering his education or establishing himself in a vocation or career, and he liked flirting with women. I realised that I wanted different, meaningful things to happen to me in life. I wasn't prepared to compromise. After about six months of dating, he started to talk constantly about sex. He was flabbergasted that I was still a virgin at my age. I think he wanted to prove that it was true. I did give in, and it was the worst experience of my life. I truly regretted that decision, especially as I couldn't face my mother, who eventually guessed what had happened. She never relented in expressing that she was truly disgusted and disappointed with me.

The time for my trip to London was getting closer and closer. My decision caused quite a stir in the office. My work colleagues could not believe that I was leaving my cushy job to go to London to study nursing. I had already been promoted twice in two years, so my job for life was certainly guaranteed. Despite the shock, they were all genuinely pleased for me and wished me luck. They begged me to keep in touch and keep them informed about the motherland. I was humbled and felt honoured by the office leaving party and the many gifts I received from my work colleagues. My friends were also interested in my choice of going to England. Normally, America and Canada were the countries of choice for pursuing academic studies, but I explained that England was the best for nursing studies.

Around the same time, my best friends were all busy establishing their careers as well. Carol decided to go to college in New York. She was sponsored by a family, which I understand was the simplest way to gain legal status in the country. Vera went to New Hampshire to study law. Esther was halfway through her nursing training at home. Pat, the most brilliant and clever of us all, had secured an Island Scholarship to study medicine in Scotland. I was the last person in my special group to begin work on establishing my career. I always seemed to be the one saying goodbye and seeing people off at the airport. It was now my turn to go.

I have realised that in all my descriptions of my life, I have not mentioned my dad's brother, who lived in London. I had never met him at that point, because he left Trinidad as a teenager to join the army to fight for Britain during the Second World War. I learnt that he actually joined the Royal Air Force and was stationed in many different locations around Europe. My dad was his younger brother and he was not married when my uncle left. Our only contact with him was the cards he sent to us on all special occasions. He never wavered from this and our whole family looked forward to these special cards. We did have a telephone, but any calls from him were occasional. What fascinated me was that he and my dad never saw each other again after the time he first left home. My uncle had a wife and two sons, so there was also the sharing of family pictures between him and us. Uncle never returned home or ever brought his children to visit his homeland. It may have been that, because his wife was an English woman, she would not visit or allow her children to travel.

Once my birthday was out of the way, my mother started to talk about my trip abroad. She started to sew and this took on a whole new meaning to me. I researched what the weather would be like and the type of clothes most suitable to wear. Inside, I was frightened to death about what I would be facing. It was so far away from family and friends. I was asking myself more and more questions, most of which I couldn't answer. Was it going to be worth it to go so far away to study, when I could stay at home and do the same? I had to remind myself that I had a dream to train in the motherland, because that would open up so many possibilities if I wanted to live and work anywhere in the world. I also had the dream to travel and explore different parts of the world. I imagined it would be easy to do so from a similar part of the world. I particularly wanted to visit France because of my love for the French language. I was a great fan of the subject of geography, so I also wanted to experience some of the phenomena recorded in different parts of Europe and Asia, for example, the Black Sea, Suez Canal, the Eiffel Tower, the fjords in Sweden and Norway. I decided that I was ready, as I had made up my mind that this was my way forward and I should be embracing it and get prepared for the journey.

CHAPTER TEN:

Getting The Key To The Door

My departure date had to be after my twenty-first birthday, as this was a milestone I wanted to share with my friends and family. This I did in great style with lots of my family and friends, from my school, my office, church and dance class. They were everywhere at home – in the living room, dining room, garden and garage. My mum made me the loveliest outfit of a red wrap long skirt and a white sequined blouse. My aunt, the chef, made most of the wonderful food we served, including my birthday cake. My brother's band played some of the music we danced to.

I had an interesting incident during the party, in that my so-called boyfriend did not turn up until very late. I was furious, but I refused to let it interfere with my happiness on the night. He probably realised that I would soon be gone and didn't care. My dear friends rallied around, as they were equally annoyed with him. They asked another potential suitor who was trying to win my affection, and he readily agreed to cut the cake with me. Cutting the cake was an important tradition, especially at a significant birthday like your eighteenth or twenty-first. It signified that you were capable of attracting a partner who was special to you and had the potential to be a serious part of your life. At the time of your party, if you didn't have a boyfriend, it was your choice to find someone you liked who was unattached and who would agree.

We had an amazing time, and it was well worth waiting the year for this experience. I was thrilled and so honoured when my darling Uncle Tony put an announcement about my party in the daily newspaper in the social column. This was wonderful for me, as this is not normal for mere mortals like me, but is for the rich and famous.

I was booked to leave for my training to start in May 1969 the following year. I was still feeling high after the excitement of my party when I realised I needed to start my preparations. I need not have worried, because I could always depend on my incredible mother to pull a magic trick out of the bag.

You will remember my horror when she demanded money from me when I started my job. Well, she suddenly appeared with this bank book and presented it to me, saying this was the rent that I had been paying to her for the last two years. It showed several thousands of dollars had been paid into an account in my name. It just seemed like so much money, more than I ever gave her. She stated, "I didn't want your money, but I wanted you to be aware of how important it was to save and put money aside for a rainy day."

I was shocked and so humbled by this. I thought she was the most remarkable and visionary person I had met. I was so delighted, as I had money to buy necessary clothes and items for travel, such as suitcases. I was also able to pay for my airline ticket to London via New York and have spending money in New York and still come to

London with some cash. I felt so proud to be able to do this for myself and not be totally dependent on my parents. I would never have managed this without her help.

However, this was not the end of this saga. I had informed my grandmother, who lived with us, about my impending trip to London to study nursing. She was so happy for me and thought I was very brave. One day she asked me to come to her room, as she had a gift for me. To my astonishment, she too presented me with a huge roll of money. She was a pensioner and I was intrigued and asked where the money came from. She said she had been saving it since I told her about my trip. I was truly lost for words, but I felt so very privileged and humbled and special that she thought of doing something so amazing for me. I hugged her and thanked her and cried for hours.

The first part of my celebration farewell was deciding to 'play mas' for the whole carnival weekend. Playing mas means taking part in the masquerade, by dressing up in costume. So, I was given the freedom to stay by my friend Gemma in town to take part in the carnival weekend. I had explained to Mum that I didn't know when next I would return home, so I wanted to have a long and lasting memory of playing mas for the first time, and I believed at home was the best place to get this experience. A few friends and I attended the Dimanche Gras show on Sunday night. This was the big, elaborate finale show of the carnival season where there were performances by all the finalists across two genres for the winner of the crown. There were calypsonians and the Kings and Queens of Carnival. The other genre is the steel band competition, but this final was held the night before.

Then we went back to Gemma's home to rest and eat and get ready for J'ouvert, which is French for "the opening of the day". In Trinidad, it starts about 4 a.m. as a celebration of our ancestors and as a celebration of our freedom from slavery. Those taking part always cover themselves in mud, paint, and oil as a symbol of remembrance to their slave forefathers. There are also traditional characters including blue devils and Moko Jumbies, who all represent and re-enact different aspects of a life of slavery and the subsequent emancipation of slavery.

After playing until about 8 a.m., we left for home as we were playing in a costume band in what is called Monday mas. We had to meet the band for 11 a.m. I remember we had such a job washing off all the mud and paint from our skin. We got dressed in our fancy sailor costumes and left to join the band. Costumes on Monday mas were much less elaborate than on Tuesday. Masqueraders can wear anything chosen by their band, from fancy sailors or T shirts and hats and shorts and crop tops. We were well looked after, as the band provided a package which included food, drink, music and security for its members.

After a few hours, we had to go home. We had not slept since Saturday night and had to get some rest to survive playing mas on Tuesday. We had an early start, as we had to meet the band at 8 a.m. Our costumes were much more elaborate and colourful. We were signed up with one of the popular costume bands. We had the most amazing time, dancing in the streets. Gemma was delighted for the experience because she was booked to leave after me to study physiotherapy, also in England.

When we had fully exhausted ourselves and returned, Gemma asked her cousin's fiancé to take me to my home. My mother was delighted to see me after three days away.

At the same time, my parents had decided they would be moving the family over to America. You will remember that my family were blessed with the gift of a smooth passage to America by being given permanent residency, because my father worked for the Americans in Trinidad. You may remember that Prime Minister Eric Williams requested the return of the area of land on the north-west of Trinidad. The history was that Trinidad was a British colony at the time, and the British government agreed a ninety-nine year lease in 1944 with the US.

My father had planned to go to New York in May as well, because he had been given an offer of a job. We planned that I would travel to London via New York and he would show me around the city. I was so delighted and saw this as the first leg of my overseas adventure. So, after a number of farewell parties and office celebrations and quite a group of friends seeing me off at the airport, I left home for New York in early May 1969 and went on to London. I was scared and worried about my life ahead, but I was determined to enjoy the journey. I arrived in New York and was met by my father. I was very happy to see him and excited about the chance to bond with him, because I was conscious we were not very close.

New York was awe-inspiring and felt majestic and overpowering. It was covered with skyscrapers that were beautiful and elegantly designed. There were also towering blocks of flats that looked like expensive homes for the rich and famous, but there were also parts of the city that looked derelict and barren. There were many abandoned houses and mounds of rubbish around. Manhattan was the area of abundance and riches. It was full of amazing shops selling very expensive designer clothes and jewellery and shoes. It also housed all of the theatres in Broadway and had the famous Times Square.

My father was so amused by my reaction of awe and wonder, as of course he was used to it, having been there for some weeks already. My ten days in the city turned out to be so exciting with my father. He said he was very proud of his first daughter, who was establishing a career for herself and headed for training in London. I really appreciated his comments. We had a lovely bonding time together, more than we had ever had before. We planned our tourist journeys during the day, and on some of the evenings we visited family and friends. One of our visits was to the United Nations Building in downtown Manhattan. It reminded me of my earlier dreams in school when I longed to become a French-speaking interpreter working at the United Nations. We visited the Chrysler building, the Empire State Building, Times Square and Central Park. We visited the Statue of Liberty but had to take a ferry across the river to the island. We also went to Staten Island to visit his friends. This was one of the New York boroughs, but we had to take the Staten Island ferry across to the island. It was such a lovely place, so different from New York. It was so clean and green and quiet and our friends talked about going to the beach out there.

In Manhattan, we visited some of the department stores that were huge but beautiful and inviting. My father's sister had moved to New York already, so we were able to visit her and my cousins. My godmother also lived there, but she had been there for some time. This is where my dad was staying, as she lived in a huge family house that she shared with her sister and her family and her daughter. During my stay, I was able to pick up that life could be very difficult and lonely in New York. Most people worked at two jobs and lived in private accommodation. Some housing seemed of a poor standard, others looked of very high quality. Very few people we knew drove cars, so travelling around the city was a long and tiring process. Everyone travelled with their head in a book or newspaper. The subway was intriguing to me, and I soon learnt that you had to go into the city always, in order to go out again. There were so many smaller lines that ran off the main lines. You have to know in which part of the train you have to sit, otherwise you will exit the train in a completely different place to what you intended. The trains had continuous carriages, so if you realised that you had made a mistake, you could easily walk through the train from one end to the other to reach your correct exit point. This was a very special holiday with me and my father that will remain a very fond and indelibly printed memory. I was so happy to be with him and bond with him so smoothly.

CHAPTER ELEVEN:
"Leave Them To God"

Now I was suitably refreshed and relaxed from my holiday in New York, I felt ready for the hard work of training as a nurse and midwife in London. I arrived at Heathrow Airport and, after collecting my luggage, I sat and waited to be picked up. This was an early morning, as all flights are overnight ones from America. After a while, I was beginning to become concerned, as no one had come for me. I checked the papers I had, but there was nothing with any instructions and there were no contact details for the hospital. I was approached by this black man who sounded Jamaican, called Fitzroy. I knew the accent because, at home, I had friends from Jamaica who were attending the university there. He said he had noticed me there for a while and wondered what the problem was. I explained I was waiting for someone from the Whittington Hospital to pick me up, as I was starting my nurse training there the following week. I was relieved and delighted when he said I shouldn't worry. He knew the hospital well and had a close friend there. He would take me if I was still there when his fiancée landed from Los Angeles. When his fiancée arrived, I was still there, so he took me to the hospital via west London, where we stopped to have lunch.

When we arrived, he took me to the reception in the nurses' home and went to find his friend who was training there. At the reception, I was met with shouts of joy and relief. I learnt they had been worried and panicked about me, because I was supposed to have taken a coach from Heathrow Airport to Victoria, where officials from the hospital would have met me. They had made several trips to the coach station looking for me in case my flight was delayed. They were so relieved to see me and I was so embarrassed about causing such confusion. I could not apologise enough for my stupidity. I realised that I had not read the instructions, which I had clearly forgotten in New York. The hospital staff could not believe my luck at meeting a complete stranger all the way out at the airport, who would actually know about the hospital and have a friend there.

Eventually, my friend Fitz brought his friend Evadne, who was training there. She was a beautiful and very slim woman with lots of natural hair. She gave an aura of great self-confidence and was really friendly. We were introduced and have remained friends to this day. She was very sophisticated and worldly and knew many interesting people from all over the Caribbean. Many people who have heard the story thought that I lost my mind to go with a stranger like that. I only thought about it later, but at the time, I was really innocent and naively trusting of everyone. I believed that everyone was honest and honourable and caring towards each other. I thought that I was also a stranger to this man. I could have been a serial killer for all he knew, yet he still offered to help me. He was also picking up his fiancée, so I imagined we were both safe in his hands. Of course, thanks to my fashionista mother, I looked like a million dollars as well, so I must have appeared approachable and helpless.

As we travelled towards the hospital, I began to notice my surroundings. I was intrigued by the range of housing I saw. Some were large and detached with beautiful gardens and driveways, while others seemed to be stuck together. I was told they were called terraced houses. I had never seen anything like it before. At home in Trinidad, many houses were on their own, no matter how small they were, except where there were blocks of flats. The air was dark and grey, although it was mid-afternoon. I realised my expectation of what London was like was way off. At school, it sounded like an amazing place, full of historical landmarks and impressive buildings, and long, winding roads, with constant development going on to bring the city back to its former glory.

My new friend Evadne and the hospital officials took me to my room in the nurses' home. She stayed and helped to settle me. Evadne was in the second year of her training. Born in Jamaica, she came to London with her family when she was a young teenager. Evadne was very friendly and very beautiful. She told me as much as she could about the hospital, and we arranged to keep in touch.

On the first day of training, I was delighted to meet my fellow students. We were quite a varied bunch from all over the world. There were students from Jamaica, St Vincent, Nigeria, Ghana, Sierra Leone, Ireland, Guyana, England and Trinidad and Tobago. The most amazing thing about our group of thirty students was that there were sixteen of us from Trinidad and none of us knew each other, even though Trinidad is a small place with only a million residents. There was only one student from England, and she left the course during the first three months. We spent three months in the classroom learning anatomy and physiology relating to the human body. We toured the hospital, which was spread over many buildings on three sites. The work was full-on but most of us felt happy to be there.

However, the happiness was short-lived, as we soon started to get quite lonely. Some of the group had family in London, so they were able to visit them regularly. As we became closer to each other, some of us were invited to relatives' homes. This was such a wonderful way to get some good, home cooking to remind you of the Caribbean. We also learnt to eat and enjoy African food.

I soon worked out that there was a way to see everyone on a regular basis, and this was going for meals in the dining room. This idea didn't cost anything because, at the time, money was taken out of our salaries for meals, so we could go to one or to all the meals each day. The dining room was a large, clean and welcoming space and seemed to be open all the time. I think everyone else thought of the same idea, because soon most of us met there and chatted and ate and got to know each other. It was there that we found out from each other about social events like shopping trips to the West End and learning to navigate the confusing underground system, concerts, parties and what was on at the cinema. We met at breakfast between 7 and 9.30 a.m.; coffee was from 10 to 11.30 a.m.; lunch was from 12 to 2 p.m.; tea time was from 3 to 5 p.m.; dinner was from 6 to 8 p.m. and from 8 to 9 p.m. for staff going on duty at night.

Eventually, meeting there turned out to be a very bad idea, because every single one of us became good friends, but we all put on huge amounts of weight. After the first six to nine months, I realised none of the clothes I brought with me fitted properly any more. I had gone from weighing 10 stone 10 pounds to 14 stone. It was a shock to the system to know that I had gained that much weight. The dining room was not to blame fully, because true West Indians/Caribbean people socialised around food, but of course the food at home was prepared differently and we ate a lot of fresh fruit straight off the trees. When we went out to homes or shopping trips, we also ate. The issue was that the English food was very different to food in the Caribbean. I had never eaten so many potatoes before, except in potato salad or curries, and that was about once or twice a week. We never had dessert, except on Sundays, but here you had it with lunch and dinner each day, with custard or cream or ice cream. When we had parties, we would go en masse to the dining room to make sandwiches for the party. The tables were set with an abundance of bread and butter and spreads for our enjoyment. When we had a party, we would sit on separate tables so we could maximise the amount of sandwiches we could take with us. Some of us tried to create the food we were used to cooking back home, but we had tiny kitchens in the nurses' home that were not very conducive to cooking. We also had difficulty finding the right ingredients, which was often unavailable. For example, it was impossible to find plantains, pigeon peas, saltfish and good quality rice at that time. These were rare commodities that cost an absolute fortune, if you were lucky enough to find them.

After three months, we were let loose on the clinical wards, and that is where the hard work began. My first ward was called a female surgical ward, where most of the patients had undergone abdominal surgery. The women were friendly and appreciated our work in getting them back on their feet. My greatest achievement was learning to successfully remove clips, which was a difficult procedure. Clips were placed across a wound to keep it closed so it could heal.

My next placement was an adult medical ward, but it was mainly full of older adults, who needed geriatric care. Immediately, I started hearing the racist comments from the patients, and this was horrifying for me. I have grown up with so many different races and colours of people at school and home in Trinidad. One of my closest friends in school was white. She was called Judy and we had the same birthday. Some of the patients would slap my hand away and say I was dirty. For example, "Don't touch me. Your dirt will rub off on me." They would ask if we lived in trees and built houses in them. How high did we go? Did we go to the toilet in the bushes? Did we ride donkeys to get around? What colour was my blood? I was so shocked by their ignorance and obvious lack of education. They asked where Trinidad was. Was it in Jamaica, in America or in Africa? They would say, "Why don't you go back where you came from? We don't want you here."

At first, I thought this was because they were ill and some were confused, but I soon realised they were all lucid, clear-headed and were serious with their abuse. The problem was that this behaviour continued all the time. Even when the patients changed, the new ones behaved the same way. It was very depressing, as I felt I was unable to do my work properly. When I reported this behaviour, the nursing staff were not really interested in helping, and whatever they said fell on deaf ears.

I felt so stupid responding to these ridiculous statements. After all, this was the twentieth century!

I called my mother at home in tears and complained about my experiences, which I described in great detail for her. I said how difficult it was to work and to feel useful. I said I didn't want to do it anymore and I wanted to go back home. Mum was very calm and asked me to try to be the same. She said, "There is nothing for you to come back to. You have a dream and a mission to fulfil and you should never be distracted from that purpose. Racism is other people's problem, not yours. You should never give anyone that type of power over you. You should find a way to deal with the problem, so that you can continue your training successfully."

I did feel better and reassured that I could handle these people. I kept thinking of what I could do. I spoke to other colleagues from my class. Some of them had similar experiences and they all had different ways of dealing with it. One friend was told to ignore the behaviour. Some staff told the patients they would not get care and would be sent home. Some got aggressive and used expletives. My friend Pearl, who was training as far afield as Nottingham, had the same experiences. She told me that she brought her family photo albums to the ward to show that we were very civilised, as we lived in brick houses with full living facilities, we drove cars, and we had large gardens full of fruit trees. She said her patients were shocked at her high standard of living in the Caribbean. They were oblivious to the fact the students training to nurse them were intelligent women who were educated and successful at their exams and had to meet a very high standard of education to qualify for this training. In my interview, the minimum requirement to train was six or more subjects at O level. These people clearly had no respect for the profession.

As I listened to these many accounts and responses, I suddenly had a brainwave about what I would do. The next time I went on duty, I made a firm stance in front of patients and staff. I stood in the middle of the ward and gave my speech. I said: "Please listen to me, as I am very distressed by your rudeness and racist taunts. I am black and have been black for the twenty-one years of my life. So surprise me; tell me something I don't know; tell me something new."

I was so impressed with this confident and assertive person saying these words. It was actually me. It was a pivotal moment in my life, because I suddenly felt this weight rising up from my shoulders. Everyone around looked stunned, especially the patients, who were unable to respond. From that point, the racism taunts fell on deaf ears. I never allowed it to bother me from then on, because I agreed with my mother that racism is the other person's problem. It was more important to me to know that there was no racism from the staff. They were seemingly more embarrassed than anything else. I realised there was no point struggling with such ignorant minds, as I was not starting the battle on a level playing field. Also, my upbringing did not allow me to be rude or disrespectful, even though they were being so with me. I remembered that, at home, the elders would say, "Leave them to God."

CHAPTER TWELVE:
Finding My Feet In The "Motherland"

Life took on a whole new meaning. I began to enjoy my work more than ever. I walked away when I heard the abuse or waved my hands and said, "Whatever." I was often still able to provide the care needed to these patients. The staff remained very kind and supportive of my actions most of the time. I began to enjoy my social life much more. I was lucky to have friends who had friends already living in London. One of the girls in my class had a married brother who had been living there for a while, so I got invited to dinner parties at their home and other types of events. We did lots of sightseeing around London to familiarise ourselves with the city. To date, I have been to Madame Tussauds and the Planetarium nine times with visiting family and friends.

We also had a lot of attention paid to us by many different African men who were studying in London. They seemed to have a homing device that told them there was new blood around, and through a friend of a friend of a friend, we eventually started meeting these men. They were really delightful and charming men who were young, intelligent and going to university. They were studying law, medicine, architecture and banking. All of the men we met from the Caribbean started off working in the public services like London Transport, British Rail and the National Health Service. I met Ray, Carl, Edwin and Watts, who all worked with London Transport.

Eventually, they moved on and started to study in different professions. They too had answered the call to come to London to help rebuild the country after the Second World War, so some of us got very close to the men from the Caribbean, as we had similar backgrounds. I was always teased as I got a great deal of attention from our African male friends. They were adamant that I was Ghanaian because of my height and physical features, like my prominent cheek bones, large eyes and very black, smooth skin. I was flattered but, in my mind's eye, I had resolved that I would never marry anyone but a fellow Trinidadian. Because I showed no interest, I finally expressed this to my friends, and they were highly amused by my rationale. I explained that I loved my country, its people, its culture and our celebration of the emancipation of enslaved people, and I didn't run away to make a better life. I chose to come to London to start my career and help with the rebuilding of the NHS and explore countries on this side of the world. When I chose to marry, I wanted a fellow partner with a similar background with similar views. I wanted to teach our children about our heritage so they fully understood their history and family culture. I wanted my children to have strong family ties and an appreciation of the legacy left for them and a strong sense of their identity, so they would grow up to be solid, all-round citizens.

My friends were staggered and concerned for me. They said most West Indian men, never mind Trinidadians, were either too old, married, spoken for or just unattractive. They wished me luck, as they didn't understand where I would find someone suitable. I didn't know how it would happen either, but I just knew that, somehow, it would.

I reunited with my friend Pearl, who had travelled to England a year before to do her training, but she settled in Nottingham. Pearl came to London to visit me as often as she could, even if I was on or off duty. She was a lovely person who was very stylish with her clothes and hairstyles. She had been my brother's girlfriend back home and they continued their relationship by letter and phone calls and visits to New York when he returned there from the navy. I was happy for her and excited to see how they progressed. We were just happy to be close with each other as friends from back home.

We loved dancing and became well known in social circles, as we were party animals. I was also flavour of the month for another reason: I was a non-drinker, so I would volunteer to drive. The guys were in disbelief with my offer, but would happily allow a woman to drive their cars. I just had to be shown the way to our destination and I could accurately take us back home. So I became the designated driver for my friends, with the satnav in my head, way back in the early 70s! I was truly lucky to have nurtured a group of amazing friends around me, from my own group of students to several others from more senior and more junior groups in training. I continued my friendship with Evadne, the first person I met at the hospital. Julie went to the same school as me at home but she was in a higher class, so we have known each other since I was 12. Jean was a special friend in my class. She was the person who lived closest to me at home, but we had never met. She met her partner Ray almost as soon as we started training. They became serious very quickly and she moved out during our training. It was lovely to go to her home to hang out with them. We have remained friends to this day and she and Ray have been married for fifty years.

Donna was a beautiful friend from Jamaica. She and Julie and Elsa were close, as they were in the same class. Pat was also one in the group and she met and married Carl during our training. Gail was already married to Andrew when I met her. She moved out of London toward the end of her training, so she had a lot of travelling to do. We devised a plan for her to maximise her study time, so I would test her regularly on past papers. She would come to my room in the nurses' home and we would study, either before she started a shift or at the end of her shift before she set off for home.

As time went on, our friendships developed into solid ones and we were involved in each other's lives and growing families. My closest friend outside of my nursing colleagues was Pat, who was studying medicine in Scotland. She was a true scholar. We went to the same school, but she stayed on to do A levels. She had gained an A grade in every exam she ever did and won a government scholarship to do medicine in Scotland. She, too, met her partner at university. As she progressed in her studies, she became engaged to him and they got married soon after.

I continued my training with pride and enthusiasm once I dealt with the abusers. I started to date a lovely African from Sierra Leone who was doing postgraduate work in architecture. He was a patient of mine, as he was admitted on my ward for treatment of malaria.

He was so handsome and tall with a mass of curly hair, as he was mixed race with a Lebanese father and African mother. He had also just moved to London, so it was fun exploring some of the city with him and meeting his family and friends, especially his sister, who was a beautiful and gentle person. I knew we would never be life partners, because we both had the idea that we wanted to marry someone from our own country, but it was a wonderful way to socialise and meet new people. I was invited to many African weddings and celebrations throughout the time I spent with him.

During my first year of training, I learnt that my brother Arthur had moved to New York to join our dad. Immediately, he was extremely lucky to find a good job. He was recruited to a job in Wall Street as a dealer in stocks and bonds. At that time in the 70s, America was heavily invested in the Vietnam War. It was mandatory for all young men to register at the selector service as the army was drafting to fill vacancies. They would send him to train immediately and, once he was finished, he would be shipped off to Vietnam. I remember that my parents and my brother were very scared about him going to war. In the meantime, our dad knew a senior official in the navy, who advised that my brother should apply to the navy as well so he had more options. We all secretly and consistently prayed that his navy application would be processed quickly. Thankfully, this is exactly what happened and he was able to join the navy the day before he was supposed to start in the army. We were all grateful and so relieved. He spent two years of active service in the navy in Nevada and four years' inactive service, during which the armed forces could call him back to serve. During his service, he worked for the Construction Battalion as a driver and mechanic of all types of cars, equipment and machinery.

Once he became inactive, he returned to his job on Wall Street. The law at the time stated that if someone had a job before he was enlisted, the employer had to keep the job open. My brother was never called back to active service, so he remained working on Wall Street until his retirement.

I had an enlightening experience in meeting a wonderful woman called Sheila. She had restarted her nursing training and had joined me on the first ward I worked on. We became friends immediately and worked well together. One day she asked me to share a double room with her in the nurses' home. We were successful in acquiring the room and we spent many happy months there. She had to give up her training several years before because she kept getting repeated bouts of bronchitis that were affecting her health. She was advised to move to a warmer, drier climate for her lungs to heal. She chose to work in southern Italy as a nanny. She had now returned to complete her training. My black friends were curious about my association with this white woman, but I saw her as a lovely human being who could probably give me more insight into white lives in this country. I had no problem being her friend and learning from a decent human being, regardless of their colour.

We had an amazing time. She was very knowledgeable, so when we hitched rides around the country, she knew exactly which offers to accept. She was the only person I trusted to go hitch-hiking with. We hitched to Middlesbrough, Bristol, Bath and Birmingham, all areas where her fiancé's family and her family lived. I got used to people staring at me and asking her who I was and where I came from. We travelled in a wide range of vehicles, from lorries to luxury cars.

My next overseas adventure was when Sheila and I went to Libya in North Africa, to visit her fiancé, who was teaching English there. We chose to break up our journey to reduce the cost of the airfare, so we flew to Malta and spent a day there before flying on to the capital, Tripoli. While in Malta, we met a lovely local who showed us around the island and shared dinner with us. We left the next day for Tripoli, which was an experience on another level. It was 1970, the year after the coup led by Colonel Gaddafi, so the country was in a strange political flux. They were suspicious of everyone. The country is Muslim and no one was allowed to drink alcohol. The Libyans could not mix with the Americans who lived and worked and travelled from the American air base of Wheelus on the Mediterranean coast, near Tripoli. The Libyans knew that the Americans supplied drinks to the British teachers living in the city, but they could never prove it. Instead, they would try to harass normal civilians like us on the road by stopping our car so many times along the road and searching it for alcohol. It was tedious but funny as well, as most of us were very tipsy at those times, as we were usually travelling to and from parties. We stayed with a wonderful couple, Pete and Gay, and this is where I discovered Simon and Garfunkel, the most wonderful musicians I had heard for a long time. *Bridge Over Troubled Water* was their hit album at the time, and everyone I met in Tripoli was going crazy about it. I heard the album every day for two weeks and soon knew all the words to the songs. As soon as I returned to London, I bought my own copy.

The next year, I was honoured to be asked to be Sheila's bridesmaid at her wedding, the first black bridesmaid seen in the north, as Sheila was married in her home town of Middlesbrough. We hitched up the motorway to Middlesbrough to Sheila's parents, Ted and Ruth. I was first measured, then a few weeks later I went back for a fitting. It was a lovely experience, including all the staring from the local people and from some guests at the wedding.

My friend Pearl and our African friend, Tony, were invited and we planned that Tony would pick us up about 5 a.m. to drive us up the motorway to Middlesbrough, taking about four to five hours. It seemed like madness, but I was determined to make it happen. I couldn't let my friend down. I couldn't get time off and I didn't want to lie and go on sick leave. To make it worse, I had to work the night before, but I persuaded my colleagues to let me off at 5 a.m. Tony and Pearl stayed at a party until the same time. We all got ready in my room, and then set off to drive for five hours to Middlesbrough. We just made it at 11.45 a.m. for a noon ceremony. There were four of us as bridesmaids – Pattie, Christine, Jane and me. Our dresses were in a lovely lilac colour and we looked gorgeous. We partied until midnight, when we left to drive back to London, via Nottingham, where we had to drop Pearl off at her hospital. I managed to catnap for the few hours to Nottingham. We all got there feeling and looking like death warmed up. So we had options – sleep in Nottingham by Pearl or in the car, or I would have to drive to London, while allowing Tony to get some sleep, as he was passing out with tiredness. I was equally tired, but I chose to drive, so my designated driver status kicked in again. I agreed to wake Tony up after an hour, but I drove all the way into London about three hours later. He was staggered, but grateful for the sleep. I think I was even more grateful and thankful to have survived it all, bearing in mind I did all this on a provisional driving licence. I could drive since I was 18, but it was not recognised here. With a provisional licence, I could drive for up to a year, if I had a registered driver with me at all times.

As soon as Sheila completed her training, she travelled out to Libya to live with her husband, who was still teaching there. Some years later, she returned home via London because she was expecting their first child. We had a wonderful reunion, catching up with life since we had previously met. I was delighted to hear that she had a baby boy some months later. I saw pictures of him, but time and distance caused us to lose touch with each other.

After a few months of settling down and dealing with the racists, I contacted my uncle, who was my father's brother. When he left in the early 40s to join the air force, his brother, my father, was not married. I remember through my childhood that we received countless cards and pictures of his English wife and mixed-race sons for all our birthdays, Easter and Christmas. When we met, he looked very much like my dad. He was very tall and quite thin and not at all how I expected him to be. He was lovely but quite eccentric. His sons and his wife were very friendly. His younger son was gorgeous and looked exactly like Jimi Hendrix, hair and all. He picked me up to take me to his home. They lived in a terraced house in Mornington Crescent, an area that has now been demolished, as the houses were old and becoming derelict. The house was full of memorabilia and many pictures of our family and my cousins. I was really impressed at how consistent he was in keeping in touch with his family.

On my first visit, I realised there was no bathroom in the house. I was very surprised and very discreetly, I asked my uncle about it. He said that they washed at the kitchen sink, which was a huge, deep ceramic one during the week, then went to the community baths on Caledonia Road at the weekend. I was shocked that someone from the Caribbean didn't bathe every day, because I still had the old-school mentality about the way we lived back home. I had to realise that my uncle had a different way of living that suited his lifestyle. He was so delighted to see me and hear about Trinidad and his brother and my family, his sisters and mother. He told me stories of his life in the forces and how scary it was going to war and not knowing if you would ever return.

He and his wife took me to Petticoat Lane to see the Pearly Kings and Queens, and to Southend-on-Sea, where I enjoyed the legendary fish and chips eaten out of newspaper. On my first visit to Southend, I was a total embarrassment to everyone. We ordered burgers for lunch and I proceeded to get generous with the condiments. I smeared the mustard on as I assumed it was the French mustard I used at home in Trinidad. My uncle kept asking me if I was sure and I said I was. I also put on salt and black pepper and tomato ketchup. I was drooling at this point and I tucked into the burger. The shock in my mouth was immediate and overpowering. I spat the food all over the table and my aunt and uncle, as I had never tasted anything so awful. Then my uncle explained that I had used too much mustard. English mustard was different, and only a small amount at a time has to be used. To this day, I dislike English mustard intensely. The French mustard I was used to was mild and tasty. That was a really harsh lesson.

CHAPTER THIRTEEN:
Cause and Effect

My final exams were looming in June 1972. We were given one month's study leave in January and February before our exams in May. I decided I needed a holiday instead, so I went home for carnival for some rest and recuperation in between the fetes and carnival shows. My mother felt I should have stayed to do my studies, but she stated that she had a few things to tell me, so she was actually happy to see me.

First, she wanted to tell me about this amazing new way of life that she had been practising called Nichiren Shoshu Buddhism. She had been introduced to it by one of her nursing colleagues and had found strength and purpose in it. They were the only two people embarking on this practice, so they were actually founder members of it in Trinidad. When I asked why she had given up our Anglican religion, she explained, "The Anglican church seemed to have little meaning for me anymore. I think that the behaviour of many people in church left a lot to be desired. I believe that many of the people who profess to being pillars of the church behave in a most unholy way."

This form of Buddhism originated in Japan and their mantra is "Nam-Myoho-Renge-Kyo", which means the true essence of life. It is the Chinese translation of the Lotus Sutra. The lotus grows and blossoms in muddy waters and symbolises the blossoming of normal life. The mantra represents the eternal and unchanging truth, and advocates the principles of cause and effect. This Buddhism teaches that, in order to change the world, you have to change yourself first. It teaches that knowing ourselves by lighting up our lives will make us aware of our full potential rather than just our limitations. It teaches that Buddhism is all about your daily life and whatever causes you make in your own life, you will experience the effects later on. It seemed such a fascinating concept, and so different to the Anglican religion.

My mother's other piece of news was devastating, because she had discovered a lump in her breast some weeks before and was advised it may be cancer and she should have surgery as soon as possible. I immediately offered to look after her and the family while I was there. Of course, she hesitated and finally decided that it would be too stressful for me, and too difficult to organise in the time. Despite my attempt at persuading her, I had to leave before her surgery could be organised. I should not have been surprised by her selfless attitude and her concern about disrupting my holiday. It would have been a massive honour to help her, but I understood her thoughts that I should concentrate on my upcoming exams.

As well as my family disaster, the carnival itself was cancelled while I was there, because of the rising levels of cases of polio in the country.

I returned to work with a heavy heart, knowing that my mother was dealing with the possibility of having breast cancer.

I worked hard and prayed hard for the next few months until my final exams were over. In the meantime, Mum informed me that they had agreed to move the family over to America and she was busy planning the move. Her surgery was also imminent. One week after my exams, I was visiting Jean and Ray and my mother called, because they were recorded as my main contacts. She told me that she had completed the surgery and was recovering well. The surgery was called a radical mastectomy, which was a removal of the lump and half the breast tissue on the affected side and removal of the associated lymph nodes up into the armpit. The biopsy showed that she had cancer and she would need chemotherapy and radiotherapy.

She said to me that the family's move to America would help facilitate her chemotherapy, which she could have there. I was so relieved that I cried uncontrollably for a while. I knew Mum was very strong and was able to cope. She asked me to organise the delivery of flowers to the nursing home to say thanks from me for all that they had done for her. Mum was well known, as she nursed many private clients there or worked as a staff member for them. For her surgery in this very upmarket private facility, they waived all the charges for her procedures and her post-operative care. This was a magnanimous thing to do and the family was eternally grateful for this. It was a great pleasure to send them the flowers, with my undying gratitude. I just wished I was there close to her to give as much tender loving care as I could manage. I spoke to her as much as I could during her recovery. My master plan was going according to plan. I passed my final exam, so I became a bona fide nursing professional, and I was equally delighted to know that most of my friends passed as well. Those who didn't pass were given the opportunity to repeat the exam three months later. This meant that my place on the midwifery training programme was secure for February 1973.

I continued to work in neurosurgery, which was the speciality I enjoyed. One day, I took an unconscious patient to the examination room for a brain scan. I was bending over for a long time, attaching leads to his head. The head of an unconscious person is very heavy and difficult to hold up, so I could feel the weight in my back and legs. I had never been taught any techniques for back care of any kind during my training. As I stood up, I experienced a sharp, continuous and excruciating pain in my lower back and I couldn't straighten my back. I couldn't stop screaming and the whole department rushed to my aid.

I managed to sit in a wheelchair and was taken by ambulance to the A & E department, which was in another building on another site. I had never felt such pain before. I had to be heavily sedated and admitted to a ward. After different tests were done and X-rays and scans, I was told I had severely shattered the discs between L4 and 5 and L5 and S1. L stands for lumbar and S for sacral, which are the names of the bones in the lower spine. This meant that I had permanently damaged my lower back. The pain was unbearable, but there was very little to be done at that time. The pain and swelling had to subside before the doctors could decide the best way forward. I had to beg the staff to allow me to go home to rest in comfort. I had moved into a flat with my friends, Evadne and Pearl, so I was in the best hands possible.

Pearl had moved down to London after completing her training. She was about to embark on a theatre training course at Lewisham Hospital. I had to ask the landlord for a piece of wood to put under my mattress that would work as a fracture board, which allowed the mattress to remain immobile. When this was set up, I was allowed home with medication. For some time I was taking Fortral for pain relief and Valium, which is a muscle relaxant, like they were Smarties. These were strong, controlled drugs and the only ones that seemed to work for me. I was off work for many months and I was seriously concerned that I was at risk of missing the start of my midwifery training.

I saw the orthopaedic surgeons, who showed me the X-rays of my spine. The discs were so shattered they looked like they had exploded like confetti between the vertebrae. I was offered surgery called spinal fusion, which would fuse the vertebrae L4 to L5 and L5 to S1. The problem was that my spine is very long and curved, and this surgery only had a 40 per cent success rate. It was likely that the surgery would cause increased pressure on the other vertebrae above and below the fusion. These odds were certainly unacceptable to me and not worth the risk, as damage to my spinal cord during the procedure was a high possibility. I refused to consider the surgery as an option.

The other option was to be measured for a boned corset that would fit from my lower back at my coccyx to under my breast bone. I would have to wear this continuously when I was up and moving around. So this was how I started my training, wearing this awful garment in which I could hardly move. My midwifery tutor was very angry with me for not informing her of my injury, as she would never have allowed me to start my training. The pain was relentless, but I had no intentions of giving up at that stage. The first half of my course was a real struggle, because moving around the classroom and the clinical areas only seemed to aggravate the pain. I had to sit around a lot before the pain began to subside over a few months.

As I was struggling with my pain, my mother finally moved to New York with my brother Phillip and sisters, Patricia and Penelope. They were really excited to start their new lives, but very sad that they had to leave Granny behind, but I was told she was even more excited for the family to move abroad and was happy to stay behind with her other children.

I certainly didn't waste any time visiting my family in their new home. On the first holiday in my training in 1973, I visited them in New York. Of course, this was my second time there, so New York felt familiar. I was cheeky, pretending I could give them advice about settling in the city. We had such fun with this. I learnt even more about the city and managed to meet with some friends from school who had moved there previously. It was wonderful to reconnect with them and, in turn, connect them with my family, so they could provide advice and support. Thankfully, the pain from my injury remained subsided, so I could get around fairly easily.

One of the highlights of the trip was attending a Buddhist meeting with my mother. She was excited about developing her practice and knowledge of the religion. She encouraged me to start practising, so I went home willing to consider the practice as an option.

As my training progressed, my back pain lessened and I felt normal again for most of the time. I was able to remove the corset for long periods.

I made friends with other midwives, who remained friends for a long time. One of the highlights of my training was attending my friend Joy's wedding along with other midwives in the unit. Joy and I met during my training and worked well together.

I also had a funny and interesting conversation with one of the midwifery sisters in the unit. We were having lunch and she stated she was glad of the opportunity to talk to me. She said that she was shocked to know that I was an actual nursing student. When I started my training, she saw me with groups of people, which I think was when my class was given a tour of the hospital. She thought that I was a model or actress, working on a documentary to promote the NHS. When I asked why, she said, "You are so tall and beautiful and elegant. You stood out from the rest." I was relieved that she wasn't disappointed, as I didn't intend to disappoint.

My injury really took a negative toll on me, as I struggled to concentrate and work hard. I had considerable pain at times, but I had to manage it the best that I could. This resulted in me failing my exam in part two of the course. I was devastated and vowed to do better. I was not prepared to fail or give up on my dream. I was blessed to have the support and help from one of the midwifery sisters I worked with. Pat was a bubbly and really caring person and an experienced midwife who had worked in the unit for some time. I was worried and feared failure again and I was talking to her about it. She immediately offered to help me and we put a plan in motion. I would study, then I would go to her home for tutorials on the work I was studying. She was firm and relentless with her teaching and I was eternally grateful for her help and support. As I approached my exam, I felt confident of my success. On my second attempt, I knew that I had excelled at my oral exam because the examiner told me so. I was delighted to have passed the full exam and made sure I showed my gratitude and thanks to my friend Pat. We never socialised because she had family commitments, but we have managed to stay in touch to date.

I did consider that maybe my socialising and travel was not entirely conducive to studying effectively. During my training, I had travelled to Malta, Trinidad and Tobago, Antigua, New York, Germany, Belgium, Spain and France. My friend Evadne was always there for me and she also introduced me to her friends. She had some very intelligent and successful friends who were well qualified as architects, doctors, journalists, professional artists, lawyers and accountants. She discovered my love for live concerts, so I was always included when her partner and group of friends bought tickets for these spectacular shows. The first big show I saw was The Jackson 5 supported by the Fatback band. Throughout the years of my training and continuing into life, I succeeded in attending thirty live concerts of various celebrity artists like Dionne Warwick, Anita Baker, Lionel Ritchie, Ella Fitzgerald, MC Hammer and Bob Marley and the Wailers.

During my visit to New York, my mother continued to sow the seed that I should join them after my training was complete. It made sense, as my plan was always to return home to my family. As it turned out, home was now New York. I said I would consider it, although I was not particularly impressed with the city on the two occasions I visited, as I felt I would be isolated and stressed living there. I decided I would continue with my plan to study psychiatry, in case I decided to take the State Board Exam. This exam is mandatory across all states in America, as it allows an individual to practice. It is done in four parts: medicine and surgery; paediatrics;

obstetrics and gynaecology; and Psychiatry. Our plan was that I would join the family for Christmas 1974 and stay until I completed the first three parts of the exam in February 1975. Then I would return to London to complete the psychiatric course from March to September 1975, after which I would plan my final move to America around Christmas time.

CHAPTER FOURTEEN:
"And What Did You Say Your Name Was?"

They say life is what happens when you are busy making plans. After passing my midwifery exams, I offered to do night duty until I left for New York in December 1974. On one Saturday morning in November, I decided to do my shopping straight after work at 9 a.m. There was no urgency to sleep because I was off duty until Monday night. I met Shirley, who was a friend of a friend, and she invited me to join her in cooking and entertaining some friends who were visiting from Germany. I graciously accepted, as I knew she was an amazing cook and I wouldn't have to do it for myself. After a few hours' rest, I arrived at Shirley's home and met her friends, who were two young men living and running a business in Hamburg. We were all from Trinidad and were enjoying reminiscing about the place. I was intrigued that we had nationals living as far afield as Germany.

As the evening progressed, the guys invited us to join them at a birthday party they were attending that night. To my great delight,

I knew the birthday boy, Johnny, and where he lived. His wife had trained at the hospital and still worked there. He was a lovely, flamboyant character who drove an American Cadillac. He was pleasant and friendly and everyone knew him, especially when he was dating his wife, as he came to the hospital every day in his flash car. We agreed, and they left us about 7 p.m. to go to the shops to get drinks to take to the party. I left for home as well and they were meant to pick me up between 10.30 and 11 p.m. I waited and waited and finally changed my clothes to go to bed about midnight. Shirley herself was frantic and concerned that they were lost in London. They arrived about midnight, apologising profusely, as they were unable to find an open off-licence in the local area. They had to make their way from north London to central London before they found an open shop that sold alcohol. We were sorry, too, that we didn't know or we would have advised them differently. They begged me to reconsider, as they wanted to show their gratitude to Shirley, and she would not go without me. I relented and got dressed again, and we finally arrived at the party at 1 a.m.

It was an amazing party, and I connected with many friends, and the birthday boy and his wife. I was dancing up a storm when I realised I had not seen my friend Shirley for a while. I set out to look for her in the gorgeous, rambling house. I entered a room and saw her chatting with a tall, elegant man who was standing next to another man in a green, silk shirt open halfway down his smooth chest, and bottle green trousers and brown shoes. I froze when I saw him. He took my breath away. I had never seen anyone like him before. He had class, style, good taste and charisma personified. I was not holding my breath, but I couldn't breathe. My stomach was churning and it felt full of butterflies. I didn't understand what was happening to me, but I knew something major was going on.

Shirley saw me and waved me over. She introduced me to the man she was talking to, who excitedly told me of his recent travels and movies that he had been involved in. Neither of them introduced me to this mysterious man, so I knew that I had to find a way to speak to him. I was totally mesmerised by him. He had not spoken a word, but appeared to be so self-confident, even arrogant, yet assertive and gentle all at the same time. I thought that he had to be a Trinidadian! Suddenly I spoke, and turning to him I said, "And what did you say your name was?"

Without hesitation, he replied, "Well, actually, I didn't."

Wow! How rude and arrogant, I thought! I was so embarrassed by his response that I said sorry to him and cheerio to my friends and left the room. I realised that I had really fallen for this person who remained nameless. I didn't believe in all this love at first sight rubbish, but I am living and breathing proof that it exists. Who was he and where did he come from? As I got downstairs to the room where I was dancing, there was a tap on my shoulder and the person said, "May I have this dance, please?" When I turned around, it was him! This was Saturday the 23rd of November 1974. He casually said, "By the way, my name is Vernon."

I said, "So you do have a name, after all."

Everything seemed a blur after that. I felt like I was in a dream, floating around on air, not understanding what was going on. I felt as if I was inside a love story in a novel. From that moment on, we danced the rest of the night until the rigours of working the night before attacked me and I became truly exhausted. I said I needed to find my friends to ask when they were going home.

Shirley was in the kitchen and she was making bake and buljol. Bakes are a form of fried dough and the buljol is made from salt fish. This was one of my favourite dishes, and she urged me to stay for breakfast. In a timely fashion, Vernon interrupted and said, "I am happy to take you home, if you wish." Yet again, my trusting nature kicked in and I accepted the lift home.

We got near to my home, and I casually said, "We should have stayed for the food, because I am so hungry now." Vernon then invited me to have breakfast with him. I was gobsmacked about my first breakfast date! I had never been taken to breakfast on a date before. We drove to the West End and had breakfast at a hotel at Marble Arch. It was an ethereal experience for me. I was finding it difficult to contain myself and focus. I didn't know that it was possible to feel these emotions all at once. I had no idea if he was single or available, but I felt that he was. He was so honest and genuine.

Somewhere along the way, I confirmed that he was Trinidadian, and I thought I had died and gone to heaven! When he finally took me home, he asked for my number. I tried to be so together and cool, so I said to him, "Don't call me, I'll call you!" I wanted to disappear, but he was equally cool and said, "That would be fine. I look forward to hearing from you." We couldn't find a pen or paper, so he wrote his number on my hand with my lipstick!

I got inside and my flatmate was going demented. She hadn't seen me all day and I returned home at 11 a.m. When I explained to her what had happened, from shopping after night duty, cooking at my friend's, attending the party, meeting this man and being taken to breakfast, she was astounded. I was hysterical with joy, and we laughed and shrieked together.

I desperately wanted to call straight away, but I had to exercise some type of decorum. I tortured myself and waited for several days before I called. It was Wednesday afternoon by then, and when he heard my voice, I felt like he was holding his breath too. He came over immediately and took me to work. He picked me up in the morning as well. He took me to work and picked me up every day after that and, when I was off duty, I spent all my time with him. This was a whirlwind affair that sent me into orbit. I was so happy, and even happier that he seemed to feel the same way.

My mind was in full turmoil, as I was due to leave for New York on the 20th of December, as I planned. He too said he was going on holiday to Trinidad for the month of February 1975. The week before I left, he took me to his flat, which was beautiful and so stylishly decorated, with built-in wardrobes and shelving and a feature wall covered in brown leather wallpaper. He showed me one half of his wardrobe and said, "This side is yours whenever you are ready." He was asking me to live with him three weeks after meeting me! *Is he for real? Am I asleep and/or dreaming!?*

It was a magical time of my life and way beyond my wildest dreams. My heart was on point, and told me this man would be my life partner. Our relationship developed in such an organic and pure way that it took me by surprise. It was so easy and stress-free. He anticipated everything and made things happen so smoothly. There was no chasing or unresponsive phone calls or disappointments. I learnt about his life history. His parents were black but they lived in

Venezuela for a time. He had four brothers and a sister. He was very active and creative and had lots of friends who were artists and dancers whom he socialised with. He was a strong believer in carnival and, in his late teenage years, he became a band leader and produced elaborate costumes for his band. Some of the designers who became famous and well known internationally were his friends, who played with him before starting their own bands, for example George Bailey and Harold Saldenah.

He came to England to train as a dentist at Leeds University. He left his wife and daughter behind, fully intending to have them join him at a later date. He also had two other children during his teenage years, but they were looked after by their mother. After two years, his money ran out and he came to London to work and save and return to his studies. Like any creative artist, he was consumed by the bright lights of the city. This was in the 1950s and everything was developing at the same time. Vernon got involved in singing, acting and dancing and playing music. He never went back to his studies in Leeds. His life turned into one big adventure. He formed a band and started playing across London and several countries in Europe. His interest in acting saw him become a member of Equity. He had parts in various films, like a few James Bond films, the Saint and Hammer House of Horror films on television. Even now, our children and their friends still see my husband in his roles in these films. They are so proud of him and his creative talents. His most prolific part was as a dancer in the film *Cleopatra* with Richard Burton and Elizabeth Taylor. He talked about meeting them and being witness to their many fights that often delayed shooting of the film. The delays allowed him to explore Rome, where he found an amazing tailor to make him and his friends an abundance of suits and shirts.

He lived the longest in France and Turkey, and subsequently learnt to speak French and Turkish. This was a sad time for him as well, because despite much pleading, his wife refused to join him in London, and they subsequently got divorced.

In 1964, he was in London on a break, and he went to his local pub, where he was part of a group of musicians who did a jam session every Sunday. On one of these Sundays, he and his friends were asked to play music in the streets for a children's carnival. They all secured their instruments around their necks and set off for Ladbroke Grove, playing music in the streets, and gathering a huge crowd of locals following them. This occasion has been designated as the founding of the Notting Hill Carnival in London. This was a milestone that has been indelibly printed in the history of black people in London, and my Vernon was an integral part of this history, as a founder member of the Notting Hill Carnival. When he told me that he could play percussion, I scoffed and thought he was showing off. When he took me to hear him play, I was truly blown away at his skills and dexterity.

I was spoilt rotten by Vernon and I lapped it up in spades, but equally I was brought up to be kind and loving and caring and respectful to others, so I dished that out in bucket loads too. It is true perfection when you feel loved and respected and cherished.

I took off for New York and knew it would be difficult on one hand, but exciting nevertheless. He knew of the plans my mother and I had made and he simply said it was a decision for me to make, but he wanted us to be together forever. My mother was beside herself with joy at the thought of me finally being able to join the family, but I had a heavy heart about telling her what was happening, even though it was the stuff of dreams and fairy tales.

I got home in New York three days before Christmas and was so happy to see my family. It was the first time for five years that we were together at Christmas. In the bedroom, my mother showed me the space she had cleared for me to use during my two-month stay. She was chatting about plans to find a bigger house when I came to live. Suddenly, she looked at me and said, "What's his name?"

I became very coy and said to her, "Whatever do you mean?"

She said, "Ally, I'm your mother. I know you well. I spent ages persuading you to join us here after your training. Now that you are here to set the plan in motion, you have become hesitant again. Something or someone must be confusing you."

I was staggered that she was so spot on. I said, "Well, I have met this man and I am totally besotted with him and he with me. He's from Trinidad and I'm crazy about him. I know he's the one and so I could not leave him in London. I have to stay and see what happens."

She was astounded. She said, "But Ally, I have talked to you every week for all these years and you have never talked about being so serious about anyone. How long has this been going on?"

Very proudly, I said, "Oh, not long. I only met him three weeks ago."

My mother was hysterical with laughter and bewilderment. "Are you saying that you have dismissed all our plans for your future here to be with a man that you have only known for three weeks? Are you crazy? What if you are wrong?"

I said, "I know that I'm not wrong. He has changed my life and I know I will be with him forever. However, as a plan B, I promise that I will complete the psychiatric course, so that I can do the full exams for the State Board, should the need ever arise." I continued, "Also, I don't think I will be doing the exams this time around. I am really sorry to say, but I would like to go back early, as he is going to Trinidad for a month and I would like to see him before he goes."

Mum was so disappointed. She sat down in a dejected way and said, "Clearly, there is no point in trying to persuade you anymore. I am truly amazed that you are so confident about your future with this man. If this works out, then I think you must have the greatest instincts and judgement in the world and you must always follow your mind in the future. I wish you all the best in the world."

CHAPTER FIFTEEN:
Life, Love and Laughter

So that was that! I had her blessing to return to London and follow my dream with this person. We had a wonderful family dinner at Christmas and we, the youngsters, were out for the night on New Year's Eve. Mum was very pleasant and willing to talk each time Vernon called. I continued to enjoy the sights and sounds of the city for a few more weeks, before returning to London in mid-January, before Vernon left for Trinidad at the beginning of February. Wow, what a whirlwind it was and I was cherishing every moment, while being very aware that I was jobless.

While waiting for my course to start in the middle of March, I needed to keep busy and find agency work, so I was sent to the maternity unit at the University College Hospital, much to my horror, as the unit had an awful reputation. Despite my fears, I thrived, especially on the delivery suite. I was newly qualified, so I was up to date and quite expert and on point with my practice.

I quickly understood the reason for the unit's bad reputation. Many of the midwives were wonderful women who are friends to this day, but many of their practices were out of the ark. The staff had been there for many years, so there was a sense of déjà vu. Of course they were never happy about being questioned, so I was always getting on someone's last nerve. The doctors, on the other hand, thought I was the best thing since sliced bread. They demanded that I took the lead in many procedures that were not yet fully practised on the unit by the midwives. For example, I was up to date on managing several medical procedures and I demonstrated a strong sense of advocacy for the women and their families. I certainly was not better than anyone, but I think my high standard of practice was evident, only because of the reasons I have outlined already.

Without my knowledge, several of the doctors had approached the head of midwifery asking her to ensure I joined the staff after I finished my course. True to her word, she discussed with me the possibility of joining the staff. I felt very pleased with myself to have come to the attention of the doctors, and I promised to contact her in October. I did enjoy my work there, and I could see the potential for change and development in this clinical area. I was excited to take on the challenge, but I knew it would be difficult under the circumstances.

In the meantime, Vernon returned from his vacation. I eventually let my cool down and agreed to move in with him. Actually, I was slowly doing it anyway, because I was staying at the flat while he was away. My flatmate used to visit me regularly and was excited for me to move in. She was more than happy to return to her family home.

Meanwhile, my psychiatric course was quite an experience. I had no experience whatsoever of this speciality, as I chose to study neurosurgery instead. This course was designed to give an overview of signs and symptoms and treatment of mental illness and behavioural problems. It was interesting and meaningful to put a label or give a name to many signs and symptoms I had observed in people along the way. I had the great fortune to have been assigned to the behavioural unit that deals primarily with obsessive compulsive behaviour. This was a baptism of fire, as I had never heard of this condition. I thought it was normal to be a clean freak in your home and obsessive about having a place for everything and everything in its place. This condition, however, was on a different level. I joined doctors and nurses who were treating these adult patients for whom the condition was seriously affecting their daily life. The unit provided one-to-one treatment, mainly in their homes, so we travelled regularly around London to visit our patients. These patients led very difficult lives, because there is no cure for this condition. It was such a contradiction to see patients obsessive about cleaning their hands constantly, but as a result they lived in filthy conditions because they could not get their hands dirty, so they couldn't clean their homes. It could be managed, but it took a lot of hard work and determination. I had a lot of empathy for these patients and thanked God every day for my healthy sanity.

I returned to the maternity unit in October to meet with the head of midwifery. She was very happy that I was interested in joining the staff and took me to the uniform room herself to be measured. So this move was the start of my long and passionate association with the unit. I was there from October 1974 for more than twenty-eight years.

My love life was progressing in leaps and bounds. My mother was particularly intrigued, because I think, deep down, she expected the relationship to fail. However, I was absolutely sure it would not. We were besotted with each other. We had so much in common regarding our culture and beliefs and morals and ethics. Vernon always had friends hanging out at the flat and all my friends eventually met him, as we often hosted dinner parties there. In June, July and August, he introduced me to his cousin, who was a band leader who produced costumes for a costume band at the Notting Hill Carnival. We became regular volunteers at this workshop on a yearly basis during the carnival season.

My life continued at a roller coaster pace. We had so much fun attending the theatre, the cinema, many R & B concerts, restaurants and museums and dinner parties at our home and the home of other friends. To my delight, Vernon asked me to marry him after only six months. I was fit to burst and so happy. I also realised that I never had asked him his age, so I did. He said he was in his forties, and that was good enough for me.

My mother was ecstatic and happy for me. When I set the date for December the 31st, I was so disappointed that my mother couldn't come, because she was doing the State Board exams herself. Remember, we were both taking the exam, but because of my shock decision to return to London, she didn't proceed. She was now going ahead a year later and wasn't free until the end of February. I would never get married unless my mother was there with me, so the date was changed to March 6th, 1976.

It was at this time that I found out my mother and father were separated. I was staggered that neither of them had spoken of it before, but I didn't feel sad. I loved my dad dearly, but I was never close to him. I was more worried about my mum. I was sad and upset that I wasn't close to her to comfort her. I was talking to her about the wedding invitations and she then said, "You will have to send your dad's invitation separately, as he doesn't live with us anymore." Despite my questions and pleas to find out what was going on, she refused to explain. My brothers and sisters also didn't make any sense when trying to explain. Mum was adamant that I shouldn't worry about her. She said I needed to concentrate on organising my wedding and planning for my future. I did talk to Dad, and he explained to me his side of the story. I really respected him for talking to me. He said he was sorry not to have explained himself, but he didn't need anyone's approval to make his decision. He apologised that he was unable to attend my wedding and wished me all the luck in the world. I was really annoyed as well, as everyone was so tight-lipped about the breakup. It was sad to break up after being together for so long. Many years later, I found out Dad had cheated on Mummy, hence the tight lips and lack of discussion..

Everyone I knew was in awe of this whirlwind courtship, because it was my dream that was coming to fruition. I felt so blessed and at peace. It was just before Christmas when we had dinner with my best friend and her family. I was telling them about having to change the date of my wedding when my friend Pat asked if I had stopped my contraception. I had not given it a thought at that point. With her obstetrician hat on, she explained the possible difficulties of getting pregnant after long term use of the pill. She suggested I stop immediately, as it could be many months before the drug was out of my system. This advice was based on her own experience. Well, it was unbelievable. I took my last pill three weeks later and never had another period. I didn't even realise, because of the excitement and activity of planning the wedding. Vernon was beside himself when I told him. I was six weeks pregnant when we were married, but no one knew at the time. Vernon had three other grown-up children in New York who were older than me! He was estranged from them for many years, although he had been in touch with his ex-wife about their divorce papers from 1965. I told him that I thought it would be a good idea for him to try to reconnect with them, as they needed to know his new family.

So I started my plans for a simple but stylish affair. Vernon was now firmly settled back in London and had gone into the fashion business with two of his friends. I was able to go into designer showrooms to look for an outfit, as I didn't want a traditional wedding dress. This was a massive thrill, and I chose an embroidered gown by famous designer Janice Wainwright. I was even allowed to have a metre of the raw material to make a head wrap.

So I went full on with my wedding planning duties. I baked my own cakes but had them decorated by a friend. I had caterers who prepared the food. My friends and I decorated the hall. We were very lucky that Vernon's friends that we used to visit at the American air force base in RAF Lakenheath and the Trinidad High Commission in London helped with the supply of drinks. My mother showered me with wedding presents, for example, the cost of my wedding dress, a gold-plated full cutlery service and serving spoons, embroidered tablecloths with napkins and sets of bed linen.

We were married at the registry office in Hampstead, which was prettier than our local one. We used the address of Vernon's friend who lived in Hampstead Garden Suburb, as you had to live locally to get married there. Both our churches, Anglican and Catholic, rejected us because we were non-practising at the time. They both demanded that we retrain in the ways of the church and create a record of our attendance. I was devastated that this was the way that churches treated their members. It was no surprise that people had stopped going to church if priests had this attitude. Well, our comments about this rebuff were not repeatable, so we went with our plan B. My mother arrived to stay with us and brought my beautiful niece, Abbegail, who was living with her. Mum finally met the love of my life. They hugged and behaved like old friends.

I was bowled over. They realised that they had met before. I was totally gobsmacked. They started to reminisce about their younger days on the social circuit. They had mutual friends who were famous dancers, artists and academics. For example, they knew brothers Geoffrey and Boscoe Holder, dancer Beryl McBernie and academic Jeff Henry. I had heard of these famous sons of the soil. It's important to clarify that, during the course of this adventure, I asked Vernon to explain what he meant by being "in my forties". I discovered that he was 49 when I asked and was about to turn 50. When I met him I was 27, and about to turn 28. On doing the maths, I realised Vernon was twenty two years older than me. Of course, he was in my parents' age range, but I didn't care and it didn't matter to me. He was a fitness fanatic and looked really youthful and seemed in good health. He was a typical example of how difficult it is to guess a black person's age. The famous saying in the community is "Black don't crack."

Soon after their meeting, my mother called me aside and said, "I know him as one of the guys who partied all the time when we were young. Do you realise that he's as old as your father?"

My response was, "Take it from me, Mum, he isn't."

She laughed and said, "Child, you can't talk to your mother like that."

Then I said, "But you know exactly what I mean," and we both laughed out loud. I often wondered, if she was living in London with me, how much pressure she would have put on me about Vernon and his suitability to marry me. However, she was so delighted to hear my news, and she insisted that I saw a doctor. I assured her that I would, right after the excitement of the wedding was over.

Our wedding was a spectacular event with many friends and some family enjoying lovely Trinidadian food and lots to drink. My designer dress was greatly admired. I was blessed to have my mother and niece with me and all my special friends. We got married at midday. We returned to our flat for a champagne reception with a few canapés and snacks and photographs. Then we all left for the reception, as Vernon and I had to be there before the guests arrived at four o'clock. My mother had a wonderful time meeting my friends and she had many offers of outings with them.

There was an unpleasant incident that almost spoilt the occasion. I was sitting chatting with my guests when a friend came to say that someone had brought the pot of rice and peas and curry from the kitchen and placed it on the table with the cakes, and he was shouting, "Come and get it."

"What should we do?" She suggested I had to go and sort this out.

When I got to the table, it was Vernon's cousin who had done it. He was clearly tipsy and we stared at each other, and out of nowhere I said, "What do you think you are doing? The refreshments for my guests are none of your business. The caterers know exactly what to do. Do you not have any class or finesse about you? You are a disgrace."

I was so upset, and my friends were incensed that he could be so divisive at my wedding. I just walked away and they took all the food back to the kitchen, where the caterers were waiting.

I was sitting with my friends, who had calmed me down, when he came to me saying, "I don't know why you are so upset. That's the sort of thing we would do where I come from."

We are both from Trinidad, and I had never seen anyone behave like this. With great control, I looked up and said, "Well, that's the problem. Where you come from and where I come from, are two completely different places!"

The kitchen problem got back on course and everyone was served and happy. We partied into the wee hours of the morning and everyone left feeling happy.

CHAPTER SIXTEEN:
Bringing New Life Into The World

We fast forward to October when I was nearly ten days overdue. Vernon had bought tickets for us to see Marvin Gaye, and I was thrilled and looking forward to it, as this baby didn't want to come out. I had been booked to be induced so I knew there was an end in sight. As the day progressed, I started to feel odd, but with no pain or sickness. I just wanted to rest. I insisted that Vernon should attend the concert, and luckily, he got twice the price for my ticket. The contractions started soon after he returned and, in the early hours, we went off to the hospital. After twelve hours, I delivered a bouncing baby girl we called Symone. I will always remember this day as the one that I missed a Marvin Gaye concert.

Now that I was on the other side of the coin, it all made sense. It was like nothing I had experienced on earth. The pain of labour was excruciating and relentless, but my bundle of joy at the end was all worth it. Vernon was barely holding on by the end. He said he had developed a new-found respect for women after that experience. I was determined to be the model patient, employing all the training and advice I had been taught and all that I had taught the women in my care. I was adamant I would never say again that labour was just a bit worse than a bad period pain. What a big fat lie that is!

I loved caring for my baby and breastfeeding her. It was hard work and took all my energy and resolve to feed through the sore nipples and swollen breasts. I had milk enough to feed two babies. When Symone clamped down on my nipples, I felt the pain shooting through my whole body, my brain, my shoulders, my chest, but the miracle of it was that it never lasted long, so once I got over that initial shock, I could feed. Thankfully, the soreness didn't last either. She fed like a trooper and enjoyed her food. I used to tell women that once they were confident in their minds that they were going to breastfeed, nothing should put you off. It was important to say "this too will pass" and work through it. My midwife and my health visitor didn't believe that Symone was only having breast milk. She had reached twice her birth weight at six months, when this should have happened at a year old. I used to tell my patients the same thing. You could never over feed a breastfed baby, even though they feed constantly. They don't develop extra body cells like a baby that is overfed on formula milk, and they level out into a normal weight range as they grow.

Although my baby was such a joy and was thriving beautifully, I was exhausted beyond measure. I didn't believe that anyone could survive on less than eight hours of sleep. I had to learn fast that it was the quality, not the quantity of sleep that you had, that was important. My other strong mantra was that you cannot spoil a baby by giving them so much attention. This is what they need at this time.

My solution was to feed Symone in bed, just moving her from one breast to the other. Often, one feed would run into the other and she would be in bed with me for hours. It's quite safe, because instinctively, you will know she is there and you will never smother your baby. It was such a wonderful experience. The secret is to listen to all the advice you get from family and friends, then decide on your own course and never be deterred from it.

It is another experience altogether being a mother and a midwife. Being a midwife has no bearing on what you are like as a mother. I had the same amount of pain and lack of sleep as everyone else. I was even trying to be a super mum and failing miserably. Every time I managed to get Symone to sleep, I would go crazy with cleaning and cooking and doing laundry and getting more and more tired. It was my health visitor who rescued me from this scenario. She visited me when I was in the middle of a frenzy, and she made me sit down and stop. She was rational and calm and asked me to be the same. She demanded, "You must go back to bed with Symone at least once a day or you will never enjoy your baby and any problems will seem insurmountable, and you will be far too tired to cope. I urge you to leave the cooking and cleaning to your husband. Tell him that's how he can help you, as he can't do any feeding at this time."

I followed her advice and slowly began to cope and feel better. Of course, Vernon was not happy to come in from work and find there was work to be done at home. But he understood the rationale and acknowledged it was his way of helping me.

CHAPTER SEVENTEEN:
The Ups And Downs Of Family Life

I remained on maternity leave for almost a year up to August 1977, returning to work part-time and on night duty while still breastfeeding. Symone was a beautiful baby and growing into a lovely toddler, who was thriving. She was very friendly and wanted to chat all the time, so reaching her milestones came thick and fast.

I was enjoying my work on a part-time basis at night. This allowed me to continue to look after my daughter, as she was far too young to go to a child minder. This worked well, as I worked alternate days, so there was no urgency to sleep when I came off duty. Vernon was in his element looking after her at night, except in the beginning when I returned to work. I had a freezer full of milk, but Symone refused to take the breast milk from a bottle. Vernon would ring me at work in a panic that she was going to starve to death. I reassured him constantly that she wouldn't. He just had to keep offering the feed to her, or I suggested he give her water or baby Ribena, until something worked. When she was hungry enough, she would feed. After about a week, she readily took the breast milk from the bottle and never looked back.

On my return to work, I was successful in breaking up my days on night duty so that I didn't have to sleep when I came home and could have more quality time with Symone. Vernon and I talked about longing for a vacation in Trinidad, as life had been quite a whirlwind for the previous few years. We got very excited about taking Symone with us.

In February 1978, we took Symone with us to Trinidad. She was only sixteen months old and none of the history would have made any sense to her, but I saw it as my first attempt at introducing her to our culture and our strong sense of identity. She was treated like a doll as she was so pretty and was trying to talk in such a mature way. She was lapping up all the attention she was getting from our friends and family.

My friends Ray and Jean had returned to Trinidad from London after Jean completed her midwifery and nursing training and Ray had finished his training as a telephone engineer. Ray was also from the Windrush generation who came to London to help rebuild the country after it was ravaged by the wars. We were delighted they offered us accommodation in their new home on our vacation.

When we took Symone to the beach for the first time, it was a very funny event. We started running across the beach with her to go into the sea. She started to scream, saying, "I don't like this, Mummy. It is so nasty. I don't like this thing in my toes," referring to the sand. So the little diva had to be lifted in and out of the water! We started our habit of taking her everywhere we went, so I noticed her curiosity about the carnival costumes she saw, and interestingly, she enjoyed touching any that were close to her. She had many grown-up cousins so, of course, they spoilt her and took her to many places around the town.

Then, without so much as a by-your-leave, I discovered I was pregnant again. I was ecstatic with joy and so was Vernon. I worked out that I would be due on the 20th of February, 1979. Thankfully, I had a normal, uncomplicated pregnancy, although it was not easy to be caring for a two-year-old as well. The greatest thrill was that my son was born on his due date, which is a very rare occurrence, and different from his sister, who was ten days late. Many women get their due dates wrong because they have irregular menstrual cycles or they simply did not remember their dates. In most cases, the doctors step in and request a dating ultrasound scan, which is based on the baby's measurements. I refused to have one, as I wanted to prove a point. I was confident about my cycle, so I was believed and my dates were accepted. I was so thrilled that my own calculations were spot on.

Looking after my son, Kevin, was a piece of cake. He was a delightfully calm baby and I was pretty chilled myself. All he did was eat and sleep, so unlike his sister, who was fretful, active and insatiable.

Actually, I think this scenario must be typical of a new mother. In my experience, first-time mothers always have many highs and lows in working out how to provide the best care for a new first baby, and finding a strategy that works well. By the time the second baby comes along, most mothers have everything down to a fine art. We quickly forget the excruciating pain, the insane tiredness and lack of control of our own bodies. I certainly found this to be true. I found that I was so much more relaxed when he cried, not going into a frenzy. I seemed to be able to identify what was wrong from his cry. Even if he cried, I knew when he was fine, and I could listen to that cry without feeling guilty.

Our flat was beautiful, but it still had only one bedroom and we were privately renting. Now we were two adults and had two babies in it. So, I got the bit between my teeth and started to think about finding a home of our own. Vernon and I talked about this option, but we had not had much time to do anything about it. We were busy having two babies instead! Our first action was to go to the local estate agents and ask them to send us suitable listings for the sale of homes in the surrounding boroughs. Vernon insisted we went to the council housing department to ask to be rehoused, although I knew we didn't stand much chance. We had no problem issues with our housing or our health, which I knew were two of the key issues. They took lots of information from us, especially about the state of our health and that of the babies. The officer seemed highly amused and politely sent us on our way to make our own arrangements and find our own home. He said, "Mrs Williams, you are a professional nurse and midwife and Mr Williams, you are a businessman. You don't stand much chance of getting social housing. You would be at the bottom of the pile, because you have no problems socially or health-wise that would give you any priority."

Although this was exactly what I had said would happen, Vernon was deflated, primarily because we had no money saved. I reminded him that he had a beautiful car that he always said was an investment. He was a committed car enthusiast and his knowledge was unsurpassed about luxury cars. When he got used to the idea of selling his precious car, he was confident it would command a top resale price. So, we started looking for a home and for someone to buy the car.

CHAPTER EIGHTEEN:
Buying Our Own Home

House-hunting was a long and tedious business. It was a sharp learning curve finding out how other people live and what they presented for sale to the public. Some homes were well presented while others were horrible. Finally, we found a lovely house in a state of disrepair, which we loved, as it showed a lot of potential to decorate in your own style. So, six months after Kevin was born, we signed on the dotted line to obtain the deeds of our home on 7th September 1979.

When I digested the cost of the mortgage and the work needed to bring the house up to a decent standard, I thought I would never be able to feed the family again. I was working part-time, which was perfect for being with the kids, but the financial pressures were mounting. On the other hand, I was so pleased with the way we were transforming the house. Kevin was a superstar at this time, and we used to go to the house every day, while Symone was at nursery school. I would pack food and snacks for us and have a wonderful day, with him sitting in his high chair, and me sitting on the floor reading newspapers from the 1960s or stripping wallpaper, or painting walls or removing dirty carpets.

On the weekends, the whole family came to the house and Vernon often managed to rope a friend or two into giving us a hand. We had no money to employ professional tradesmen to do the work.

As usual, I would cook for us and any friends there as a way of saying thanks. It was exceedingly hard work but I think the days of watching my uncle and his men while they were building our house in Trinidad certainly paid off, as I relished the jobs and became very competent at DIY.

We worked on the house for three months to make it liveable, before we could move in, two weeks before Christmas. We had no living room furniture, so we used the dining room chairs and large cushions on our bed as furniture. We managed to get a good deal from a carpet showroom, so we had a beautiful new carpet laid for us. We spent many hours rolling about on it and having fun. Our pride and joy was the elegant, tall and rather large coffee table in the room. It was beautifully and stylishly carved from mahogany and had a dark brown, shiny finish. Vernon and I almost waged World War Three over it. I was shocked and horrified that he had been so casual about spending from our limited budget. I was furious, but his horizontal approach kicked in and he described his luck in getting it, through bartering, as the Swedish furniture shop was closing down. He had paid £250, which was one third of the price. (This would be worth thousands today.) With a glint in his eyes, he said, "I promise you, you will never have to buy another coffee table ever again." He was so right, as the table has remained in use with the family since then, more than forty years ago. The kids used to swim across it, slide over it and play hide and seek under it.

The icing on the cake happened about a week before Christmas. This large box arrived with the postman, much to our surprise. It contained four authentic Japanese kimonos, one for each of us. They were absolutely exquisite. I had never seen anything like that. The beautiful embroidery was in the shape of a dragon for the male and the female ones had embroidered flowers all over. I cried because, yet again, my mother was thoughtful with her timely presents. When I spoke to her, she said she wanted to send us something special at Christmas to enjoy in our new home, after her return from a Buddhist convention in Japan. It was such an honour to have her as my mother.

It was very liberating to know that we owned our own home. I felt it was a wonderful start toward bringing up our children in a safe and comfortable environment. I wanted their experience to be as wonderful and interesting as mine. I was brought up to be principled and independent, so I never worried about the increased financial burden. My philosophy was that I had the ability through my profession to work and manage our finances, including debt. So I got myself ready mentally to take on the responsibility of keeping the roof over our heads, especially as the mortgage was being paid from my bank account.

My husband's business was doing very well, but his income was inconsistent, and this made him frustrated. He had left his partners in the wholesale business and opened a ladies' fashion shop near our home in Maida Vale. It was very tastefully decorated and had the most amazing clothes, mostly made in France and Italy.

Together with friends, he was always using us to model the clothes and posting pictures of us in the shop window. The shop was popular and I enjoyed helping out and examining all the clothes whenever a new shipment of orders arrived. I wanted to see what lovely stuff I could earmark for myself. This was a turnaround for me, as Vernon was the one who used to bring me clothes all the time. I used to feel so blessed when he brought me items of clothing during our courtship. I used to be the envy of my friends and I treasured them greatly.

So, I became the financially stable force. I suppose I was stupid and irresponsible but, truthfully, I preferred to be showered with love, kindness, pride, respect, understanding, support, empathy and laughter, all of which I got in abundance. I believed that those assets go much, much further in helping to create a happy and loving home The situation reminded me so much of my dad and how he seemed to me when I was growing up. It seems that this laid-back, horizontal approach to life is a trait prevalent among West Indian men. The women always seem to be in control, in an often quiet and determined way, without emasculating the man. I believe, however, that my father and my husband were very proud of their partners and showed great admiration and support for them in their own special way.

I can only speak for myself, but I was besotted with my husband from the day I met him, and I know he felt the same. Vernon and I had a running joke that we said to each other. I was the "How? Why? Where? When? What if?" type of person, always questioning everything and getting on everyone's last nerves. Vernon would say, "You are so cantankerous with your questions. You must have an answer for everything." I would say in turn, "You are so laid-back, you are almost horizontal. Someone must have an opinion around here." We both knew it was true, but we always said it to each other in humour and with laughter.

I cannot express what a joy it was to have my daughter and son to look after. They were adorable, and their dad loved them so much. He would talk to them as if he was talking to an adult. They laughed a lot together.

CHAPTER NINETEEN:
The Birth of Genesis

During these years of having our children, Vernon continued to help his cousin with his costume band for the Notting Hill Carnival. He also continued to take part in the carnival competitions and win prizes as well. His friends had always acknowledged his experience of being a young band leader in Trinidad, so they began to encourage him to start his own costume band. We managed to achieve this in August 1980. It was imperative that band leaders applied for funding from the Arts Council, because it was impossible to design and make costumes for members of your band out of your own pocket. I became the band's administrator, responsible for completing all the relevant paperwork and funding applications required. It was a huge amount of complex work, but it had to be done. My other role was as chief cook and bottle washer for the volunteers who helped us on a daily basis. I would go from work in the community, then to the workshop where the volunteers and Vernon were working on costumes. I cooked for our volunteers almost every day during June, July and August, as providing food and drink for our volunteers was our way of showing our appreciation and thanks for their help. My husband also offered travel expenses for anyone living a distance away.

The application process was not done or signed off until after the season when I completed progress reports, summaries of activities and schedules of finances, which were sent to the funding body.

Our band was called Genesis and it was a huge success, with a large number of players and supporters. One of the difficult issues around having a workshop for the carnival season was that we had to find somewhere different each year. Early in each new year, Vernon would set out in the surrounding boroughs to find empty spaces to rent that were safe. We would then get involved with the cleaning and setting up of the space. The most important feature of each space was ensuring there were bathroom facilities and a kitchen with running water. This process has carried on for more than forty years of producing carnival costumes, except the few times when we were able to stay for several years in one place. The issue is that most band leaders have full-time jobs, as carnival for them was a hobby, not a full-time occupation. It was therefore impossible to own property that was used solely for this purpose.

The carnival season was always such a hectic time, which I thoroughly enjoyed to a point. Most people forgot that I had a full-time job, as I was everywhere and always there. I was responsible for the refreshments at the yearly band launch, where I usually sold it all. Then there was more of the same after the season, when we would hold a thank you party, to say thanks to all our helpers, supporters and volunteers. Our thank you parties were legendary and quite unlike any other, as they were free to everyone. Vernon was adamant he could not say thanks to volunteers and supporters

TELL ME SOMETHING I DON'T KNOW!

while charging them an entrance fee to a thank you party; it would be a huge contradiction.

CHAPTER TWENTY:
The Pursuit of Financial Freedom

My response to dealing with our financial constraints was to try to work full-time. Symone was at nursery school and I found a West Indian child minder across the street from our home who would look after Kevin until he was ready to go to nursery. I applied for a sister's role in the unit, but I was unsure of this possibility, as I had worked part-time for so long, and I wondered how I would physically manage the shift system.

> I decided that I would go for broke and work it out, if I was given the opportunity. At the interview, I was questioned at length about my thoughts on community midwifery. This was my favourite time during my training, because I enjoyed working with and caring for women in their own homes, through all aspects of pregnancy and childbirth. I was able to discuss this with some knowledge and passion. To my delight, I was offered the role, not on the labour ward in the hospital, but in the community, sometime in

the future. The role was just being created as the community was being reorganised, and my enthusiasm and passion for the community was recognised as being a huge asset in the development of the community midwifery services. I felt very special that I was chosen to participate in this development.

The arrangements to take up this role included returning to day and night duty for a month to update my skills in all areas. I was apprehensive about taking on this role, but I was reassured by Vernon that I would have control of my practice, and the hours would be flexible and more conducive to having a young family. I also knew that Vernon would have my back with his caring and loving support, even though this level of childcare was new to him because he was never fully involved in the upbringing or the daily lives of his other children. He was so good with children that I prayed that he would have a warm and meaningful relationship with Symone and Kevin. He didn't believe in smacking children (we call it "giving licks"). He always said that the greatest discipline a child needed was lots of love, because if you then have to give them licks, they will know they deserved it and it was not because you didn't love them.

The community midwife job was a dream, because there was so much to do to develop the changes that were suggested at interview. I worked for several months with the community midwife, who was retiring after many years of service. She would tell me that it was important to get involved with families, but it was not helpful to get personal. Also, she would say, "As far as your clients are concerned, you are always busy at work. Whether you have two or twenty-two clients, you should never disclose this to your clients. This gives you freedom to plan and prioritise your day, and helps you avoid conflict and disappointments. Never promise to visit by a certain time. You must make them aware that circumstances change all the time within the community, but they will always be seen that day." This was the best piece of advice I had received from a senior colleague, and it would stand me in good stead throughout my career in the community.

For several years before I joined the community staff, postnatal care was the only service provided in the community. I joined a team of four midwives across the area, so there was no capacity to do any more than postnatal care. Over the next few years, many more midwives were appointed, as we worked toward the introduction of antenatal care in the community, working alongside GP's and establishing our own midwives' clinics in GPs' surgeries giving normal midwifery care to women. I was lucky to have developed a good working relationship with some doctors in my patch. It was important that we did our homework first, because not every GP was amenable to any changes to their practice. I made sure that I targeted the GP's I knew were enthusiastic about getting involved and expanding their services in midwifery. We also had it in mind that we would develop the home and domino delivery services, which meant that the GP's involvement and support was imperative. This service meant that women could labour at home, under the care of a GP and community midwife. After delivery in hospital, mum and baby are able to return home within six hours.

One exciting event happened to me that put a smile on my face. When I first started as a community midwife, our office was on the ground floor of the hospital. I arrived at the base after working a full day and was in the office sorting out visits for the next day. The door was ajar and I heard voices coming along the corridor. Suddenly, a voice spoke from the doorway and said, "This looks like this is where the real work happens." I turned around to see Lady Diana step into the room. I stood up and she said, "Hello. Tell me what happens here."

I said, "This office is the base for the community midwives, and we meet here each day to sort out our work for the next day."

She said, "Thanks for telling me. Keep up the good work," and she stepped back into the corridor and moved on. I was so dumbfounded and honoured to have spoken to Princess Diana about our work. I stood there and watched the entourage of people following her along the corridor. I had forgotten that she was there to open the new neonatal unit.

My mother hadn't seen me for a while, so she encouraged me to visit the family with my children for my forthcoming 35th birthday in July 1982. This would also allow my dad to see Symone and Kevin for the first time, but unfortunately, I didn't have the money at the time. Mum wanted to send the cost of our tickets, but I refused. Although she did not comment, I felt embarrassed, because I thought that I should not have been going on vacation, with the tight purses we both had at the time. The bottom line was I felt that I needed a break. My travel agent was very supportive and suggested I try to get a loan at my bank. I had no idea this was possible, but she said this was common practice in society. She explained that the English feel strongly about family and this is how they manage to take their families on summer holidays. They would take the year to pay off the loan, only to start again the next summer. She said, "This is how you create a good credit score, which dictates if you are a good or bad risk to borrow in the future."

To my delight, I secured the loan straight away and went back to the travel agent. She was delighted and booked our flights for the next day, as I then had to go to the American embassy for a visa for us. Once I received the visas, I was off with the kids. The children had a busy and exciting time. The start of their vacation didn't go well, as they were covered in a heat rash for several days. New York was unbearably hot at the time. I was so happy that I made the effort, because my dad was able to see them and talk with them and take them shopping and to dinner. He made our trip such an enjoyable one.

Sadly, he became ill in October and died in November 1982. He had been suffering with chronic leukaemia for some time and was often in hospital for transfusions. He was working in a factory handling chemicals, and my mother was convinced it was this exposure that brought on this disease. He had just reached 60. As you would imagine, I had to return to New York for his funeral. My uncle, his brother, was upset and shocked and indecisive about attending the funeral, so I made my own arrangements and went alone. To my surprise, he arrived in the middle of the funeral service, having been picked up at the airport by his nephew. I was really glad he was there, but it was so sad that this was the first time that my uncle would see his brother since he left Trinidad as a teenager.

At last, the day came when my precious daughter started primary school. She was excited to wear a uniform. Until then, she and her brother were attending the same nursery back in Maida Vale, where my husband had his shop. Symone and her brother Kevin had also been involved in the carnival since they could walk. Thankfully, I found a child minder near their new school whose daughter attended the same school, around the corner from our homes. She was a lovely mother with a large family, including a disabled daughter. Our families became quite close over the years and her children and mine remain friends to this day.

Symone was progressing well and getting involved in many activities. Her first report was a joy to receive. Vernon and I went to parents' evening to get this report. The teacher reported that Symone was very smart, kind and supportive to her friends and always willing to help them. She concluded in summary, "In fact, Symone would organise everyone's life for them if she was allowed to do so." This was wonderful stuff which made me very proud of her.

In 1984, we were blessed with a new head of midwifery called Anne. None of us had heard of her but we were told we were so lucky to have her there. When she arrived, we had to move our base, as the space was needed for her secretary and office equipment. Her appointment was so welcome, and I could see that she was fully aware of the task in hand. The unit as a whole was still behind the times and needed further modernising. On discussion with her, she seemed to have a clear vision about where we should be going as a unit.

Our new community manager was appointed almost immediately. She was a breath of fresh air, as she was supportive and always ready to give hands-on support. She was knowledgeable and experienced and also let me fly with my ideas about the service. She was based at the Middlesex Hospital, so our office base moved over there. We enjoyed more space for meetings and, more importantly, there were now beds available for use as part of the community service we were developing. This was open to women who had a normal pregnancy and antenatal care.

They were not confident to have a home birth, but they would deliver in hospital by a midwife, then return home after six to eight hours once the mother and baby were discharged as fit by a doctor. As we proceeded, we made significant progress, which was very satisfying and rewarding.

The main concept I was working hard to achieve was the establishment of a normal midwifery service. Until then, the women were treated as if they were ill, and all of them came into hospital to be seen by doctors and midwives. I was so excited about our work. I took the lead on many projects regarding creating policies and guidelines to facilitate good practice. We were soon finding out how important this was. Our unit was not a training school for midwifery, so we had to streamline our own way of managing our daily practices, as there was the potential to carry out the same procedure in a hundred or more different ways.

In order to improve my finances, I had started to work occasional extra shifts, usually at night. My agency regularly sent me to a cottage hospital called Perivale Maternity Unit, which was part of the Ealing Hospital Group. It was a wonderful place that was quaint and quite busy at times. My rota in the community was for normal shifts of nine to five, including being on call for emergencies, so I was able to map out my schedule for many months in advance. Over a fortnight, I would be off on a Thursday in one week, then the next week I would be off on Friday, Saturday and Sunday. That meant I could be available on Wednesday night one week and Thursday, Friday and Saturday nights in the next. I started off slowly with this schedule. Soon, I was offered a lot of work there on a regular basis because they were impressed with my level of expertise and seemed to want me there all the time. I became very familiar with the unit after a period of time, and that was so important to me. It meant I wasn't sent somewhere different each week, which can be very unsettling, especially as it was not my primary job. I also had Vernon's support with caring for the children. Naturally, I became chronically tired, and I began to get frustrated and resented the level of pressure I had.

I could see improvements in our finances, so I carried on. Occasionally, I would have to refuse, because my own work in the community was expanding, and I also had to ensure that I spent quality time with the children and Vernon and that we did things together as a family. I was booking more and more women for midwifery care. Our homebirth figures were up and our midwife clinics were also growing. I had a habit of always being one of the last people to leave the office. I hated to think that any work was left undone, so I always tried to make sure there were no outstanding issues missed. Usually, we would have all the work allocated for the next day, so I would check the visits were covered. It was not exactly my job, but I wanted to look out for the women. My boss used to call me "the fixer". She actually used me as the calm and collected one when my fellow midwives had conflicts with the women they were looking after. She was very discreet and could trust me to be the same. As you would expect with strong-minded women, there were clashes between midwives demanding women did as they were told and clients who didn't want to be told what to do.

My strategy was to go in, seemingly having no idea of what was going on, and being my usual sweetness and light. I would explain that our boss had to reallocate clients' visits due to workload issues. The women then felt they had free rein to express themselves. I would always apologise for their distress, but never apologise for the midwife's behaviour. I would usually get to the bottom of the problem and was always successful in resolving their issues, as I felt it was important to support a new mother who was already struggling with a new baby. Also, it was so important to resolve problems amicably, rather than face a potential formal complaint. I had to report back to my manager about the incident, and we would agree that either she or I would discuss the matter with the midwife. I had to be very careful with my approach to my peers and my suggestions regarding giving advice, if they experienced similar incidents in the future.

CHAPTER TWENTY-ONE:
My Life Changing Situation

During the carnival season in 1984, I was busy making costumes at home, because we were all invited to a wedding, but Vernon couldn't leave the mas camp, so the kids and I were going to represent. The kids were playing in my bedroom while I was sewing, when suddenly I felt a bang to my head and realised the mirror had fallen over and shattered over my head. The mirror was very large and set in a natural pine frame. There was glass everywhere and I saw stars of all colours. Blood was gushing from several areas on my body, my head, arm and foot. The children were screaming with fear so I sent Symone next door to get our neighbour. My neighbour, Auntie Agatha, was my rock and called for an ambulance and they took me to hospital, while Symone and Kevin stayed with her. There were no mobile phones at that time, so I had to inform my husband by sending a message to him through a friend who lived near to his mas camp. He came immediately to the hospital. He was so shocked and scared, as he knew the size of the mirror and thought I was unconscious or seriously injured. I spent some time in the hospital as they had to clean up my injuries. I had stitches in my hand and foot and my head.

Unfortunately, I made a serious mistake, as I returned to work, as no one told me I should stay at home until the stitches were removed from my foot. A week later, when the stitches were removed, the wound opened and copious amounts of foul-smelling pus oozed from it. In the long run, I had three different courses of antibiotics and was left with a permanently swollen leg. The doctors said the infection in my foot had permanently damaged the lymphatic drainage in my leg. From then on, I had problems getting my shoes to fit. Over the years I have had to live with the problem. At one time, I ended up spending a week in hospital on antibiotics through an infusion. I had cut my toe on the damaged foot and my whole leg became infected. It was a painful and scary time. From that time on, I have been warned that I must only use professionals to do my pedicures.

Vernon and I continued to experience huge financial difficulties over the next few years, and it really put a strain on our relationship. At one point, I asked for a divorce because we were constantly fighting about money. I heard a lawyer say that most married people fight about money, so I suppose we were typical. I felt I could go out on my own, but I was actually scared of the thought and sickened to think about the effect on the children. They adored their dad, as I did, and were close to him, and he never faltered from caring for them.

My lawyer was a different breed himself. He was amazing, as he tried to get me to think seriously and to change my mind. He actually said, "After talking to you so much, I don't believe that this is what you want." My baby sister, Penelope, was devastated and said the same thing. The children loved being with their dad, especially during the carnival season. He would take them with him every day after they left school, then I would get them after work. We were living separate lives at the time, so I didn't really care or listen to the gossip that he was seeing someone else.

This particular day, I went to collect the kids from the mas camp, but my car keys mysteriously disappeared. I got the police to try to pick the lock and they couldn't, so I had to go home for my spare keys. Vernon offered to take me home. Neither of us said a word on the way there, but as we were returning to the workshop, he stopped. He said, "I am going out of my mind at the thought of losing you and the children." He truly poured his heart out in a way I had never seen. He talked of feeling he had let us down and put so much pressure on me, because his business was so erratic. He acknowledged he had taken his frustrations out on us, which was unfair and selfish. We both said we loved each other so much and didn't want to break up our family. We agreed to talk in depth. We did this later that night, and it was liberating and fulfilling. I used the opportunity to speak openly and truthfully by putting everything out on the table that was troubling me – and I mean everything.

I often wondered if I was a control freak, wanting to have everything my own way, and not being prepared to listen or accommodate any other opinion. The situation forced me to look inwardly at myself.

From that point on, our marriage progressed on a different level. Our communication was the best ever. I would stop and think before reacting negatively to any given situation. I didn't think it was possible to be so vocal and honest about life with a partner until that point. I was so relieved and delighted to have changed my mind, and so was my lawyer and family.

My dream was always to have a loving and close-knit family and to teach our children all the best family values I could. I wanted the reality of the fairy tale to continue indefinitely. I knew that my love for Vernon and the kids would never die. At the end of carnival Tuesday, we arrived back at the mas camp, and he fell asleep almost immediately, as he was so tired. When I went to find him, there was this woman trying to wake him by rubbing his face and back. I was so grateful that the music and general noise drowned out my screams and foul language. I just threw her out the building.

After the traumas earlier that year, Vernon wanted to go home to Trinidad in November to do some business with a friend who had a ladies' clothes shop. I was happy that he could go away and unwind. At the same time, the teachers were planning strike action for better working pay and conditions. It became quite difficult at this time, because parents got very short notice of this action, like a few hours, and Vernon was not there to help me. I was often called to pick them up from school either midmorning, lunchtime, or mid-afternoon. This, in turn, was disruptive to my community work, so I was paying extra for childcare or asking friends to help me. I spoke to Vernon about this and he suggested they should go to Trinidad. Their head was very supportive and fully in favour. She said, "You are welcome to take them on holiday. They will learn much more than they are learning at school at the moment."

Vernon arranged their airfares, so at the beginning of December, I put them on a plane, in the care of the air stewards, and they travelled to meet their dad. The plan was that I would join them for the carnival in March 1987.

I was regularly in touch with Vernon and the kids. He was delighted they were so settled and enjoying life. Vernon's niece got them enrolled in school for a few weeks before Christmas and they loved the experience. He had lots of help with them, as his side of the family was a large one. My friend Carol also helped by keeping them for weekends. I missed them terribly too, but it was a great opportunity for me to work hard and unwind at the same time. I could work extra to my heart's content, but was also able to sleep undisturbed. I used to cook for three or four days at a time or eat at the hospital as much as I could, just to have more time to rest. Don't be fooled, though – I still managed to attend a few wonderful parties during the Christmas season and New year.

I was on duty for Christmas Eve and, as luck would have it, I landed on the labour ward in the early hours with a woman who was having a domino delivery. She was progressing very well, and I hoped she would be delivered that morning. I also contacted one of the GPs, who wanted to observe the delivery. She was new to the practice and it was part of her induction. She agreed to join me and, when she arrived, I introduced her to the woman. I also called another colleague for help, as I had many women to see. Around mid-morning, the woman delivered normally of a lively and healthy baby boy with an intact perineum. She was delighted and so was the doctor, who had now witnessed her first normal delivery since becoming a GP. After I ensured that both mother and baby were well and safe, I went to the midwife station to complete my records.

The GP was talking to a gentleman I presumed was a new doctor I had not met. She returned to the room to chat with the mother. This man came to me and said, "Are you the midwife who just delivered a woman with the GP observing?" I said that I was. He stated, "She was telling me what an amazing experience it was. She said your skills and expertise were outstanding and she was very impressed with your manner and the care you gave to the mother. Well done to you." I said thank you and proceeded with my records.

Then he said, in front of an area full of midwives and doctors, "Excuse me, but I have to say something to you. I think you are the most beautiful black woman that I have ever seen. Your eyes are extraordinary, and your cheek bones are exquisite."

I was shocked and taken aback. I simply said, "Thank you, but I don't feel beautiful at the moment. I am just tired and hot."

He said, "That's to be expected, but take it from me, you are. I know what I'm talking about."

Everyone around was in shock and there was silence before the wows and cheers when he went away. I too stood up and said, "My goodness, who the hell was that? He's very brave."

One of the midwives then said, "Don't you know who he is? Have you not met him? He's our new consultant obstetrician."

By the next day, the incident had travelled all around the hospital. When I came in for lunch on Christmas day, we had a discussion and a great laugh about it. I was called "cheek bones" from then on. My husband was highly amused by the story, but he said he knew that anyway!

The months went by and I arrived in Trinidad at the beginning of March. My husband was there to meet me, but there was no sight of the children. They were staying with my friend Carol and were so excited to see me when I finally arrived. The first thing my daughter said was, "Mum, why are we living in England when it is so warm and beautiful here?" It was a good question that I had asked myself several times, but moving was never an easy option. Personally, I wanted a career and was not ready to consider giving it up. We had discussed this at length and the cost of moving seemed prohibitive. We would have to find suitable housing, and suitable jobs and schooling. I weighed this up against the home we already had, the free schooling and healthcare that was available to us, and honestly, at that point in our lives, it seemed like going backwards.

CHAPTER TWENTY-TWO:
Learning About My Son's Hyperactivity

It was another eventful year in 1987, as I started being called into the kids' primary school because they said my son was becoming disruptive in class. The teachers emphasised that he was never rude or aggressive, but he chatted all the time and disturbed the other children from their work. I attended some of his classes and watched him and often couldn't see what the problem was. I had many discussions with the head and, finally, she agreed to have him assessed so that we could plan the way forward. A child psychologist was assigned to do a full assessment and his report was quite thought-provoking. He concluded that Kevin was bordering on genius. He was highly intelligent, very creative and had the behaviour of a classic lateral thinker. Everything around him must be precise. He recommended that Kevin should be moved to a higher class which would stretch his ability further. However, this excellent report fell on deaf ears. The system could not accommodate these suggestions. They could not move him, as it would mean that he stayed in one class for two years. They suggested this was only possible if he went to a private school, which was not an option for us.

I was devastated that we had no financial means to support our son. The option chosen was to send him to a school called Vernon House, which was a smaller school that managed boys in particular who had emotional, behavioural and social difficulties. I was devastated and heartbroken, but I wasn't defeated. I developed lots of headaches because I was so worried. I prayed for guidance. I talked to some friends I had in south London who often invited us to dinner. Jocelyn trained as a nurse and she was the sister of my friend Carol, who worked with me at the Ministry of Education in our teenage years. Jocelyn, a nurse, had arrived in England before me, so I never met her at home in Trinidad. She met and married Andrew and they lived in a gorgeous house in Battersea. Andrew was a teacher, so I was able to ask for help. I was totally reassured by Andrew that Kevin would not be disadvantaged by this move. He was so caring and explained the school system in much clearer detail to Vernon and me. He gave us examples of students of his who experienced the same fate, and ended up going to secondary school and university in the normal way.

It was such a weight off my mind that my son was not strange or weird or seen as a monster. I was gutted that we didn't have the means to help him achieve his full potential by putting him through private education. He was a potential genius and certainly capable of achieving greatness and I loved him so much. I was so pissed off that the normal school system was so intransigent, unwieldy and unhelpful. I was determined to make sure he got the best of the present system and didn't become part of the statistics about black boys that underachieve.

It was always a pleasure visiting my friends, as I felt great empathy and support. I talked to Kevin at length about what was happening. He said he was scared, but I cuddled him and encouraged him to see this as a special move to give him space and time to focus on his school work. I promised him I would be there at the school as much as I could to make sure he was all right. I warned Kevin he would see boys very different to him, but he just had to focus and do his work well and continue to behave well and listen to his teachers.

I joined the governing body of the school so I had a presence there, and Kevin could see and connect with me regularly. The teachers in the school were very supportive and very impressed that I could find the time to work with them. I wanted to understand how the school was run and to make a positive difference that would support my son. Kevin told me he was careful not to mix with the bad boys because their behaviour was foreign to him. He would talk about his shock of how some boys behaved. He said he worked hard because he wanted to return to a normal school. To this day, I still have the toolbox he made for me in his woodwork class. I was truly intrigued by the toolbox, because it had two large circular indentations in the handle. I asked him why he had done that to the handle. He said, "I did it for you Mum, so you can carry the box easily." He also learnt to play the clarinet. Even until today, I worry and wonder how much of a detrimental effect that school must have had on him, but I know how much love and support and kindness he got from the family.

Thankfully, Kevin spent only two years there before he secured a place in the same secondary school as his sister. He always said that he talked to himself and promised himself that he would work hard, as it would get him back to a normal school again.

Later that year, around the carnival season, Vernon got busy early on looking for premises and we were lucky to be allocated a huge space that had been part of a school that had closed down on St Mark's Road in Ladbroke Grove. It was clean and spacious, with kitchen and toilet facilities. We also had access to a large, empty room that excited Vernon, because he could make his large costumes there in peace and quiet and in secret.

Soon after, we realised a steel band was also moving into the front part of the building. We were introduced to the players and band leader, who made it very clear to his players that they were restricted to their own space and should not encroach on ours. As we continued to work together, I noticed that Symone and Kevin showed a keen interest in the steel band. They would both go to listen to them practising. Kevin in particular would find himself between the players to watch them play. After a while, the band leader found an old, unused steelpan called an Invaders pan and gave it to Kevin to practise on. He wanted to keep him from distracting the players with his endless questions.

One day, in the height of activities in the place, the band leader, Vernon and I were having a chat over a cup of tea in the kitchen, which was next to the empty room. Suddenly, we heard the tune that the band was learning being played by someone and it was coming from the room. As we listened, I commented that the person had learnt the tune really well. Vernon agreed and so did the band leader, but he said, "Yes, the tune sounds great, but I told the players not to practise here where you are working. I will get the person to stop and move away." As he opened the door, he said loudly, "Oh my God," and we all ran out to see what was wrong. When we looked in the room, it was my son Kevin playing the entire tenor section of the tune.

I asked him, "Who taught you to play the tune?"

He said, "Nobody, Mummy. I learnt it by myself by looking at them."

I was so in awe of him. I gave him the tightest hug I could manage. I thought he really showed a genius streak there. The band leader and his dad were staggered by his intelligence and musicality. The band leader asked us to allow Symone and Kevin to join the band the following year. Vernon and I were delighted to agree. There were many other youngsters in the band and the adults looked after them well.

My delight was also in experiencing how genuinely interested the children were in the music and culture of Trinidad, especially as they had already fully embraced the rigours of our costume band and the making of the costumes.

The time had come when Symone was about to start secondary school. It was a busy process up to that point, because there were many visits to schools around the borough, during the previous terms, to make a selection of the school of your choice. I had my heart set on one school that had a good reputation, but which was difficult to get a place in if the child didn't have connections or siblings at the school. I was confident that Symone would be recognised as a well-behaved child who was hard-working with good results. I was very pleased when I learnt that Symone had secured a place at this school, which was her first choice. She had an amazingly active school life. She was very athletic, so got involved playing five-a-side football, netball, basketball and running. I always made it a point to attend all her fixtures to give my support and encouragement.

I was so lucky and blessed to have my very flexible community midwife job, so I was always juggling my life, including meetings and evening events, as I had also joined the governing body. It was always important to me to have a strong presence in my children's lives. On several occasions during her school life, it was so wonderful when Symone came home and said, "Mummy, were you in school today? Three different friends told me they saw you." It was what I saw that my mother did for me and it made me feel so special, and loved and valued by her. I wanted my own children to feel the same.

CHAPTER TWENTY-THREE:
Life Begins At 40!

By that time, I was 40 years old and feeling like I was 50. Vernon and I organised a party for me to celebrate the start of my life, as they say "Life begins at forty". I had a party at home with my nearest and dearest and it was a wonderful experience for all on a warm summer's day in July. The highlight of the party was opening the jeroboam of Moet & Chandon champagne that satisfied all my guests. Up until that point, the champagne had been a wedding present from one of my husband's celebrity friends, and we agreed to open it on a special occasion. So it just sat in our home for ten years waiting on this special occasion. It's my favourite drink and it tasted divine.

Life beginning at 40 certainly didn't take into account my existing busy life, my hectic job as a community midwife, doing regular agency work, looking after my husband and my home, raising two children through school and holidays, sitting on boards of governors, cooking every day between June and August for volunteers in our mas camp, being the band administrator and sewing costumes. I am not complaining, just saying. I loved every minute of my life. I was truly enjoying my life, and everything I did I believed was important and necessary to my family life and career. I wanted to make a difference to the women and their families in my care. I wanted to be an excellent midwife and a true advocate for these women.

As for my children, I couldn't do less than my mother did for me. I wanted to support them every step of the way. It certainly wasn't easy in London to care for children, because there was no support from an extended family like there would be in the Caribbean. As the proverb says, "It takes a village to raise a child." My village was not family, but great friends, amazing childminders and me and their dad. Both my children already were developing an active social life. They enjoyed attending concerts and after-parties. They especially liked attending concerts where artists sang the soca and calypsos, which are traditional at carnival time. I felt it would be selfish of me to say no to them because I didn't want to leave home.

We took them everywhere with us, for example to dinners and carnival events. They were regularly invited to birthday parties and I made sure I was available to take them. Symone especially had her friends visit for the weekend. I felt like I won the lottery one day when I heard her talking to her friends in her room. She was talking non-stop about the wonderful time she enjoyed when visiting Trinidad. Then one of her friends said, "Please let me ask you. I am so confused because I don't understand. How do you know so much about that place? Exactly where are you from?"

Symone replied immediately, "I am not confused at all. I am a Trinidadian. I just happened to be born in London."

I couldn't believe what I had heard. I ran downstairs to her dad and was jumping around with joy and punching the air. I explained what I had heard and I just kept saying, "Yes, yes, yes." I had fulfilled another dream of exposing my children to the legacy of their parents.

My husband was pleased Symone had a special friend called Charmaine who was a regular visitor at the house. She was lovely and I knew her parents, although they were separated. Charmaine had what she called "an embarrassing experience" at our house that was so funny. The first time she came to stay, she went into the bathroom and became immediately confused by the two "toilets". She had never seen anything like it and got more and more confused about which one to use. She was getting quite desperate, so she had to call Symone to help her. Symone laughed and explained they were not two toilets, but a bidet and a normal toilet. The bidet is there to wash your private parts after you use the toilet. We still talk and laugh about it to this day. She said she felt very stupid and uncultured at the time.

Life dealt me another punch below the belt when my sister called to tell me Mum was in hospital. She was returning home to New York from her yearly trip to Trinidad. While coming off the plane, her legs gave way and she couldn't stand up. She was taken to hospital from the airport, and after an MRI was done, she was diagnosed with spinal cancer. This was devastating news to us all. I spoke to her in hospital and she was so cheerful. She said, "I had dodged the bullet fifteen years before, so something was bound to happen sooner or later."

Now in hospital, she said she was having her fifteen minutes of fame, because she was told she was such an anomaly. She had lots of doctors and cancer specialists coming to see her for her story. There were different schools of thought about her diagnosis. One camp said her spinal cancer was metastases from her breast cancer. The other camp said this was impossible because, if she had metastases, it would be in many more sites and she would have died within seven years, according to agreed scientific research. Another camp said that her spinal cancer was new and different and not at all related to her previous breast cancer. Another camp said it is rare for one individual to get two different types of cancer. In the end, they went with her cancer being new. Surgery was not an option, so they gave her massive doses of radiotherapy, which worked. Within six months, she had moved from being in a wheelchair, to using a walker, to using two canes, then one. She was a giant of a woman, with the strength and resolve and determination of many. I admired her greatly. I remember when she was diagnosed with breast cancer, she said she was not ready to die. She was on a mission and had too much work to do. Within months of her release from hospital, I made the first of many trips to visit and comfort her.

At the same time, I also learnt that my sister, Pat, was not in the best of health. Pat was the third of five children and was in her early thirties. She had been diagnosed with lupus a few years previously. Lupus is an autoimmune disease where the immune system overreacts and produces antibodies that attack the body's tissues and organs. It used to be called a silent killer, but almost all sufferers survive now, with good treatment. The most significant damage done to the body is kidney disease. Pat started suffering from severe tiredness and painful muscles and joints, which were the most prevalent symptoms of the disease. She seemed to have suffered from an acute form of the disease as, before long, she had to have surgery to remove her damaged spleen. Then she started to have trouble with her kidney function. She was put on a waiting list for a kidney transplant. She adamantly refused to have any of the family tested for the possibility that one of us could be a donor. She was resolved that she would never disrupt our lives to that extent, although the doctors were very clear that an adult could live a good life with one healthy kidney. She eventually started on dialysis, which she managed to do herself at home. She had to stop working for a while, but she continued to do the dialysis twice a week. When she began to have difficulty, she had to go to hospital three times a week for dialysis. She returned to work and was picked up from there for her hospital visits. She managed this procedure well for a few years.

You may have noticed that I have not said much about the carnival season, but it never ceased to have a dramatic impact on my life. Vernon was self-employed, so he was flexible and mobile and doing his usual business activities leading up to June, July and August, the crazy and busy summer months before the carnival. My work was equally full on at the hospital, and it took every ounce of my being to stay focused and sane during this time.

The season started with Vernon looking for premises to produce the costume band. In 1988 and for three years after, we had the great fortune of being given space at St Clements, a local community charity in west London where there was a youth leader called Nat King. Vernon took Nat under his wing and he began his mas-making apprenticeship. My role as usual was to complete the funding application on time. When the season started, I would start my role of hostess, cooking for and feeding all the volunteers at the mas camp. In the early months, I would then clean up and I might leave for home, because of course I had already worked for nine hours.

Together with St Clements, we made some incredible costumes for adults and children. I was ultimately responsible for the sewing of the costumes, especially the children's. In the beginning, I had to find seamstresses to help me, so I would take materials and measurements to them and agree a date to collect the finished garments.

Over the years, I truly admired my husband and his skills. He was legendary for producing historical themes with elaborate and distinctive materials. He certainly made an impression on the community, but if the truth be told, all I could think about most of the time was how tired I was and my longing to go to sleep. I started a countdown about a week before the carnival weekend, which Vernon acknowledged and found amusing. Every day in the last week, I would announce loudly, "Don't worry everyone: by this time next week, it will all be over."

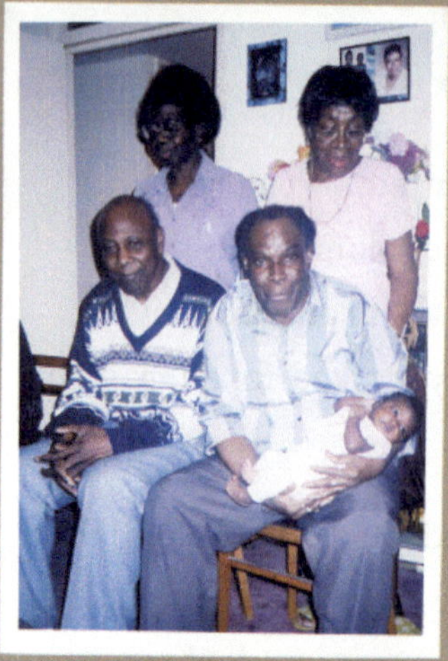
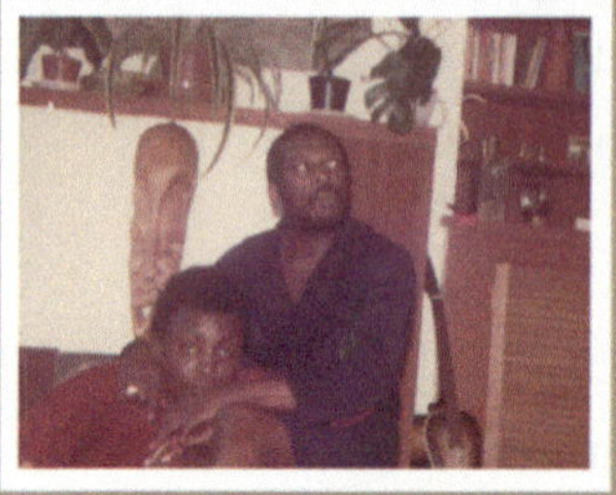
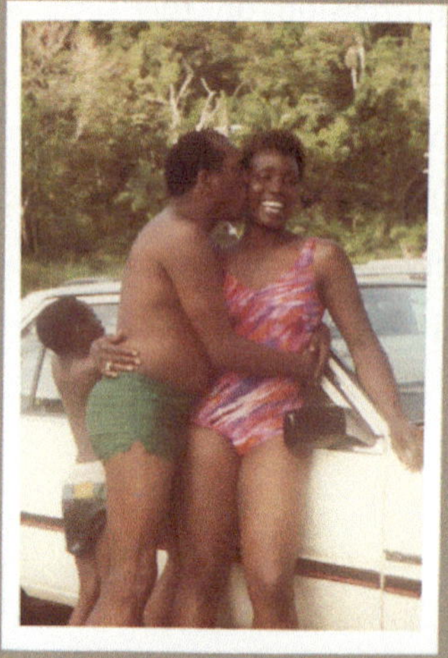
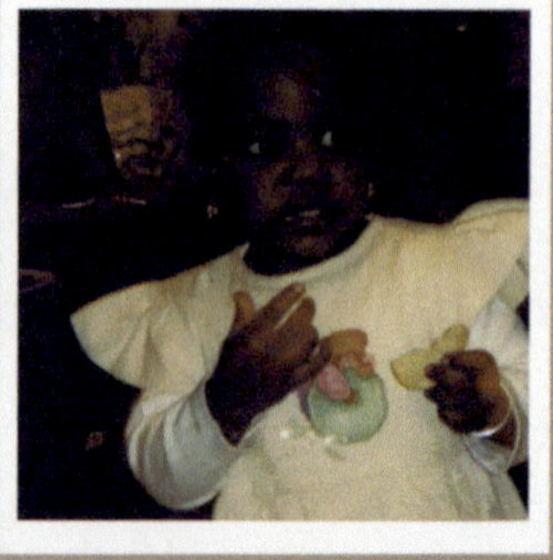
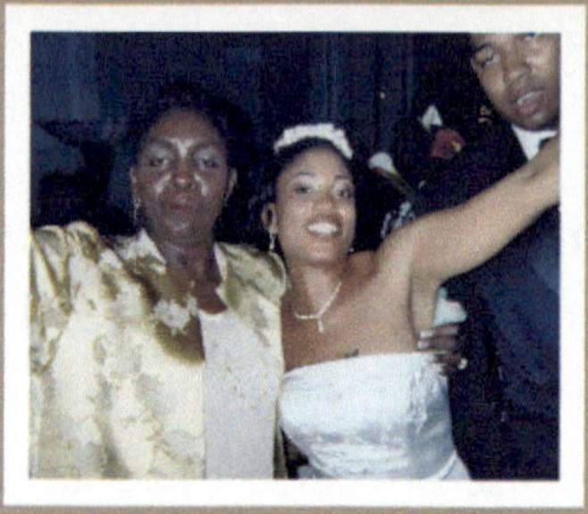
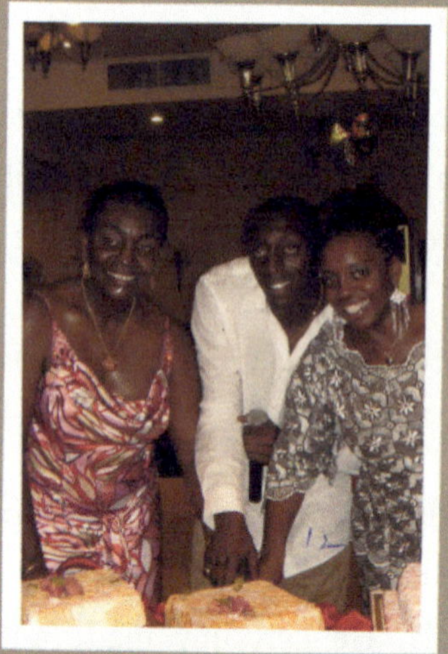
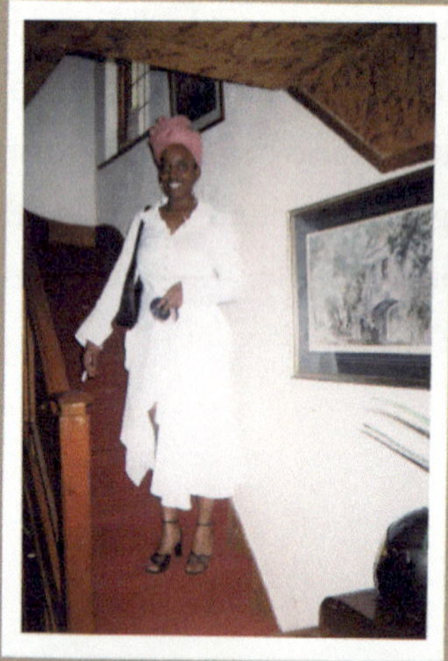
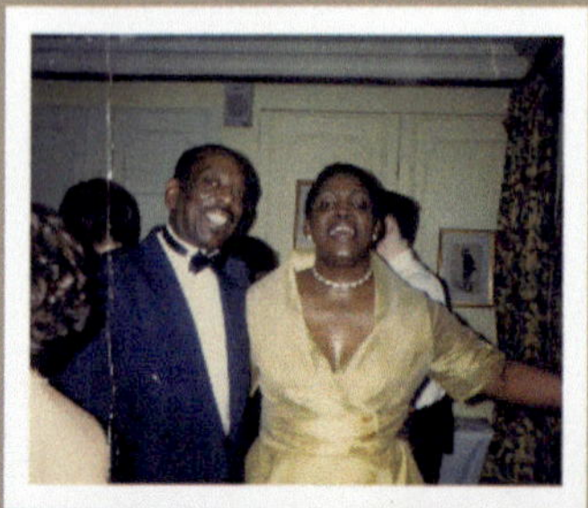
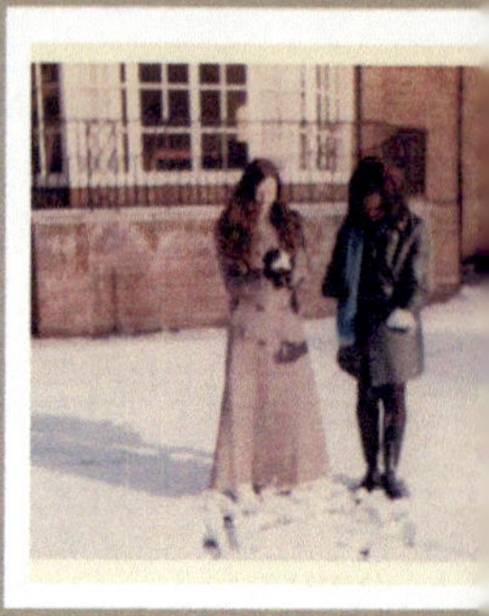
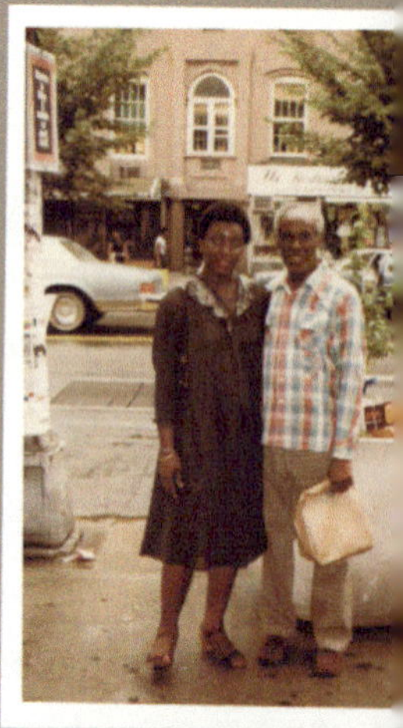
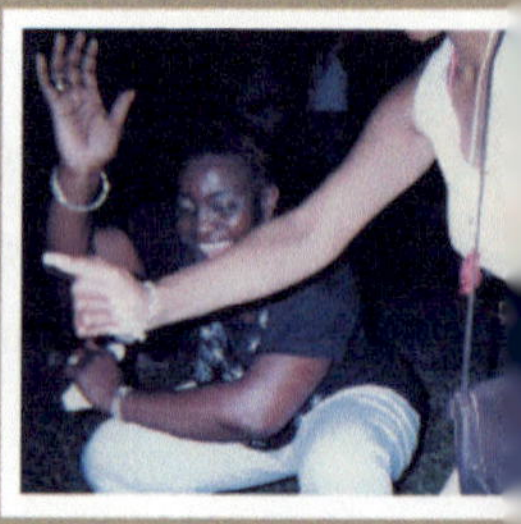
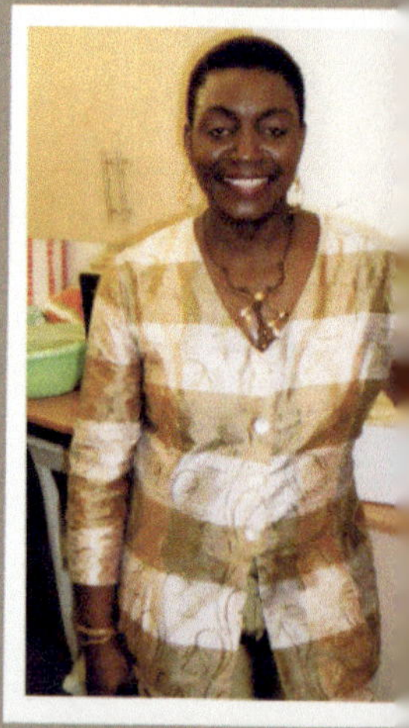

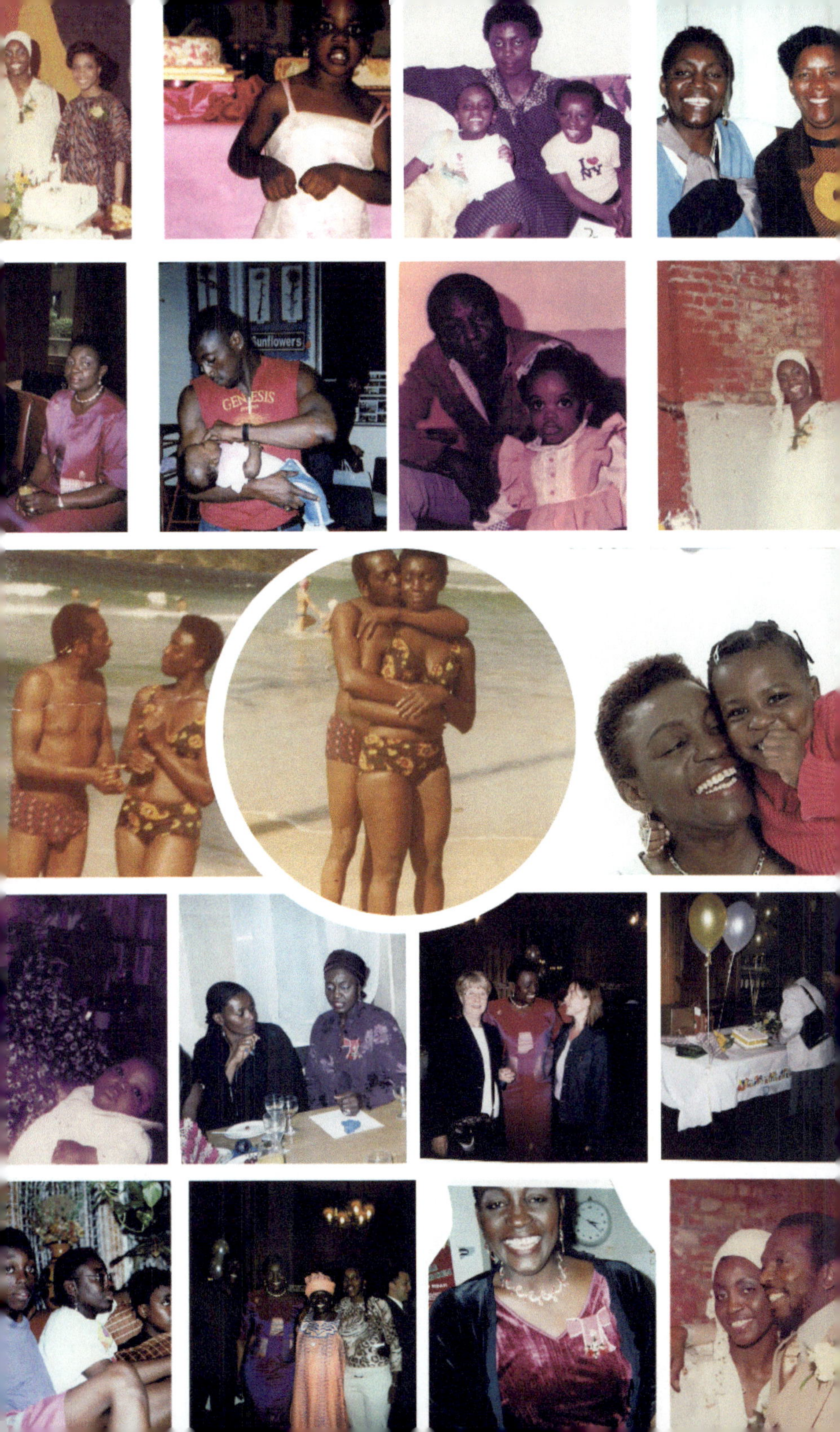
Sunflowers
GENESIS
NY

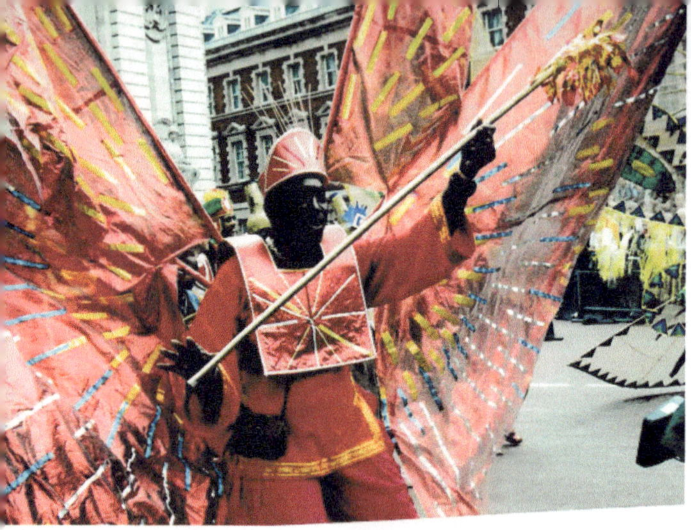
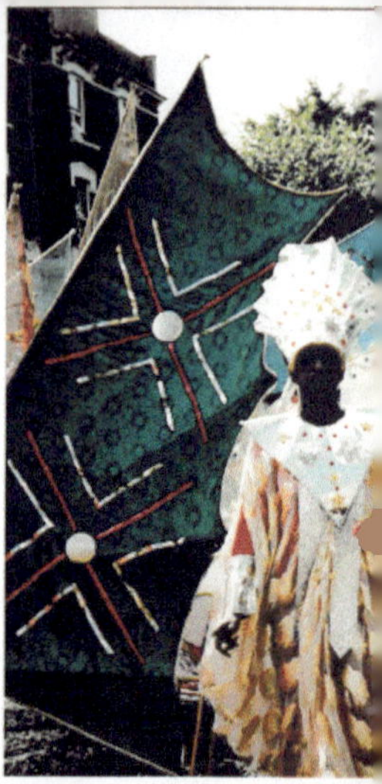
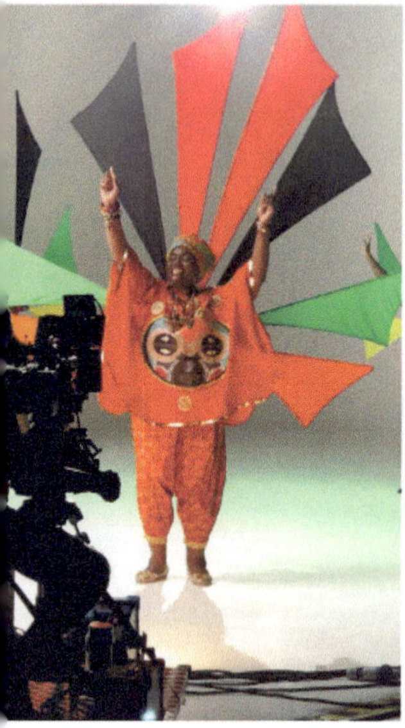
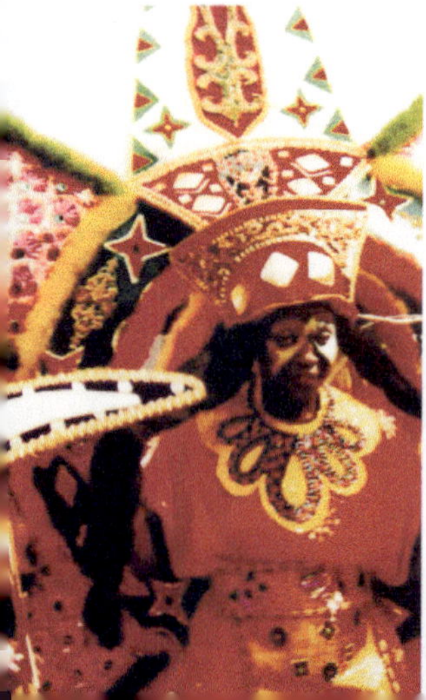
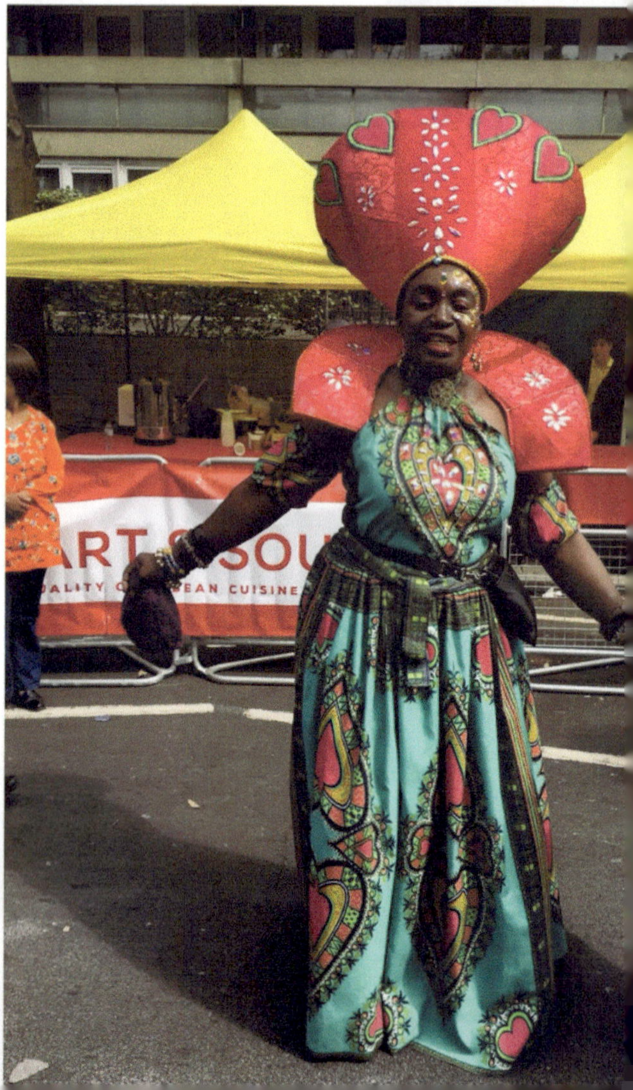

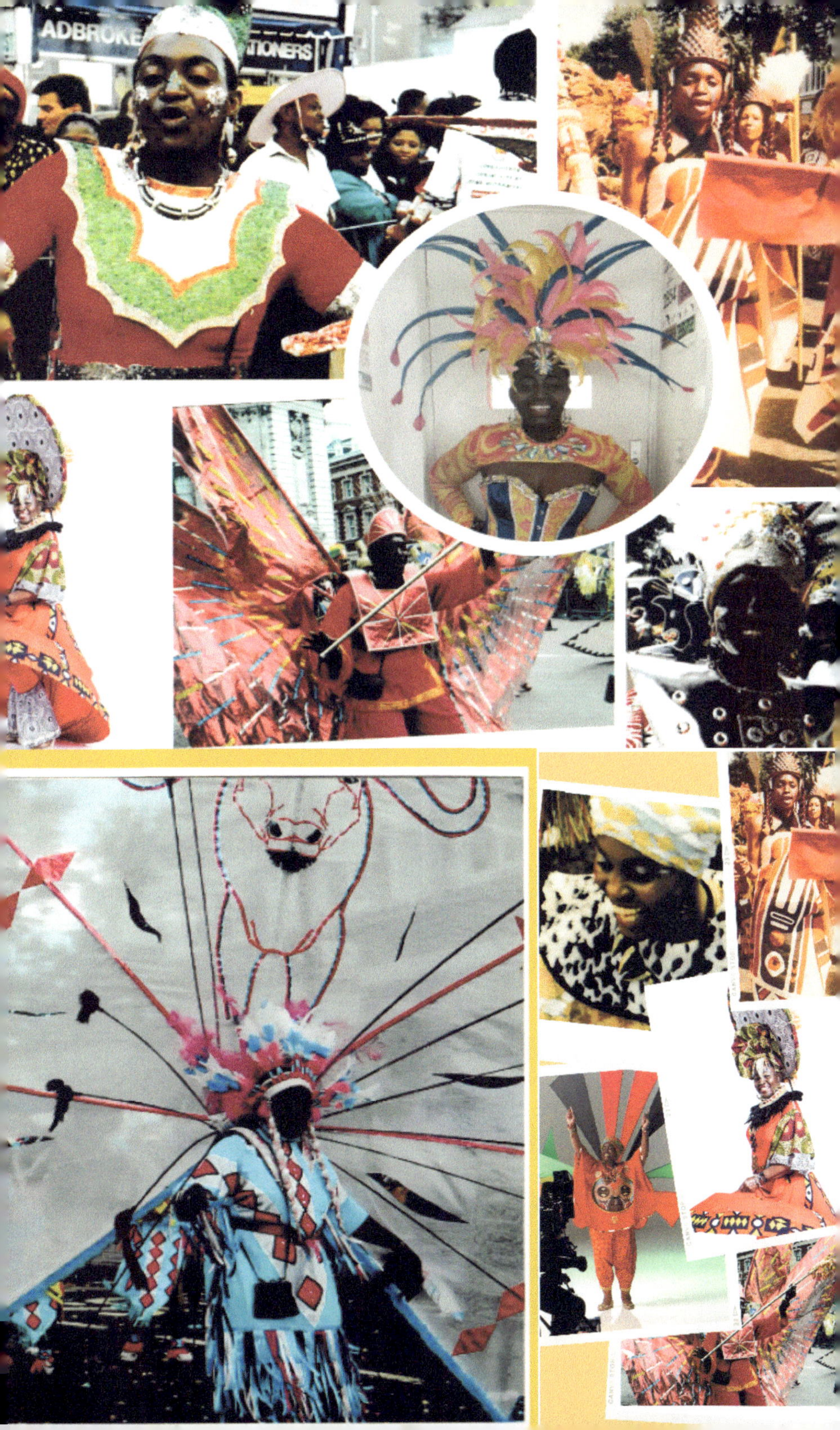

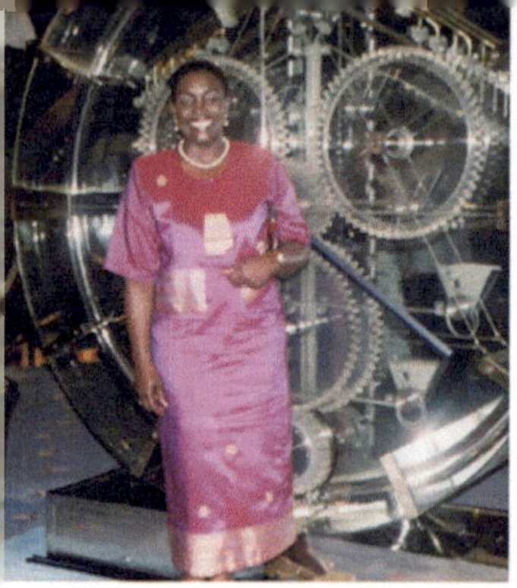

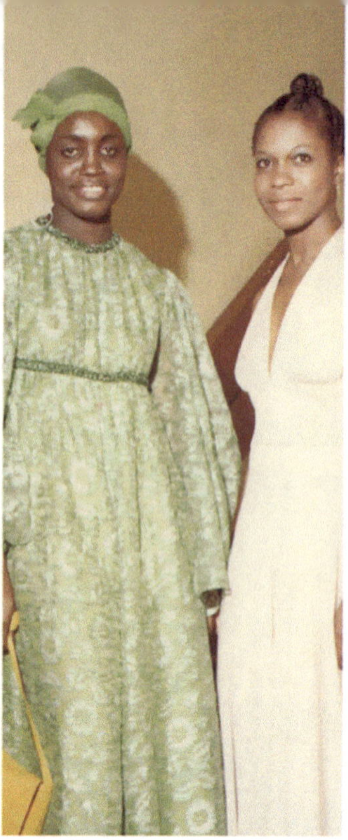

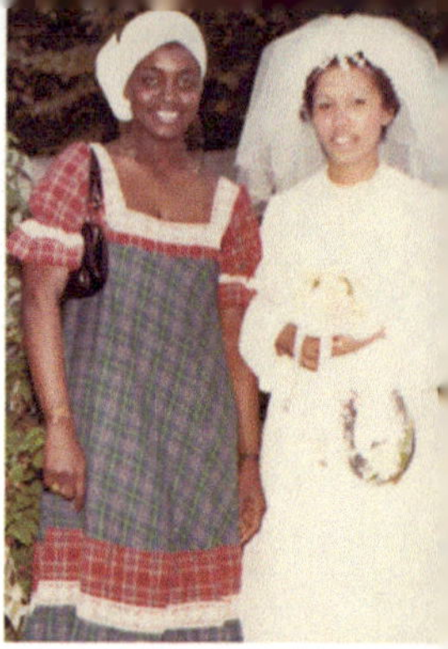

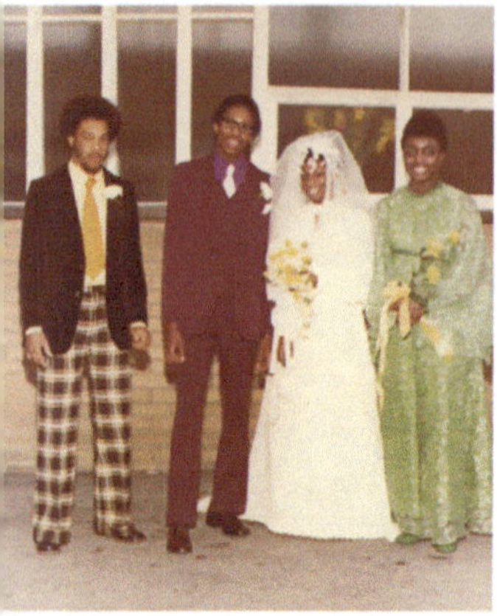

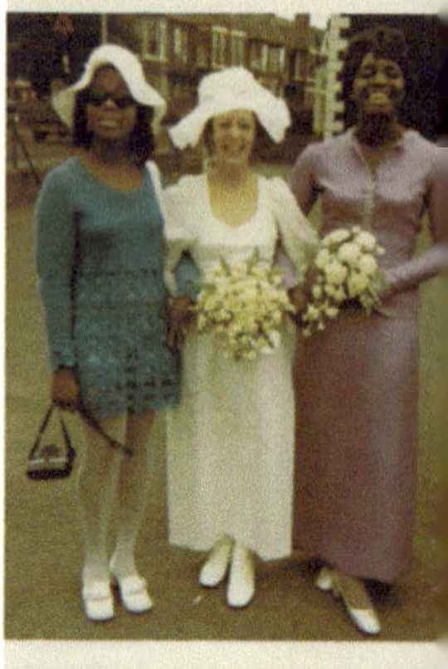

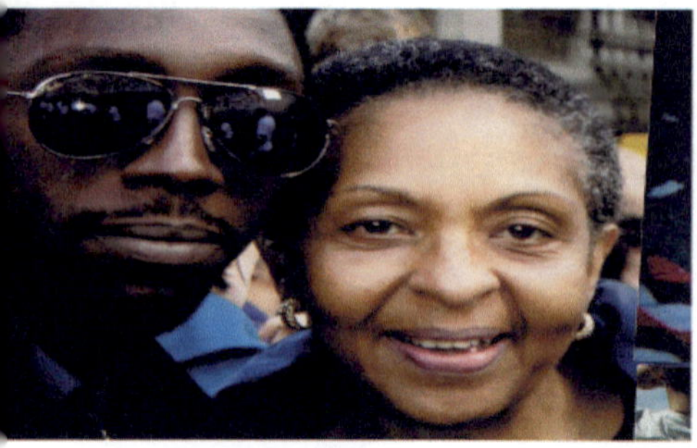

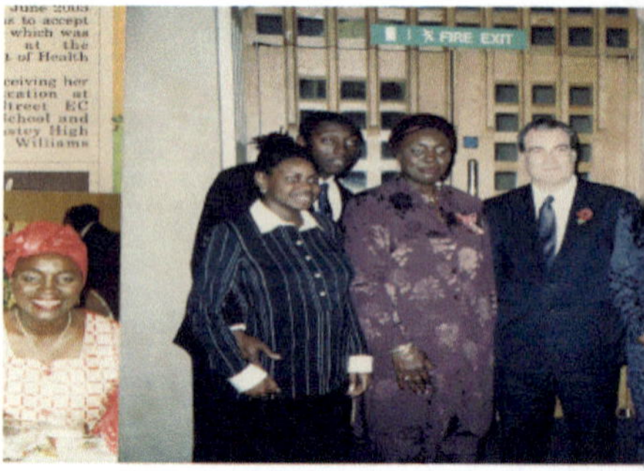
FIRE EXIT

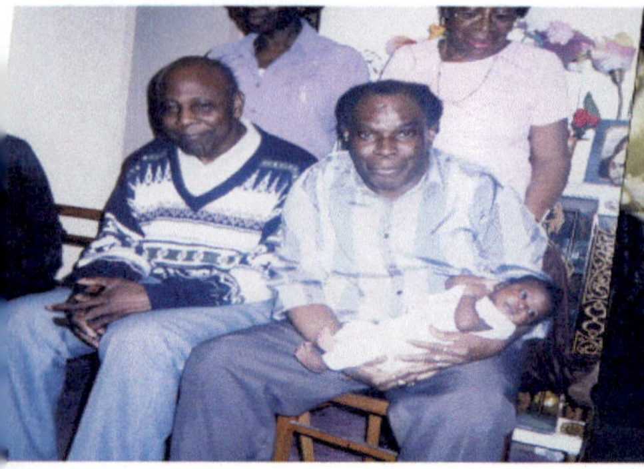

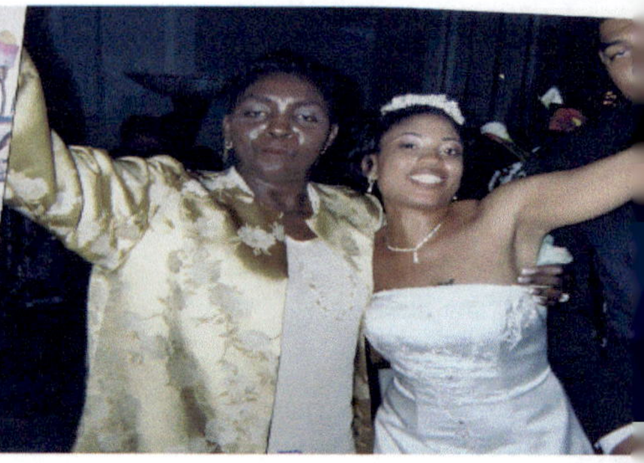

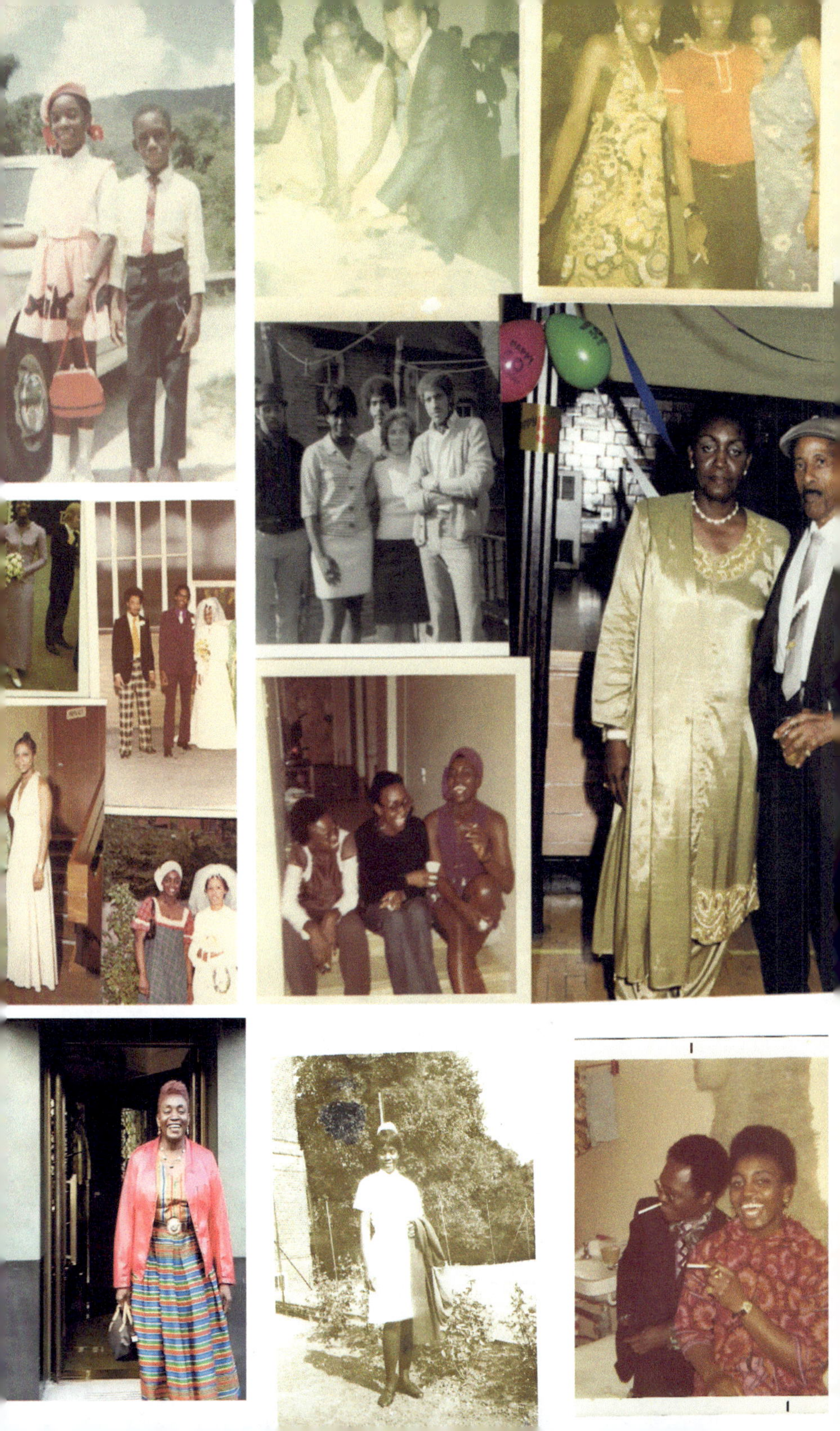

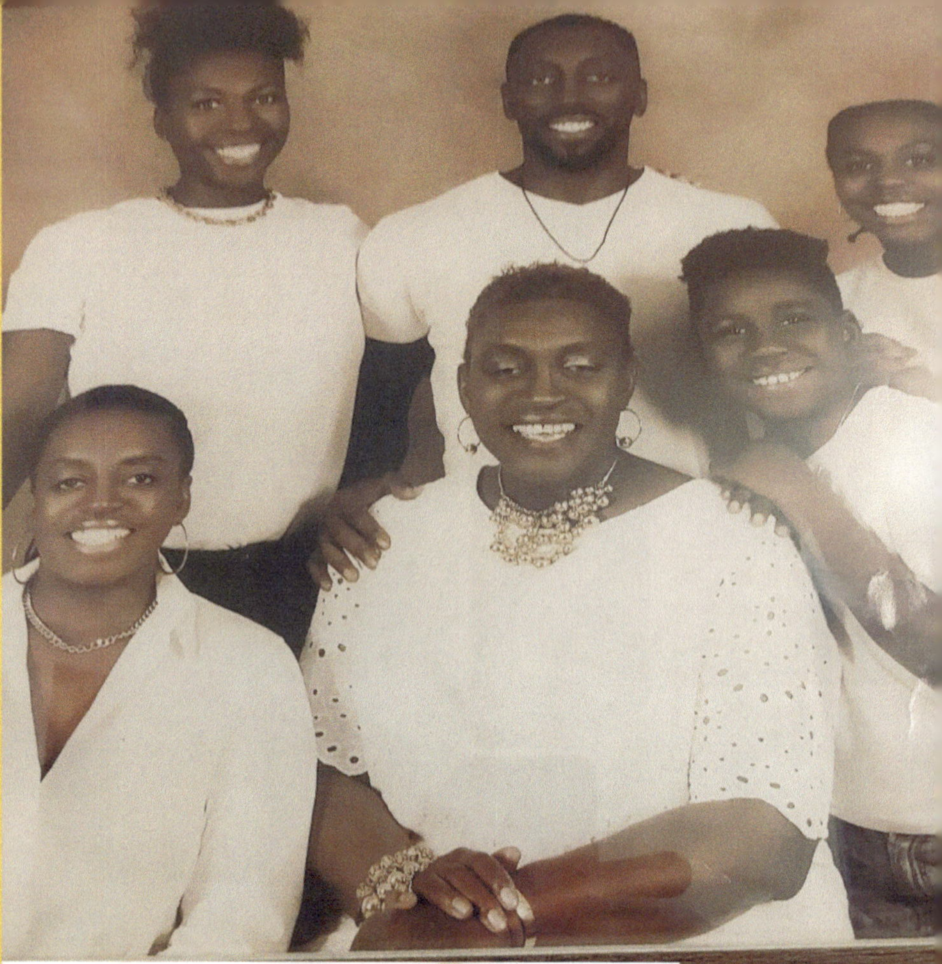
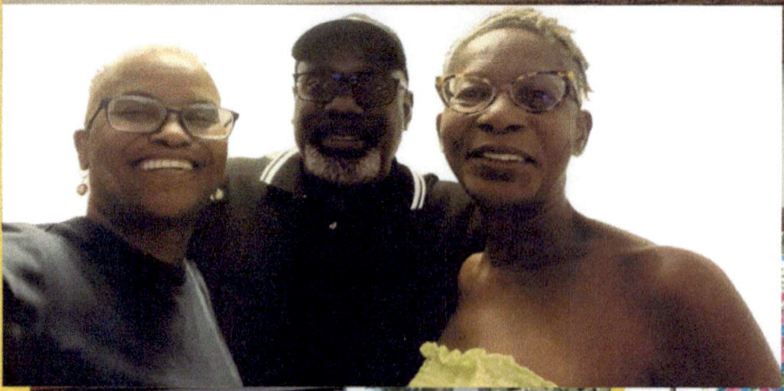
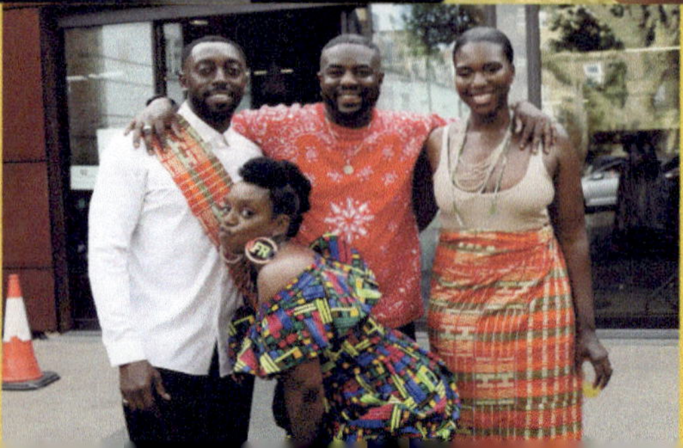
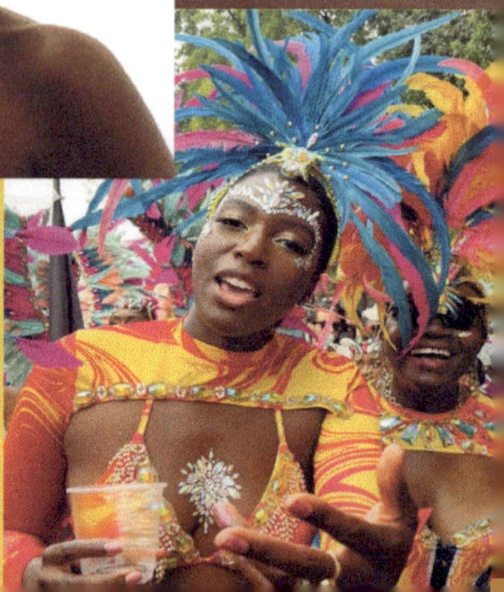

'THEY CALLED ME NAMES'

Allyson Williams, MBE, 74, former hospital services manager, from Trinidad

I arrived here when I was 21 after my mother, who was also a nurse, had been told about the British recruitment drive for nurses.

I hadn't expected racism here. Trinidad and Tobago was the most cosmopolitan place in the world. I went to school with white girls, black girls, Asians, Indians, Chinese and Syrians – you were just human and great friends with each other.

'I told patients, "I am black, so tell me something I don't know"'

When I got on to the ward the patients were very scathing about black nurses. They called you names, said, "Don't touch me, what are you doing here? You come from the jungle." The staff who were white did nothing about it. It was relentless. After nine months, I rang my mother and said, "I can't stand it, they're so racist."

She said, "You have a dream and an ambition to qualify, don't let them put you off. The racists, it's *their* problem, not yours." That made quite an impact on me.

Once I said to the patients, "I am black, so tell me something I don't know," they stopped. They were taken aback. But when a new lot of patients came, it was the same.

The racism continued – I'll always remember when I got promoted. One of the doctors came to me, straight up to my face and said, sarcastically, "I never noticed your blue eyes, how did you manage that?" He was trying to say that it is only white midwives who get promoted.

INTERVIEWS: SHERNA NOAH

---

son, 'Trini to the bone', gets MBE

ALLYSON WILLIAMS

...ni to the but some- be some- ...ppy hu- ...e when ...lliams was ...mbership of ...ers of the ...mpire in ...November

...son Layne in 1947, ...igrated to ...gland to training ...ittington ...n north ...ualifying ...later as a ...ered Nurse

...ved and ...England ...her adult ...othering to ...tion. ...at when ...as offered ...n recogni- ...outstanding

contribution to the development of midwifery services for women in London," she graciously accepted and then discovered, to her surprise, that she could not receive the honour because she was not British and would need the permission of the Trinidad and Tobago Government.

The British Foreign Office wrote the Trinidad and Tobago Government via the British High Commission in Port of Spain and permission was received in June 2003 for Williams to accept the honour which was presented at the Department of Health in London.

After receiving her early education at Quarry Street RC Primary School and Bishop Anstey...

worked for three or four years" at the Ministry of Education beore going off to London to study nursing.

Qualifying as an SRN, she "did midwifery for an additional year", becoming a State Registered Midwife.

Over the next five years, Williams worked part-time as a midwife, married Vernon Fellows Williams (a founder/member of London's Notting Hill Carnival) and bore two

children, Symone and Kevin, who are now both at university in England.

Williams and her husband (who died two years ago) presented their own carnival band, Genesis, for 24 years at the Notting Hill event.

In 1981 she became a midwifery sister working in the community.

In 1987 she was promoted to Hospital Manager (Midwifery) at the University

College of London Hospital, where she remained until her retirement in July 2002. She managed all aspects of the maternity services and was successful in encouraging midwives to develop autonomy in their clinical practice.

Williams is an accomplished speaker on many midwifery topics and writes on professional issues for professional magazines and lay publications.

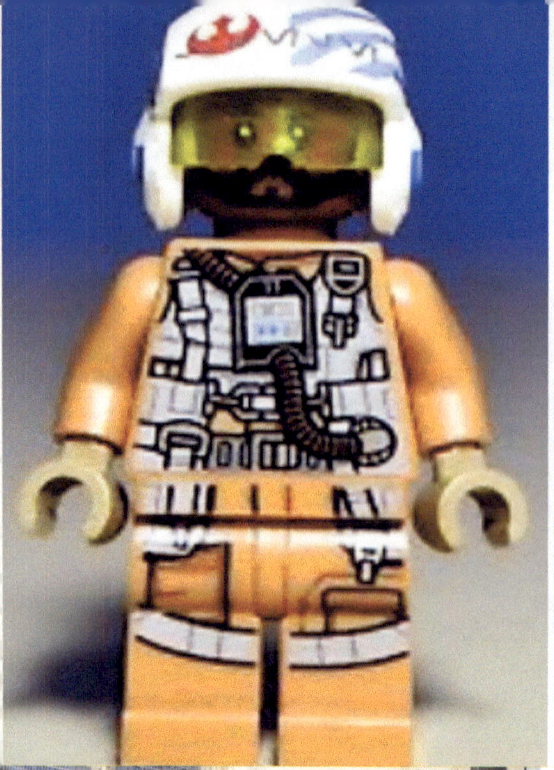
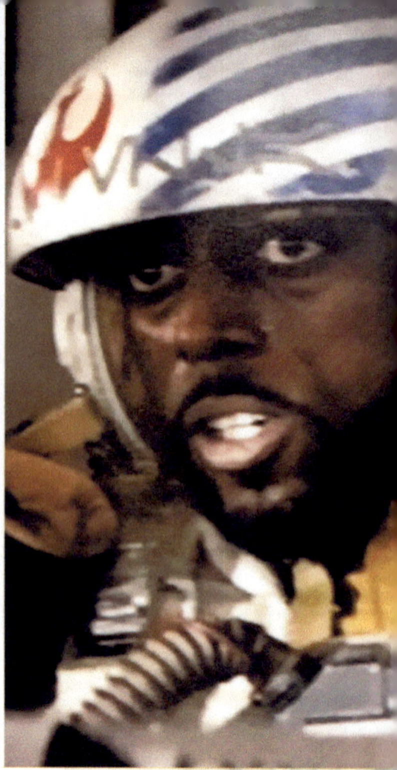
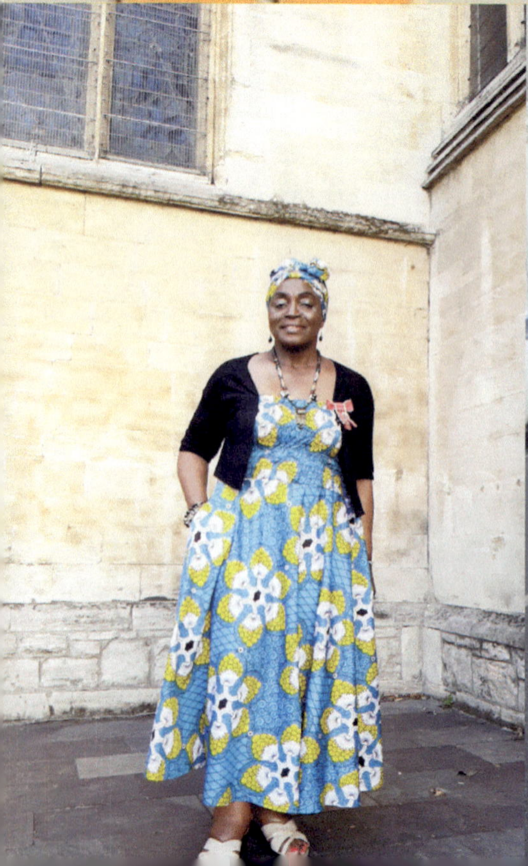
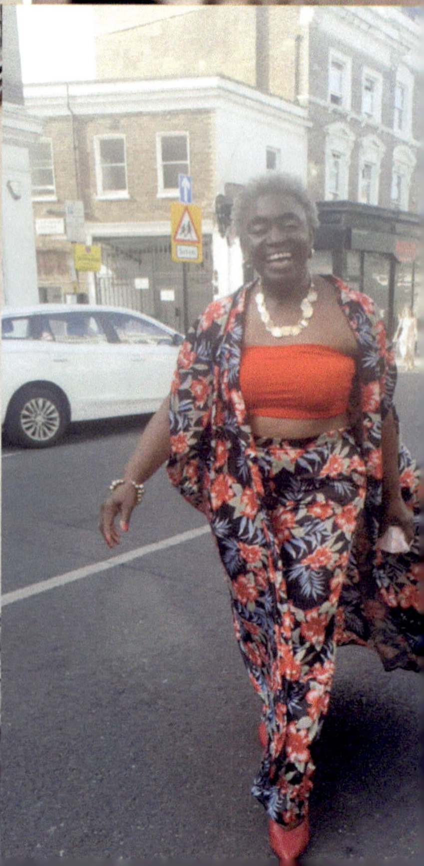

CHAPTER TWENTY-FOUR:
The Developing Community Midwifery Service

My work in the community continued to flourish. We were successful in setting up community midwife clinics across the borough. We did identify GPs and their surgeries where they were interested in providing space to accommodate a midwife. The idea was to develop the fact that midwives were trained as experts in normal midwifery and able to provide full antenatal care to normal, healthy and pregnant women. The women themselves relished this idea, as they felt normal, were seen immediately and didn't have to endure the long waiting times in a hospital setting. The doctors in hospital were experts in the abnormal, and midwives are trained to recognise abnormal changes in pregnancy and transfer care to a doctor. We had to be very careful about the care we provided because, as you would imagine, we were being watched carefully by the doctors in the hospital.

In my experience, most hospital obstetricians believed that midwifery was only normal in retrospect, as I was told this so many times. This was a difficult pill to swallow, and so illogical, so we had to set about proving them wrong. We had to prove that a profession that has thrived since the 1500s, and was regularised in 1902, could not be built on retrospect. It would be impossible to sustain that premise. It was built on strong, skilled women who practised to the highest standard in all aspects of clinical midwifery care. The creation of the NHS in 1948 came at a time of an increasing birth rate and the rise of hospital maternity care. The midwifery profession became the only profession in England that regulated its own practitioners. This practice ensured that midwives were up to date and current in their clinical practice. Interestingly, doctors and other health professionals have followed suit in more recent times, as they recognised the importance of keeping their clinical staff up to date.

I was so blessed to be part of an amazing team of community midwives, and led by a spectacular head of midwifery who had vision and passion for the profession. We worked well together and socialised well together, although I was not a fan of going to the pub. I cannot stand the feeling I have when drinking. I think it's such a waste of energy and I hate the feeling of being out of control. Our favourite night out was going to dinner. In central London, there was a plethora of interesting restaurants serving a variety of food. We would go to celebrate many different occasions, like birthdays, anniversaries, Christmas or just simply to de-stress at the end of a hard week. At one occasion, I was truly honoured when the midwives agreed to hold a Christmas party at my home for all community staff.

After some years, I was part of a very substantial home delivery and domino delivery service. Our numbers of community midwives were increasing and we had a large number of very satisfied clients.

I thoroughly enjoyed being part of this new initiative that was bringing a lot of job satisfaction for the midwives involved. I was also involved in training student midwives. I was allocated several wonderful women who were equally passionate about the profession and who successfully qualified at the end of their training and went on to become sisters and senior managers within the profession.

After many years of hard work and joyful successes, my manager informed me she was leaving her post and returning to her home in Cornwall. She was confident I would be suitable to take her place. This was a shock to my system, and I was humbled she thought so highly of me. I immediately refused and said I was not management material. She disagreed and asked me to promise her I would spend some time writing my CV. She explained to me what the process was like, as I had never done one before. She would look at its content and give me an honest opinion of my chances of promotion to a managerial post. A CV is a personal statement that outlines your achievements throughout your career up to the time of use. It gives you the opportunity to sell yourself to prospective employers. So I went away to complete the task for the first time, to appreciate my career path and acknowledge the contribution I had made. The new post also came with several changes to the service, including the relocation of the community midwifery services back to the obstetric hospital, which was near the main hospital site.

I had never considered working at a managerial level until that point. Although I was good at organising meetings and our daily workload, I always did it for the benefit of the women and their families in our care. My boss's faith in my ability was very encouraging, and I began to give the idea some serious thought.

Once I had finished my CV, I passed it to my manager for her scrutiny. When we met again, the first thing she said to me was, "Seriously, have you read your own CV? I would give you the job, just from reading the document. It is well written and very comprehensive. It clearly demonstrates your skills and potential to be a good manager. I highly recommend that you should apply for the post."

I applied and immediately set about preparing for the interview. Our new head of midwifery was a wonderful, visionary leader and I started to relish the thought of working closely with her. She was so bright and intelligent; I always thought she was way out of my league. I had nightmares about the questions I could be asked. I certainly made sure I could explain all aspects of my work, as I had described on my CV. I even thought of new ideas for future development. I got a great piece of advice from one of my colleagues, who said, "You should keep smiling no matter what and keep talking. Never allow them to drag responses out of you."

The day came for interview, which was conducted by the head of midwifery, her assistant, and a head of midwifery from another hospital. I will never forget my first impression of the panel. My head and her assistant were dressed beautifully in the standard blue and white uniform, but the outside assessor looked stunning. She wore a plaid dress of red, green, blue and black squares, with a large white collar with a bow. I breathed a sigh of relief and said to myself, "Wow, they are human and look warm and friendly, so just enjoy yourself."

I took my friend's advice and never stopped talking, always checking that I understood their questions. I think they acknowledged that I would never hesitate to tackle difficulty head-on. In the back of my mind, I was confident I did a good job, but realistically I thought I didn't stand a chance, as I was up against three very accomplished white women. When I returned later in the day for the results, I was blown away. My head of midwifery said, "It is clear that you have little managerial experience, but your potential to succeed and become a good manager is so great. You were the only candidate who understood how to manage conflict and difficult scenarios. We are very pleased to say we would like to offer you the job of senior midwife manager."

I was ecstatic and accepted the role immediately. I didn't believe the way people looked could have such an impact on me, but I realised as I grew up and went along in life that I think first impressions are so important, as they leave lasting memories.

I suddenly realised that, after working in the community for eight years, that over a weekend I would become the manager of my peers and be in charge of them instead of being one of them. When I came out of the meeting, I was thrilled and delighted and shrieking with joy. The first person I saw was one of the consultants in the team. I was almost hysterical when telling him my news. We hugged and he congratulated me and offered me any help I might need. I called Vernon and he was delighted and said that I truly deserved it.

The joy of my success and my rising career coincided with my strong desire to visit and comfort my mother. My first holiday was spent with her. She was so happy for me and my promotion and quite resigned to her latest diagnosis. She had been receiving radiotherapy, with the hope it would shrink the tumour and give her a chance at surgery. She had lost her appetite, so my sister was encouraging her to take liquid meals. After spending some time with her, I had to return, but I was happy she was more comfortable and making slow progress.

Back at work, the changing attitude towards me was getting me down. It was actually difficult for me too, as I was never interested in power and glory. I wanted to make a positive and meaningful difference to everyone's lives. One midwife told me that their behaviour wasn't personal, it was just that I represented the establishment now, which they would always have difficulty believing in. It was difficult to put a finger on the problems; it was their general attitude. They seemed to ignore me when socialising. I suppose I was expecting a lot, but we were all friends first before I became a manager.

Another aspect of my job was the issue of working out what it actually entailed. It was confusing, and the retiring manager for the hospital services left me cabinets full of paper that didn't make any sense. I discovered that the staff under my care now had no comprehensive records. I felt I was getting nowhere fast. I went to see the head of midwifery to ask for help as I wasn't making any progress. My boss was very supportive and calm. She said that giving up was not an option. She said that she and her colleagues saw great potential in me to be an effective and successful leader, so I just had to develop a strategy to learn how to manage my job.

So, we made a plan. The first thing was to prioritise the tasks in order of importance and then decide on a time frame in which they could be achieved. She called in her assistant and we arranged that she would meet with me weekly to get a progress report on my actions and offer advice and help if needed.

This was the most invaluable advice I received throughout my career. I was able to work through most of the issues raised and, as time went on, I was able to accurately complete many of my jobs. I learnt to interact with my junior staff in a very different way and on a different level than before. I started off being very weak and unsure of myself, but I grew stronger and was able to rise above the rubbish. I had to remember that I was in charge. I felt there was definitely some jealousy or confusion in them trying to understand my role as well. I thought of my mother and I remembered her saying to us as children that she wasn't there to be liked or be our friend. She was there to train us on how to be respectful adults and know right from wrong. I also thought long and hard that I could not let down my loved ones or my supporters. I also had to try to stay calm, when all I wanted to do was scream and cry hysterically. I was looking after my husband, my home, my children, worrying about my financial situation, my mother and her developing cancer, and about my sister, whose body was being attacked by lupus, all while coping with my new job.

At the same time, my husband and I were still doing what I imagined was happening to all married couples: wanting the best of everything for their family, but completely out of their depth. His business was very slow and, to be honest, I didn't think he was a very good businessman. I used to keep saying to him that running a business was a 24-hour process, but he felt working nine to five was enough. I had no choice but to reduce my agency work drastically, because my new management role was from eight to four from Monday to Friday, with several on-call shifts during that time, in the evening and at weekends. One saving grace was that my salary was much improved and went some way to helping our situation.

After a few months of focusing on the task in hand, I was beginning to enjoy my work and contribute more sensibly to developing the services. I was put in charge of changes we wished to implement that we knew would be unpopular and controversial, especially with the medical staff. I set up a working group to brainstorm the ideas to a group of interested midwives. I was so happy that the staff I managed were made up of a group of committed midwives. We reunited as friends and continued meeting and socialising. I remember, at a party held by Debra, an outstanding midwife that I managed, where her family were astounded that the boss was socialising with the staff she managed. Debra was very clear and stated, "We know our boundaries and respect Allyson's role as the manager. She was a friend long before she became our manager."

I was once witness to a heated tirade by a group of midwives about another midwife in the office. One of them noticed me and said, "Do you realise that Allyson is here!" Another midwife quickly commented, "Never mind. Allyson is really cool. She's not the enemy. None of this will leave the room and she will put us right when she has to." I felt that was the ultimate demonstration of trust and confidence my staff had for me.

CHAPTER TWENTY-FIVE:
Condolences But A Celebration of Life

When Mum's spinal cancer was confirmed, I called her several times a week and visited her each year to give her moral support and tender loving care. She was so strong and determined to do her best. Each time she had a relapse, I was there to support her. The most wonderful thing about this time was that my boss was so calm and caring about my situation. On two different occasions, I asked for no-pay leave, as my annual leave was spent. She said, "Please just go and support your mother. We will decide what we will call your absence when you return to work. You work over and above the time for your job. You spend your time going that extra mile for the women and their families. You deserve this time with your mother."

I was so relieved and grateful for her empathy. At the beginning of March 1992, Mum had to be transferred to hospital. I went immediately to see her. I spent eight hours every day for two weeks at her bedside. She was primarily in a hospice, a very beautiful place that was state of the art. They were wonderful to me and offered me food and drink all day. I will never forget her reaction to seeing me. She groaned loudly and her eyes opened really widely on hearing my voice. She clearly recognised me but could not speak. I was so devastated. Mum was my idol and mentor and a life guru to me. I adored her and all that she represented. It was so painful to watch her deteriorate, but I chatted to her all the time, telling her of all the nuances of my life in London. Suddenly, I made a snap decision to return home, as I had to consider my family and work. Also, the thought of waiting there for her to die was just too painful. She subsequently passed away two weeks later, and I had to return to New York at the end of March 1992 to make her funeral arrangements.

My mother's funeral was conducted following the style of her Buddhist practice, which meant she was to be cremated. Her instructions were that she wished to be dressed in her Buddhist uniform, including the jewellery she wanted to wear and how her hands should look. She stated that I must do her eulogy at the time. In America, the funeral services are second to none and can be quite lavish, in beautifully decorated premises. There is an evening for viewing, when the family is host to guests viewing the deceased. It is like the body lying in state. We had an evening of viewing for my mother and it was a wonderful occasion. There were many of her nursing colleagues who came to pay their last respects, because they were not able to attend the service and cremation the next day. I did not know most of them, but they were very complimentary about her skills and talents as a nurse, as well as the kindness she showed to others. Her colleagues talked about her hard work at fundraising on behalf of the Nurses' Association. They recalled she was always knitting or crocheting or sewing items for sale.

I was truly devastated to lose my mother, who was my idol, but I realised it was more important to celebrate her life and sing her praises for making such a wonderful difference in so many people's lives. Her cremation ceremony was equally wonderful. I was so shaky and sad. I never wrote a single word down, but when I stood in front of several hundred people, the words just flowed and I spoke for twenty minutes about my mother's strength and the wonderful life lessons she taught us and how much I appreciated her involvement in my life. I will love her forever.

After returning to London, it took me some time to focus. I was uplifted by the kindness and condolences from my colleagues and from my husband, children and friends. I was also concerned about my baby sister, who was living with my mother and was then left alone in the flat. She was in her mid-thirties and had decided long ago that she didn't want to be married or have children. I always found that to be such a profound decision. As I was so far away, it was difficult to fully probe her and get a satisfactory response. Once she told me she did not want a child to turn out like her sister, and this was the only way to be sure. Our sister, Pat, was the one who stood apart from us. She was six years younger than me and six years younger than my sister. I have talked before about how much she was spoilt when she was the baby. Well, this feeling of entitlement carried on through her teenage and adult life. When my parents tried to turn it around, she brought on the tears and the tantrums and, to keep the peace, the indulgence would set in. My brother and I hated the drama and noise, so we sought comfort with each other.

My sister told me that life didn't change much when they moved to New York. As Pat's beautiful daughter was growing up, she would dish out the "licks" to her. Mum did explain to me that she was awarded custody of Abbegail because the doctors thought she was being abused. She was just 12 when she was admitted to hospital with suspected appendicitis. Because she was mixed-race, she presented with many marks and bruises on her fair skin and social services were concerned for her safety. It was at this time that Pat's mental health was assessed, and she was considered to be bipolar. Mum told me she had to beg the social services officers, as they had decided Abbe would go into care.

So Abbe had to move and live with my mother, who became her official guardian. I had to agree, because I did have experience of Pat's mental health going wrong when we were children back home. I had to get Daddy to discreetly put extra locks on my wardrobe. When Pat got into her moods, she would target my clothes. She would say that I was a show-off and thought I was so nice, wearing skimpy clothes. This was because I was very skinny when young and she was very chubby. At one time, she got hold of a lacy lingerie set and cut them up. Thankfully, in New York, Pat lived on her own, so everyone just braced themselves when she came to visit. Her daughter, Abbegail, grew up to be a beautiful young lady and, after getting married, she moved on with her husband. The rumour was that Pat had played matchmaker because she was close to a co-worker who had a son, and they put them together.

Penelope assured me that she would be happy on her own. She had a group of caring friends at church and at work and she socialised a great deal. Her friends were amazing people who were a joy to be around when I visited New York. I persuaded her to consider a vacation to London sooner rather than later. Thankfully, she took my advice and came to London for the Notting Hill Carnival in August the year that Mum passed away. Pene and I had always been great friends, as well as sisters, and I promised myself I would stay close and look after her. She came on holiday with her best friend, Paula, and they had a wonderful time over the carnival. After that, my best friend Julie and I took a five-day trip with them to visit Amsterdam and Paris.

It was approaching October 1992 when Symone reached her sixteenth birthday, and she begged to have a celebration at home. She was not in favour at the time, but that's another story. I relented so she could enjoy her journey into adulthood. The party was a resounding success. Symone and Kevin were very well liked and respected and very streetwise. Throughout their lives, they were surrounded by a range of adults all the time, for example, we took them everywhere with us to parties and dinners and award ceremonies. They socialised with their dad's friends during the carnival season, adults in the steel band, and my work colleagues. They were always teased because their friends didn't understand how they had so many aunts and uncles.

At the party, the lights were dimmed all night and the adults were confined to the bedroom. One of the nice things that happened at the party was that Symone's friends didn't want to leave. I went to the front when I heard the doorbell. It was about 1 a.m. and a mother was there to pick up her daughter. Symone begged for her to stay and said her mum would take her home. "You will, won't you?" she said, turning to me. Of course I couldn't refuse, and this scenario happened several times. So the party went on until 6 a.m. because, of course, all the neighbours were warned. Some of them even attended the party. I didn't even know until much later that Symone had one of the best DJs, Stone Love, playing the music. It was then that I found out how many children I was booked to take home. I ended up making four trips all around Wembley, Willesden and Harlesden, taking about sixteen children to their homes. Symone hugged and kissed me when I returned from the last trip. She said, "I knew you wouldn't mind. You have always said that everywhere is on the way to Wembley, so you are always happy to take my friends home."

The best thing that happened was that all Symone's friends who were waiting to travel on the first bus in the morning had cleaned the kitchen, living room and dining room and had brought all the furniture back into the house and returned everything to its rightful place. All the rubbish was cleaned up and binned. The DJ had packed up all his equipment and was leaving. The dishes were done and all the remaining food was put in the fridge. I was so impressed and thankful for their thoughtfulness.

CHAPTER TWENTY-SIX:
My Personal and Professional Development

My tiredness continued and I also had occasional headaches for no reason, so I decided to visit my GP. We discussed how I felt and, as part of the process, he checked my blood pressure. After recording it several times, he stated that it was high. He asked me to describe why I thought it could be high: "Are you sleeping and eating well?"

I said, "I was having difficulty, but maybe it's stress caused by my new job. I have just been appointed as a manager. I am so excited about my new role but struggling with the workload."

He just stopped and stared at me, leaning into my face, and said, "Wow, I never noticed your blue eyes." I was horrified and said that his comment was very racist. He said he was joking, and continued, "Sorry, but didn't you know that hospital is the most racist institution in London. You must be really good at your work. I wish you all the best. I know you will be an amazing success."

I said, "Why didn't you say that in the first instance?" I was left wondering what was in store for me, but was grateful for my doctor's candour.

I imagined the job would be difficult, but only because of the doctors' belief that midwifery was only normal in retrospect. I was not at all fazed. I just braced myself for the onslaught. Also, I was actually very proud and excited about being the first black manager in the maternity unit. It was certainly a privileged position to be in, and I was determined to make everyone proud of me. I found it so time-consuming and exhausting, always having to be so aware of being black and keeping tuned for the racist language. I always got the feeling that people were watching for me to slip up! I was also very aware of the saying that black staff have to work three times as hard as their white counterparts to achieve the same results!

As part of the unit's development, I was constantly interviewing new staff and noticing how highly qualified they were. They were all hearing about our work and wanted to be part of the journey. Many of them were qualifying at degree level, while others were coming through the normal route of training as a nurse first, then as a midwife. The degree-level course was an admirable course of study, but these graduates often lacked the invaluable expertise and the basics of training as a nurse, like a good bedside manner and basic nursing skills. Some of them would come under my care.

I began to feel I was lagging behind, so I asked my boss about further training. I felt it was imperative for me to have a similar experience of advanced study. In 1990, this led to my enrolment on the Advanced Diploma in Midwifery, which was six months of study at diploma level at the Royal College of Midwives. My boss also secured funding to cover my study leave. I met a group of remarkable and intelligent midwives with many years of experience between us all. I belonged to a group and we called ourselves "Phoenix", as we felt we were getting on a bit but still full of hope and life and so rising from the ashes. We did a lot of exciting projects, my most favourite being a full exploration of the use of alternative medicine in pregnancy. This was an amazing insight into the use of acupuncture, reflexology, massage and homeopathy. We also explored evidence-based practices and research, which was invaluable for me, because we had started to provide evidence for all the procedures and guidelines we were preparing for use in the unit.

As part of the course, we discussed the role of midwives around the world, and this intrigued me. I had heard of the midwives in the Bronx, New York, so I arranged a visit the next time I went there. The maternity unit occupied a whole floor in the hospital and was staffed by both nurses and midwives. Their motto was "pregnancy is paramount". This meant that all pregnant women were cared for in the unit, regardless of any medical issues they may have. For example, I saw a pregnant woman, who sustained a broken leg from a car accident, being cared for by the orthopaedic teams, nurses and midwives. There were women having treatment for heart disease, dialysis and type two diabetes. The deputy director of midwifery was trained in London and talked fondly of Central Middlesex Hospital. The midwives were highly respected and very well paid. They practised fully as midwives.

The most interesting aspect of the care they provided was reflected in the figures. Their statistics showed that 90 per cent of the women they cared for had a medical condition and were considered high risk. However, the midwives achieved a 94 per cent normal delivery rate. These midwives participated fully in all procedures regarding the delivery of the baby. What we called the extended role of the midwife was normal practice for them. They also conducted the circumcision of male babies on request. This experience started me thinking about extending the role of the midwife, to truly enhance their clinical skills.

One of the most important jobs I had to do was appoint a clerical officer to help with the coordination of the community service. I appointed Tom Hughes to the post, who turned out to be a proficient and important appointee. Tom had just returned to London after years of wandering around the world, including living in Australia. I soon realised what a reliable and dependable person he was. His commitment was important, as we were making some revolutionary changes to the service. The work was unrelenting, but he never complained. He soon became the go-to person as we discovered his ability to chase people and get results. We made a great team, and the midwives appreciated his skills immensely.

I got very close to him. We had a ritual of calling each other every evening as a sort of debrief and wind-down session, which was helpful to us both. My husband and children would raise their eyebrows when the phone rang, and would call out to me, "Mummy, it's him."

After attending one of his parties, my daughter asked me to explain why Tom and his friends were different. Then she said, "I think Tom would have asked you to marry him if he wasn't gay, because I think he loves you a lot." We laughed when I said that we were happy to have her dad. Tom had a wonderful sense of humour that was dry and quite irreverent at times. I had to rein him in at times, but he consistently kept us laughing all the time. He called me his Caribbean Queen and I cherished that reference to my life in the carnival in London. He was the greatest asset we had in the team, and the midwives and I praised him for his outstanding work and support.

Eventually, he moved on within the Trust to bigger and better roles. We always kept in touch and had dinner or drinks regularly. Tom was the first person to take me for a birthday dinner at The Ivy in Shaftesbury Avenue, somewhere I would never afford to go normally. It's a very popular restaurant in central London, frequented by the rich and famous, but we didn't see anyone of consequence, besides us, on that day. Also, I was particularly touched that I was invited as his special guest when he was honoured for his twenty-five years' service in the Trust.

I had the wonderful opportunity of meeting a wise and successful head of midwifery who had recently been appointed to the role at our neighbouring hospital. She visited our unit as part of her orientation, and I was asked to look after her and explain all that I had achieved in my role so far. She was blown away by projects I had achieved, like setting up midwife clinics in the community, increasing the home and domino delivery service, changing the home delivery packs to make them more efficient and cost-effective, the updating of many policies and procedures, ensuring they were referenced with evidence-based research. She was excited and determined to achieve similar progress at her unit.

Before I knew it, I was called to a meeting with my boss and this head of midwifery, where I was asked to consider holding a joint post of community midwife manager across both sites. I jumped at the chance. This was the hospital where I trained, and the thought of returning as a senior manager was mind-blowing. I felt so honoured and privileged to have been asked. I also acknowledged the confidence they had in me to make a difference and improve the clinical practice and thus the experience of their clients.

I was pleased to be able to train an experienced sister to take my role when I was away. The idea was that I would work for two and a half days at each unit, but in reality, it took a while for me to settle and get organised. The job was full-on and difficult and I was up and down from Euston to Highgate like the proverbial fly! I had to clear my diary and start again. I was initially running between both hospitals on a daily basis, which was madness. I had to plan to be in my unit for two days and the unit at the Whittington for three days.

On my first day in my new role, I discovered half the community midwives on the rota did not come in to work. On investigation, I was told they were on annual leave. Apparently, they could decide for themselves when to go off on leave, irrespective of the workload of others. They simply worked in their own patch and never shared work or offered to help their colleagues. I was horrified. You could imagine what a nightmare it was to get a working annual leave policy in operation. For some of the changes that I wished to implement, they involved the trade union representative from the Royal College of Midwives. You could imagine my name was mud for a long time, until everyone could see and feel the benefits of the changes I put in place. I had a lot of good times, too, especially reminiscing about back in the day when we were students. Many of the colleagues I trained with or worked with were still there.

I learnt a valuable lesson from this head of midwifery. As you can imagine, the two units were constantly employing staff to fill vacancies for the developing services. The Whittington had more senior roles to fill, so some of my staff applied. She had previously interviewed someone from my unit twice, who was not appointed and I asked her about it. She said, "The panel was equally shocked that they could not appoint her. Her performance bore no relationship to the CV she had presented. Someone clearly wrote it for her. She could not rationalise or think on her feet." We confirmed she was an excellent and experienced clinician, who was reliable and a tower of strength in a clinical setting. She continued, "She was not capable of becoming management material. Her skills were learnt by rote, and that was not enough to progress further in the management arena." I had to confirm the meaning of the word "rote" myself. I had never heard it used before. This was an eye-opener to me, because up to that point I assumed anyone could be a manager if they wanted to, but clearly this was not the case.

This was one of the most stimulating experiences of my career. I managed the post to the best of my ability for about eighteen months and managed to achieve most of the targets I was set. I could physically and mentally see the positive effects of the changes on the midwives in their clinical practice. I grew so much more in confidence and belief in my ability as a good manager.

Once I had settled back at my own unit, the work came thick and fast. By then we were on the map, so I was constantly showing people around the unit, and explaining the way we worked. We sold numerous booklets of our project on team midwifery.

It was a sad day when our head of midwifery retired. Together with me and two other managers, we took the unit into the twentieth century. Her arrival was timely and very welcome, as we were struggling to come out of the dark ages. To do justice to all that she achieved would be another book by itself. We certainly put the unit and our midwifery practice on the map. Our unit became the headquarters of the Advanced Diploma in Midwifery course, throwing us onto the national and international stage.

However, we were always up against our esteemed medical colleagues, but Ann always warned that if we were to succeed, we must cover all eventualities and leave no stone unturned. She taught me to pay attention to detail. She gave me so much self-confidence. I was happy to engage with the consultants, one especially who always complained about the domino and home deliveries and how I was managing that service. He always threatened to report me to my boss. I always encouraged him to do so, and I asked him to please take the evidence with him. I could not figure out if he ever went to my boss.

Our most notable achievement was organising for women to carry their own notes. She took me and another community midwife up north to lecture for the first time and sell our successful project booklets on team midwifery. Although I was terrified each time, once I started speaking, the fear and anxiety went away. She gave me invaluable tips and strategies on preparing and delivering my presentations. For example, she was adamant that you must know your subject inside out. Your facts must be in a logical order, making it easy to follow. If you don't have an answer, you must say so and say you will find out and make contact. This gives you great credibility. She delegated me to lead on the Midwives Practice

Group. This was very empowering, as it gave me the responsibility to produce agreed policies that were evidence-based in a timely and efficient manner. The buck stopped with me and I loved that.

Another practice she spearheaded was the creation of the extended role of the midwife. This was big, because we had to work with the medical staff to identify what aspects of their role we could safely train midwives to practice. We also had to agree programmes of training to get the midwives signed off as competent to undertake that procedure. This was exciting stuff, as the midwives were very clear about what they needed to do to enhance their role and improve the overall experience for women in labour. It also meant that my manager, colleagues and I had to be the first ones trained, so that we could support the medical staff who took a lead in the training. I was responsible for creating and getting approval for all the policy papers, the training programme and the relevant paperwork for this initiative in my role as chair of the practice group. Anne's drive and great humanity transformed our lives, both as consummate professionals and strong, compassionate women.

Now we had the trauma/excitement of having no leader and waiting to see who would take her place. She was a hard act to follow, but we lived in hope. My colleague, Mary, became acting head until such time as one was appointed. I was encouraged to apply, but I knew that I wouldn't stand a chance. I had experienced so many negative situations with the medical staff. My name was mud once because I allowed two of my best midwifery sisters to deliver a woman who was pregnant with twins. The doctors were astounded to learn that this woman had progressed normally under the care of midwives. Although we had successfully changed the face of the unit in terms of midwifery practice, the doctors were powerful men who had a huge influence. Eventually I did apply and was interviewed, but I did it for the experience. I wasn't appointed, but I was happy with that decision, as I didn't feel experienced enough.

CHAPTER TWENTY-SEVEN:
Yet More New Beginnings

Our new head was wonderful. She was bright and cheerful and very supportive. We worked well together and continued to sustain the many initiatives we had started. We continued to fine-tune team midwifery both in hospital and the community. We appointed more community midwives and midwifery managers to sustain the new initiatives. It was awe-inspiring to me that the community where I started working with only four colleagues had grown so remarkably to sustain work for twenty-four community midwives.

One of my greatest achievements as a manager, was leading on a project to change the permanent night staff from working nights only to being part of a normal rota of doing day and night duty. I wrote a business plan to explain the rationale. I believed that these midwives would benefit greatly from all the training and experiences they would be exposed to. It was a very difficult process, as some of these midwives had worked on night duty only for up to twenty years. I had to involve human resources, the Royal College of Midwives and a financial officer. At first there was strong opposition to the proposal, but after many meetings and negotiations, the role of permanent night staff was abolished and the midwives joined the normal rota, working day shifts and nights with their colleagues. Our evaluation of the project was a good one, as the midwives truly appreciated the changes and the numerous opportunities they had to increase their knowledge through training and thus improve their skills. This was a very rewarding and satisfying outcome.

I also found that I was interested in lecturing. During my work, I got interested in several subjects that were difficult to understand or easily assimilate. I decided to become the resident expert on these topics. After the amazing opportunities I got from my mentor to lecture, I got lucky and was asked to lecture all around the country. I worked in London, Birmingham, Stoke, Penrith, Leeds, Oxford, Cambridge and Northern Ireland, to name but a few.

As if I didn't have enough to do, I got the taste for study after completing my Advanced Diploma in Midwifery. I found it further exposed me to research which was becoming much more important in our daily practice. I was talking to one of my staff and she told me of this course she was about to start on healthcare management. I made enquiries too and went on to complete the requirements needed to start the course. The system was one of Accreditation of Prior Educational Learning (APEL), where all my prior study was accredited. After supplying all the information, I was required to write an essay that would give me the full points required to start the course. I was so happy to have been selected, and even happier to have negotiated study leave with my boss. We studied from 2 p.m. to 9 p.m. once a week for two years, with normal university holidays and study days thrown in. Although my boss had arranged study leave for me, I insisted on going to work, so I was at work from 8 a.m. until about 1 p.m. and drove like a bat out of hell to get to my class for 2 p.m. It was an amazing experience. I worked out a strategy during the course to try to maintain my sanity. We used to get study days, and I was given the time off and relished the chance to stay in bed that day to catch up on some sleep. After a while, I realised I needed to spend that time more usefully, as the work was piling up, so I dragged myself out of bed and left the house as if going to work. I would spend the day in the library working on an essay or reading. Luckily, I was at the university site near my home, so the travel and parking were easy and stress-free.

I thoroughly enjoyed the hard work, the socialising, the regular pub quizzes at the bar and the study time we spent together. It was a different kind of pressure to what happened at the hospital. Over two years, we completed twelve assignments, an exam at the end of the first year and a dissertation of 12,000 words at the end of the second year. I had a particular burden because I couldn't type and relied heavily on my secretary. I had no choice but to write out all my assignments, and the dissertation, and she typed them for me. I was thrilled to graduate in healthcare management with upper second class honours. I was so happy to have survived at this very high standard; I really don't know how I did it. I think it was sheer guts and determination, because I knew failing was not an option. I was on a mission and not ready to let go. I realised I wanted to be a role model that others could look up to.

So what did I do? I signed up straight away to do a master's degree at Birkbeck over two years. The course was called Gender, Society and Culture and explored our thinking about gender and our place in society. I was encouraged by my friend Carol to do the same course she had done some time before, as it helped to lay a foundation for providing advocacy for the women and their families in our care. This was a much harder battle on a different level. I finally understood feminism, matriarchy and patriarchy, and it confirmed to me yet again that feminism is not about hating men, but about women fighting to be recognised as equal to men. I was exposed to a different level of academia. We studied feminist writers, sociologists and academics and looked at films on the subject. We regularly attended events at the Institute of Contemporary Arts (ICA) at The Mall near Trafalgar Square.

The ICA was a whole different world for me. It was admirable and staggering how much rich and varied creative art there is out there. We enjoyed films, exhibitions, and visual art. The real killer was the number of books that were recommended reading, to complete six assignments, a group project at the end of the first year and a dissertation of 15,000 words at the end of the final year. Thankfully, I survived, and graduated with a master's degree in Gender, Society and Culture from Birkbeck College, University of London.

At the same time, my husband was bored with selling ladies' clothes and cars and wanted to start a new venture. It was his dream to open a restaurant. He encouraged his friend Ken, who was a chef, to work with him to start this venture. After securing a lease, he realised his dream and opened a shop in west London. It was a huge success. Of course, Ken was Trinidadian, so the food was tasty and fresh and very much like all we would have at home. Ken would start work at 7 a.m. and cook until we opened at noon. Then my husband would serve until 11 p.m. It was a lot of work to do, as there was shopping and cleaning to do as well. Every day, Symone, Kevin and I would work for several hours in the afternoon to help. The shop was decorated beautifully and was very relaxing when it wasn't busy.

As with all black establishments, it became a hub to hang out in at times, but Vernon was very diplomatic and handled his friends very well. I fondly remember meeting a fellow midwife, Julie who dropped in very often after discovering the shop. She was lovely and very chatty and passionate about her career. She was studying health visiting, and we spent many hours discussing her work and helping her to perfect her essays.

The weekends were another story. On Saturday, Vernon and I would go to the cash and carry for containers, cleaning materials and paper goods. Then we would come back to the shop and work. Then we would clean at the end of the day, if we wanted to have some quality time together with the children on the Sunday. Our family unit was small, so it was just us doing everything. Vernon could not afford to pay more people than the chef.

At the beginning of 1996, I had to deal with a family tragedy. My sister Pat seemed to be managing her illness satisfactorily. She was back to work and was being picked up twice a week to have dialysis, because her kidneys had failed. Yet again, she was adamant, refusing to allow any of us to become a kidney donor. When we spoke, she said she was tired and fed up. She suddenly felt unwell during her procedure and had to be taken to hospital. She was found to have a chest infection but, worst of all, her heart was suffering the effects of the lupus. Pat informed me that she was offered heart surgery to repair the valves in her heart. The doctors were confident she would make a full recovery because she was young. She asked my opinion and I thought the doctors sounded sure she would have a good recovery. She agreed and so the surgery was booked. I spoke to her when she came out of surgery and she was in pain and drowsy, but hopeful for no complications.

That was our last conversation. My other sister, Pene, called to say she had died in the night. She had a massive cardiac arrest because there was leakage from the valves that were repaired and she drowned in her own blood. This is called cardiac tamponade. I was sad because she was just 42 and had two lovely children to bring up. I had to go to New York to help my sister organise the funeral. I was so devastated for her children, who were still very young. Abbegail was 26 and married, but Pat's son Matthew was only 12. My sister subsequently became his legal guardian and he moved in to live with her. I then got the unenviable job of clearing her home, as no one else would do it. That was a long and very sad task. I was in somewhat of a mess at the time, as I was studying for my first degree at Westminster University. In my frenzy to get to New York, I forgot everything, including calling my tutor to explain about my sister's death. I didn't do it until I got to New York, by which time I had missed a deadline for handing in my assignment. This meant that I would be allowed to hand it in on my return, but I would only receive the minimum mark, no matter how well done it was. It was one of my best essays with a potential to get 65 per cent, but I was only given 40 per cent.

In the midst of our turmoil of running a restaurant, my husband and I were invited to his granddaughter's wedding. You may remember that he was not in touch with his children when I met him, but I soon got him to make the effort to contact them. His son lived in Canada with his wife. His two daughters lived in New York. One had a partner and two daughters, and one was a single mother with a daughter.

I was much luckier than him, because I made sure I contacted his family every time I went to New York to see my family. They were lovely to me and very welcoming and I was often invited to spend a weekend with them. One weekend I was there, his daughter and I were having a drink in the kitchen. Her husband was in the basement playing music with a friend. Suddenly, she called out and said, "Mike, can you come up for a moment." This friend emerged from the basement, and she said, "Do you remember meeting my dad when he was here? You must meet his wife."

I held out my hand and said, "I'm Allyson. I'm pleased to meet you."

He froze and stared at me and said, "No, no, you must be making a mistake. This lady couldn't be your dad's wife. He is robbing the cradle big time. This must be a crime." I was highly amused, and we all laughed.

I said, "Don't worry. I'm much older than I look, and we already have two children." I thought he was very rude, but he was so genuinely shocked that he couldn't speak. I don't know how old he thought I was. He just walked off and went back to the basement. Marcel and I talked and laughed together and I said they should talk to him to put his mind at rest. I could understand his confusion, as I was actually Marcel's stepmother and younger than Vernon's first three children.

We decided to go to Vernon's granddaughter's wedding on a weekend in July. It was the middle of the carnival season, so we didn't want to stay away too long. It was wonderful to be away with my husband alone, even for a short time. His daughter worked for Pan Am Airlines, so he got a free return journey as her dad. The wedding was a wonderful, lavish affair at a golf club with hundreds of guests. Vernon's granddaughter was so delighted to see him and thanked us for coming. We danced the night away and had great fun. Then, on the Sunday, we had a barbecue in the garden, to which I invited my sister because I couldn't get up to the Bronx to visit the family. We happily returned to London in the knowledge that we were successfully bonding with the family. We were so happy too that our children managed the work in the mas camp in our absence.

CHAPTER TWENTY-EIGHT:
Challenging The Status Quo

In July 1997 I turned 50, and it seemed fitting to have a huge party to celebrate. The last few years had seen some highs and lows in my family. I was left trying to absorb the events going on in my life, like my promotion, the joint managerial post, diagnosis of high blood pressure, my mother's death, sister's death, my other sister's vacation in London for the Notting Hill Carnival and our glorious vacation in Europe, the retirement of my boss and mentor, my success at graduating with a first degree and master's degree, my husband opening a takeaway restaurant, and now my birthday party. The party was a wonderful affair with lots of fellow midwives and friends across the carnival fraternity. My favourite DJ played and Vernon organised a surprise for me by inviting his "pan around the neck" friends to serenade me by playing a myriad of calypsos. It was so special. My only disappointment was that my friend forgot to make my birthday cake, but we managed with other cakes that friends brought.

One of the midwifery sisters came to see me to ask for advice about some conflict with a doctor. This way of life was constant, as we worked in a highly pressurised environment. We worked with ten consultant obstetricians who all wanted to mark their territory and keep midwifery on a medical path. I was aware this doctor was particularly difficult and sometimes rude to the women and midwives. He was very reluctant to take any advice or direction from a midwife. Of course, it was not feasible to believe that a midwife could possibly know more than a doctor in a normal midwifery setting. Each time, the senior sisters and I would suggest a plan of action on how to deal with the issue at the time. The sisters would report on speaking to him about his attitude, and although he would apologise, his attitude never changed. I tried, but he was even more offended that I dared to speak to him.

Life continued to be busy and exciting at the same time, and we faced our many challenges with respect and outstanding practice. Prior to this, I continued to be challenged by the doctors. I was involved in an incident with a sister and her patient who was having twins and who had arrived in labour at thirty-nine weeks of pregnancy. I was well informed about this woman having her twins throughout her pregnancy. I had spoken to the woman several times and she was adamant she wanted to remain as normal as possible throughout her pregnancy and delivery. The midwife looking after her was her named midwife, and she was one of the best professionals I ever met.

When the woman arrived in labour, she had laboured at home for several hours. I assured the woman and her midwife I would be there to support them. Then I had to make yet another call home to say that I would be late home. The medical staff were very twitchy. I got the feeling that they were taken aback totally because this woman had never presented to them in pregnancy. Although the rules were that pregnant women had to see a doctor at key times in her pregnancy – for example at twenty-eight, thirty-six and forty weeks – there is no stipulation that the doctor has to be in a hospital. So this woman chose to see her GP. The hospital obstetricians were incensed that I was allowing this midwife to conduct a twin delivery in this way. Even some of the midwives were concerned, and they continued to suggest that the woman should be monitored. The sister looking after this woman assured them that the woman was being carefully monitored. The sister running the labour ward had placed a series of machines outside the door of the room, but they were never needed. I was very clear that I had taken full responsibility for this case. I suggested that they leave the midwives alone to manage the woman's labour successfully. I was so happy to see this level of normality. I couldn't understand why others couldn't see it. The junior doctors called their senior colleagues, and I said the same thing. Of course I was very nervous, only because I feared the doctors would pull rank, but I was prepared for the fight.

Finally, the consultant on call came to the labour ward, and he was extremely supportive and said we should continue our care. We didn't need his permission, but it was important that he respected our decisions to practice normally. As expected, the woman delivered normally of two gorgeous baby boys, with no pain relief, no mechanical monitoring and no episiotomy or tear and with minimal blood loss. This was certainly a rare occasion, but it showed midwifery care at its very best. I was in awe of these midwives, who had the confidence and strength to believe in themselves, and in me for having their backs. I congratulated them on their skill and expertise. I also congratulated the woman on her successful and normal pregnancy, labour and delivery and on her confidence to believe in the midwives who were caring for her. After a couple of hours, the mother was able to stand up and walk out the room to use the bathroom. The doctors were actually very magnanimous and congratulated the midwives and the woman.

The sister in charge of the case and I had a full debrief after the mother and her babies were settled on the ward. We both said we were nervous and maybe even scared about the outcome, simply because there was so much pressure from other midwives and doctors who didn't wish us well. I was delighted that we all stood our ground and we were able to prove what our profession is all about. It was so sad when the doctors that work with us think of us as in competition with them. However, I was also sad, as I realised many midwives were still happy to behave like obstetric nurses and only willing to follow a doctor's instruction and not fight to develop their true skills. I think this wonderful event gave me another entry on the doctors' watch list. I heard that one of the doctors said I was very challenging and he was concerned about me. This was nothing new to me, as I had been challenged for many years about my style of managing, training and empowering the staff. I was always threatened by the doctors with a formal complaint to my boss, but none ever materialised, as I always insisted their complaint must include their research evidence that my leadership was wrong. I often got the impression some of them were happy to let us get on with it, but their power and control would not allow them.

Another sister came to me in some distress, requesting that I take further action, as they continued to have difficulty and conflict with the doctor they had discussed with me before. They documented incidents of his unprofessional behaviour that made them question his decisions. One client in labour screamed at him and asked him to leave her room and never come back. My fellow supervisor of midwives and I met to discuss a strategy of support for the staff. My management role is very different to my role as a supervisor of midwives. Supervision is all about clinical practice, and giving support, help, training and advice in matters of professional skills and competence. Supervisors make sure all midwives are taking part in continuing education. Supervisors must develop and promote good practice that meets the needs of all women.

We agreed to outline a detailed letter to the clinical director, who manages all doctors, about this doctor's unprofessional behaviour, as this was having a negative effect on the staff who were providing care and on the women receiving care from him. We included statements from the midwives concerned and from the women who complained on the day in question. We asked for a possible meeting to resolve the issues, as communication was not good and the atmosphere on the labour ward was unsettling. We discussed this at length with our head and she gave her blessing. So, my colleague and I took the letter and papers to the clinical director and explained our dilemma. She agreed she would investigate and get back to us.

After a week or two, we had heard nothing. Then one of the midwives I managed asked me to have a drink with her. I couldn't get out of the invitation because she insisted I would need a drink after hearing what she had to say. As we settled in the corner of the pub, she dropped a bombshell. Through her contacts in the medical profession, she learnt that the papers I had given to the clinical director were given to the doctor himself, so every doctor and midwife on the labour ward had seen the papers marked "Private and Confidential". I imagined they were all thinking about the audacity of this midwife who dared to complain about a doctor. The next thing I knew was being contacted by the general manager, who informed me she had initiated an investigation into my complaint. Together with my union rep, I was the only person interrogated for several hours, not my supervisor colleague, the midwives involved or the women who complained. The next step was that the general manager circulated a letter to anyone who could read explaining my complaint and stating categorically that there was no evidence to support the claim, so there was no case to answer against the doctor. The letter concluded that the matter was now firmly closed.

Over the next year, the directors of personnel and the general manager harassed me to withdraw the letter and to say I had made a huge mistake. I was horrified and disgusted and furious all at the same time. How dare they disrespect and undermine my integrity like that. I sought solace in my husband and friends outside the unit and my union representative and my friend Carol, who was our director of education. I used to smoke at that time, and we would sneak off to have a fag. We had so many meetings about their demands, but my stance remained the same.

Then the British Medical association (BMA) joined the fray. They came on heavy and requested that I should be sacked for causing this doctor such unnecessary distress. Their biggest problem, they said, was the tone of my letter. I had said that we had become intolerant of his unprofessional behaviour. The BMA stated that those words were a huge indictment because the phrase suggested his clinical practice was poor and questionable, and had the potential to ruin his career and reputation.

Well, it was the year from hell. I cried and swore consistently on my friend Carol's shoulders. I had to be strong but very discreet, as I didn't want the staff to be affected or think I couldn't cope. I questioned my actions all along the way, as I didn't expect this public reaction. I remained confident we did the right thing in the interest of the women and their families in our care. My boss was a blessing and continued to support me. The midwives involved were upset about what was happening. I reassured them I would always help and support them with any concerns, then and in the future. They were fully aware that, as a supervisor, I was duty-bound to help and support them. There was also my management role, where I had to secure their physical and mental well-being, so they should have no cause to become ill. My rep suggested I take out a grievance against the Trust, which I did, for the mismanagement of the case and for causing me great distress. The Trust was found negligent and unprofessional about the management of the case. They had to officially apologise to me. Interestingly, the doctor did leave the unit, but I never understood if this was by accident or design.

Again, I met with the double act of personnel directors, who were working as a job share! I got my letter of apology, but the BMA would not let up. To my great surprise, one fateful day, I got a direct call from the chief executive. We had met several times before over a drink with my friend, Tom, so he posed no threat to me. He asked me to go to see him, and my union representative and I did so. He reiterated the question of my description of the doctor's unprofessional behaviour. I said to him: "I was very careful with my wording. I just wanted him to be a team player, so the labour ward environment could return to being calm and productive. However, we all know that professionals who scream and shout and throw things in a clinical area use this behaviour as a smoke screen and are often insecure and questionable in their practice and often refuse to take help and advice from others. I was not responsible for their interpretation of my words."

The chief executive offered to help, by writing two letters. One was to the midwives, assuring them they did the right thing and should not be afraid in the future to express their concerns. The second letter was to the BMA, saying I was sorry for their confusion, but I was not responsible for their interpretation of the words in my letter of complaint. I agreed to accept his help and I awaited these letters. My head was hot and confused. I decided I wouldn't panic and would wait. I am very intransigent, and if I believe in something, I will never be shifted from that belief. The letters came and they said exactly what he had suggested. I sat down and got very angry, because I felt greatly undermined. I thought, *how dare they question my decision to complain; what about freedom of speech? What about my role in protecting and supporting the midwives and women that I am responsible for?* I kept thinking that my response letter had to put a stop to this harassment. Outwardly, I was as cool as a cucumber, but inwardly I was pissed and fed up with them. I couldn't help wondering, if I was a white manager, how this complaint would have been managed. I was continuously angry, but I realised I would have to beat them at their own game. After much discussion with Carol and several edited versions, I came up with this response:

TELL ME SOMETHING I DON'T KNOW!

Dear Sir,

It was lovely to see you last week and I thank you most sincerely for your time and advice in helping my representative and me to resolve this issue.

However, I am sorry that I cannot accept these letters that you have written on my behalf. The letter that you addressed to the midwives is far too little and too late. The midwives in the unit are well managed by me and communicate well with me and are fully aware of my role as a Supervisor and advocate for them and the women and their families in our care. My staff will never be afraid to express their concerns to me in the future, because they know that I will support them.

The second letter to the BMA is unnecessary. I am not responsible for their misinterpretation of my words in the letter of complaint. Besides, you will be aware of a letter sent to many different doctors by the General Manager about a year ago. She outlined the case and the investigation that she conducted, after which she stated categorically that there was no case to answer, and the matter was firmly closed. Therefore, as far as I am concerned, the matter has been firmly closed by your senior manager and remains firmly closed.

Yours sincerely,

Allyson

I took the letter to my head of midwifery and union representative, and they were happy with the contents. I also delivered it personally to the chief executive. So it was a waiting game to get a response. One week turned into one month, then two months and more. We were all wondering what was going on, but I was determined not to contact anyone about the matter. I dared to hope it was really closed. Six months later, my boss called me to her office to give me some news. She had just attended a heads of department meeting and found some time to speak to the medical director. She asked him if he had any idea what was happening with my case. He simply said, "Nothing at all. Did you not read the letter that your manager sent to the chief executive? There was simply no answer to that. The chief had no choice but to tell the BMA to go away. She is very clever and strong, your manager."

My boss was very complimentary, and yet again called me a wise owl. We always had this joke, because I would say I was a wise old owl and she would disagree, claiming I was saying it twice. She said if you were a wise owl, it suggests you are already old, and that's enough.

CHAPTER TWENTY-NINE:
On-Going Changes At Home and At The Office

At the same time, my daughter and son were growing up rather fast. My daughter didn't want to stay on at school to do A levels, although she had good grades in ten subjects. Instead, she attended college and completed a BTEC National Diploma in mass communications. She had talked at length about a career in fashion but had not really explored it fully. By that time, she had become totally immersed in the creative side of carnival. She became her dad's right-hand man and they were inseparable. She learnt to select and buy materials from specialist traders in London and the surrounding areas. She was given responsibility for certain sections within the band, so she had to ensure the production was completed to the highest possible standard. She and her brother also became important members of the steel band they were part of. Symone joined the stage side, which was a group of players who wanted the experience of doing public performances at events like weddings and parties and corporate events. That way, she had the luxury of travelling all around England, Wales, Scotland, Ireland and Europe. I used this as an opportunity to travel too. I went as a chaperone to Munich on one of the steel band's tours. It was an honour to visit the Munich stadium for the Olympic games of 1972, during which the Israeli team were targeted by terrorists, with 11 athletes killed.

Earlier in the year 1998, I encouraged my husband to go on a short holiday by himself to Tobago, because he had just been through the trauma of closing down his restaurant business. He was very sad about doing this, but he realised he could not manage this successfully anymore. I was flagging and chronically tired and trying to finish my dissertation for my master's degree. I couldn't give much help anymore. Vernon, too, was very tired and the restaurant was not making enough to employ salaried staff. Sadly, he had to sell the lease and move on. I was happy that he was able to get a well-deserved rest in Tobago. I was thrilled to learn that he decided to buy a plot of land over there as a present to me and the family and an investment for us all.

After my nightmare with the medical staff, it came that time again when our well-respected head was preparing to leave. This time, it was not her preparation to retire, but a change of career. She had been toying with the idea for as long as she could remember and felt this was as good a time as any to explore her love for the law, and maybe train and qualify as a lawyer.

So, again, there was a gap in our leadership, and another opportunity to present myself as strong management material. This time I felt truly ready to apply for the post, but I knew deep down that I would never be appointed at that unit. I was considered too much of a challenge for the medical staff and I didn't conform to the status quo. Despite this knowledge, I applied for the post anyway. As expected, I was not appointed, although I knew it was the best interview I had done. I believed that they discriminated against me, because the candidate they chose was not a practising midwife. My union representative suggested I take the Trust to tribunal. I didn't expect to win, of course. Although the judge said there was no discrimination, he said the trust had a duty of care to help me with my continuing professional development. So it was left to me to find something that was exciting for me to do.

In the meantime, I continued to work with the new head. She had a lot of experience of managing organisations, but she had no up-to-date clinical or managerial midwifery practice. I felt she was simply appointed so that they could avoid appointing me. We had to work closely together, because I was doing a long and detailed handover.

I had a very shocking experience once, as we were part of a management meeting with other midwives and senior nurses from other departments. As the meeting progressed, our head banged both hands on the table and stood up. She said, "Please listen to me, everyone. Please remember that I am the new head of midwifery, and not Allyson Williams. I am so fed up of this situation. Everywhere I turn, I am told Allyson Williams this, Allyson Williams that and I want it to stop. I am in charge here and not Allyson Williams." Everyone went silent. Our mouths fell open and no one could respond. Finally she sat down and continued to chair the meeting.

We carried on with the running of the unit but it was difficult and isolating. Working with this new head was intolerable and an insult to the wonderful and experienced midwives she was managing.

Thankfully, it was 1999, which proved a wonderful distraction. Early on in the year, there was lots of activity concerning a potential millennium bug which was predicted to shut down all communication networks around the country, on the stroke of midnight of 2000. There was so much work and systems put in place to ensure that no data or records were lost. Thankfully, nothing at all happened with the computer systems. We all had to be available to work in the event that something happened, but we moved into the twenty-first century in great style.

At the same time, my husband was delighted with his success at being offered a commission to produce two large-scale costumes for a production in the newly created Millennium Dome in Greenwich, for an international gala night to welcome in the year 2000. After the Notting Hill Carnival weekend in 1999, he began work on these costumes. This was great kudos for our band, Genesis, as part of only a few bands representing the Notting Hill Carnival. I didn't have much need to help there. The children were the important ones, as they had to wear the costumes, so my husband had to measure them and fit the costumes to them. I attended the ceremony with two friends John and Joan who were loyal supporters of the band. We felt and looked very royal ourselves. I was dressed to the nines, in a satin gown with plenty of sparkle. I felt honoured and privileged to have been part of the opening of the Millennium Dome. My children did us very proud as they danced spectacularly in their large and colourful costumes. It was a spectacular occasion and a memorable experience.

I was so happy to be taking the children home for the carnival season for 2000. They were fit to burst as they couldn't wait to play in All Stars Steel band again. Their first experience was so magical that they wanted to reconnect with their friends again. This time we agreed to take a family friend with us. She was Cati and she was from Minorca in Spain. She was my husband's protégée because she was very creative and talented and had worked with him for many years. She was mesmerised by Trinidad and its culture and lifestyle. She commented constantly about the food and how different it tasted from food in London. I would always say that it was because the food is sun-ripened. We had an amazing and memorable holiday. Symone and Kevin excelled at playing and we watched them practise night after night. The band was successful at the competition and placed second. I am especially proud, because my daughter Symone can be seen on the video of the band's performance, where she will remain in posterity.

We returned and resumed our various roles. I tried to forward-think and look at any outstanding projects that needed to be completed. Then, one day, my head of midwifery called me and said she had decided to change my title to deputy head of midwifery, because she acknowledged my experience and expertise. I graciously accepted, as I think she realised she would be lost without my support.

However, my tiredness was increasing and I was struggling to cope. I had not found anywhere interesting to go on a secondment. Soon after the Christmas and new year celebrations, I went to my GP and expressed my concern about being so tired. I said I must be anaemic and asked for blood tests to assess my haemoglobin levels. He asked about my blood pressure and I said it must be normal because I had been taking my medication regularly. When he checked my blood pressure, he found it to be very high. Even after rest between readings, it remained high. We arranged a plan that I would make a record of my blood pressure every day for a week. My blood was taken for specific tests, and after a week, I returned to see my GP with my recordings and get my test results. My readings remained high. I had better news with my blood tests. They were mostly normal, except my kidney function, which was slightly compromised but not a need for concern.

My doctor put me off sick for one month or until my readings had significantly decreased. The first few weeks, I slept continuously. I didn't remember what it was like to sleep so much. It took two weeks of sleep to make any change in my readings. I also had to change my medication, as I was clearly desensitised to it and the tablets were having no effect. Finally, I was hopeful I could return to work. Then, in March, I saw an advert in the press looking for a midwife advisor in a research and audit organisation affiliated to the NHS. It was interesting, because I would be working differently and out of my comfort zone, as I had little experience of conducting research or audit. The best part of the job was being employed as a midwifery expert and going around the country, selling the outcomes and research to units around the country. I was successful in securing a year's secondment, and arrangements were made for my transfer.

This was yet another memorable experience. I had to read, learn and understand all aspects of the midwifery research that had been done in the previous year. I was particularly employed to lectures on the eighth annual report that had just been published, as it was all about maternity research. I got booked to lecture around the country about nine times over the year. I kept up with a plan that I had devised over the years. I would always volunteer to lecture in the morning, so I could stay in a hotel overnight, lecture in the morning, then I would use the afternoon to explore the town I was in. I was the lead midwife on a project investigating type 2 diabetes in pregnancy. I also wrote a few papers on the research for the midwifery press. My colleagues were extraordinarily intelligent doctors and nurses who were experts in data collection and analysis. I learnt a great deal from them, especially when I attended seminars and study days on audit and research.

At the same time, my husband reported to me that, occasionally, he could feel a small lump on his right side under his rib cage. He had seen the doctor, but no one could feel it. I couldn't feel it, so he was happy to leave it.

During my time at CESDI, I decided that I would retire from the NHS at age 55. It was six months before my retirement that I went to see the pensions officer to work out the details. I learnt that my settlement would not be much better if I stayed working until I was 60, so I stuck to my plan of early retirement. The story is that if you have trained and worked in the NHS up to age 55, it was the equivalent of working behind a desk up to the age of 60, simply because of the nature of the work. I could certainly vouch for that. I was exhausted from the physical aspect of the work, but the mental strain is equally heavy-duty. There were also the pressures of real life for women who chose to have a career and also raise children, with all that entails, while caring for a husband and home, all at the same time, as I explored for my master's dissertation.

My husband was delighted with my decision as, technically, he was already retired. You will remember, earlier in the book, I discovered he was twenty-two years older than me, so he was longing for me to stop and have a rest. We discussed that we would get plans drawn and approved and ready for our new-build. We agreed to go on holiday to Trinidad to initiate these plans, during the carnival season.

CHAPTER THIRTY:
The Beginning of The End

Just before the Christmas holiday, Vernon visited his GP to do blood tests for his PSA levels. The GP who saw him was the first person to feel the lump he had talked about. She ordered an ultrasound scan. This appointment came in January for early March, but he had to rearrange, as we would still be abroad. To our surprise, the hospital was able to bring the appointment forward to the day before we travelled. We were assured that, by the time we returned, our GP would have the results.

We excitedly went on holiday, with plans to see the architect and also enjoy all the wonderful shows and parties and extravaganzas that are put on for the public. Early in our holiday, I began to notice that he was not as energetic as usual. For the first time, he decided to sit in the stands for some of the shows. Then, a week into our holiday, I noticed his tummy seemed to be getting bigger. I went cold and shocked because I suspected what this was. We spoke to our children and they told us our GP had called to speak to him. The doctor said if Vernon was feeling unwell, he should return to London. We immediately made these arrangements and returned home. The GP came to the house immediately and informed us that the scan had identified a large tumour that looked cancerous, at the head of his pancreas. The GP had secured a bed in hospital for Vernon for further investigations. Vernon was admitted on the Monday morning. By then his tummy was really full of fluid. They started draining this fluid and collected nine litres. By that time, I was quietly hysterical, but in private. I knew I had to be strong, and Vernon kept saying we should not panic until we had the full picture. After having a biopsy under ultrasound guidance, the consultant oncologist came to see us a few days later. She was very kind and gentle. She said the biopsy confirmed that Vernon had cancer of the head of the pancreas. It was at stage 3 to 4. She offered him chemotherapy but could not guarantee how or if it would work for him. He said he realised he was seriously ill and would accept any help that was offered to him. Vernon asked the doctor how much time he had. She said, "I would never make this type of prediction. That is up to God."

When she left, I followed her out and asked her to be more specific with me, as I was a fellow professional. She was reluctant, but I pressured her. Every time I suggested a time frame, she said no, until I said three to six months, when she said that was more realistic.

I was just coming to the end of my secondment when they asked me to stay on for another year. I readily accepted as, suddenly, I had no interest in returning to the hospital unit, as my husband's health and well-being was the priority. The literature stated that once cancer of the pancreas is diagnosed, it is usually terminal. It is almost impossible to diagnose early, because the pancreas lies directly under the stomach. If it is diagnosed early by some miracle, the survival rate is 5 per cent.

Vernon opted for having drugs each day in the first week of every month. He kept saying he was so grateful and thankful for my help and support. The children were so sad and upset by this turn of events. They could not accept that their dad was dying. My son refused to accept it. He virtually ignored him for a long time, saying he was fine and would be better in no time. I think he was in shock and total denial.

Vernon asked us to tell our friends and family, so you could imagine the phone lit up with calls of good wishes. We were inundated with requests for visits, but we had to keep them to a minimum, while allowing him to talk to his children and family abroad. The treatment was unrelenting. In the first cycle, he couldn't tolerate the drugs after three days and had to be admitted to hospital overnight. After the second month, he perked up considerably and was more mobile. He was able to drive and we attended a friend's wedding.

It was in the third month that he had the worst reaction. After the third day, he had to be admitted to hospital because he started to vomit profusely. He was made comfortable but he had to stay for observation. When I visited the next day, he was very dozy. He said he was in pain overnight and was given painkillers. He asked me to take him home as he wasn't going to have the painkillers they gave him. They made him hallucinate and have bad dreams. He said, "Darling, I know that I am dying. I don't want any more chemotherapy or painkillers. I want to be comfortable and die in peace at home." I cried so much, but I knew I wouldn't have it any other way. When I checked, they had given him morphine. This was on the first May bank holiday. I negotiated with the staff to take him home and he was very happy.

I did some research on herbs and juices that would be tasty and easy to digest. He wasn't able to eat large meals, so softer, tasty stuff was on the cards. Symone and I took turns to look after him. She turned her job to part-time to help. Her brother, Kevin, remained in total denial. He would flit in and out casually, saying hello but not spending any time with him. I knew he was scared and in shock about losing his dad. I just hugged him and talked to him and suggested he should talk to his dad in his own time.

I did my best to keep Vernon comfortable. We talked about life, death, the children and family. He would sit for long periods in the sunshine in the conservatory, as it reminded him of Tobago. He said it was his little bit of heaven. He told me, "I feel so lucky to have been married to you. It was the happiest time of my life, being with you and our children. I feel so privileged and grateful that you are looking after me. Not many wives would do this and would have put me in a hospice." He also said, "You should not grieve for me when I am gone. You have so much love to give, you should find someone to share it with."

I was so very touched by his comments. I also said, "Meeting you and being with you has been my life and my dream. I have loved you unconditionally and completely and I have been the happiest and luckiest woman in the world."

He would sit outside in the garden and watch me do some planting or weeding. When he had pain, I would give him suppositories, as he couldn't swallow tablets. I would bath him and wash him and feed him. I was terrified of being without him, as he was my life and my tower of strength.

The day he died was the most surreal of all. Symone woke to a crashing noise in the kitchen. She found that Vernon was trying to make tea and dropped the cup. He told Symone, "I wanted to make one of the lovely drinks that your mother always made for me," but he didn't know how. Kevin came and lifted him up and put him back to bed. Symone made the juice and brought it to him. To our surprise and delight, Kevin announced that he had the day off and would spend the time with his dad. Vernon was so happy and said, "I have a job for you, Kev. I need you to cut my hair. You have to help me to sue the hospital because your hair is supposed to fall out when you have chemo, and mine is growing back so quickly." We all laughed and Kevin said he would get the tools. Vernon was sitting up and asked to go back to bed. As he lay down, I could hear his breathing change. We started to cry as we could see him fading away. Kevin was screaming and asking his dad to talk to him. Vernon passed away a few minutes later.

Before we could do anything, Kevin got his tools and started cutting his dad's hair. He simply said, "This is the last thing he asked me to do. I must do it."

As he finished this job, sister Monica came and my neighbour. Kevin then had a full-blown, grand mal fit. He was holding his dad but thrashing around next to him and frothing at the mouth. I was shocked and desperately worried about him. As the fit went off, he remained clinging to his dad and wouldn't move. The doctor came as well to see Vernon and examined Kevin as well, but could find no reason for his fit except the shock of his dad's death.

The funeral home said we could leave Vernon and Kevin there as long as we wanted. Then, one of his close friends called to enquire about him and was given the sad news. He offered his help and I asked him to tell as many people as possible for me. It was midday by then and, by 7 p.m., well-wishers started to arrive.

I can truly say I have been in a daze ever since. I was hysterical and overwhelmed by it all. I felt like a robot going through certain motions. I couldn't believe that Vernon would not be there anymore. I couldn't imagine what life would be like without him. Then there was the onerous task of informing his family in Canada, Trinidad and New York before anyone else did. I had to support Symone and Kevin, who were distraught and inconsolable. The pain and distress reminded me of how I felt when my mother passed away. Every night there was a stream of friends who came to the house to pay their respects. The Noel family, in particular, came every night until Vernon's cremation. They were wonderful and it was truly comforting to have them there. I was so grateful that friends came with food and drink and also flowers and cards, so in a strange way it was distracting and comfortable to sit and chat with friends. A few times, I did have to escape to clear my head. Once I drove to the car park at Tesco and screamed and talked to myself for an hour.

My husband had the most beautiful send-off I have attended. Sister Monica took me under her wing, and I will always be grateful for the loving kindness and support she gave to Vernon during her visits to see him and to me in arranging his funeral. He was Catholic, so we arranged with a local Catholic priest and church in Ladbroke Grove to hold the service. I agreed the order of service with the priest. I ordered all flowers and wreaths from the family. Sister Monica and I secured the use of the tabernacle free of charge, as a tribute to Vernon being one of the founders and pioneers of the

Notting Hill Carnival. His children, my sister and his brother were coming from New York and Canada.

I managed to escape to a friend's office to prepare the programme. I was very particular about this, because I insisted that the entire service must be printed in a booklet. I hated people fiddling about with paper or standing looking blank and unable to follow the service. I started to receive many offers for catering, so one of my friends coordinated all aspects of the food and drink at the reception. My friends and family insisted I should do very little, and it was a joy and such a relief. When our families arrived they all insisted on staying at the house. So, for six days, my home was host to me and my children, my sister, Vernon's daughters and husbands, his brother and son and his wife. It was lovely, even though it was a sad occasion. We got closer with each other and shared so much during that time.

The midwives at the hospital were spectacular. They came to the church and set up a memorial table with memorial books and got visitors to sign. I was blown away by their gesture. The church was full to bursting, with approximately 600 people there. The service was a long one and, after, the cortège travelled along the carnival route until it reached the crematorium. The cremation really got to me and, for the first time, I broke down and cried uncontrollably as the curtains came around his coffin.

The reception was a wonderful occasion. Vernon was well known for telling his friends that, when someone dies, we need to celebrate their lives, not mourn their death. He would tell his friends that they must all wear colourful clothes to his funeral, and this is exactly what happened. His reception was a bright and colourful affair. There was an abundance of food and drink to share for many hundreds of guests. We talked and laughed and really celebrated Vernon's life. Many friends got up on the stage and paid tribute to him. I too got up to thank everyone for being there and for supporting me and the children. When Vernon's family left some days later, my sister stayed with me for some time after. She was a godsend and a great comfort to me. I was at a loss to know what to do with myself.

We paid a wonderful tribute to my husband soon after he died. The year before our band, Genesis, was asked to participate in the queen's jubilee celebration in June 2002. It was an amazing honour, as we would be representing the Notting Hill Carnival. Vernon had arranged everything with the organisers, so it was just our responsibility to get the costumes ready nearer the time. Now that he had passed away, I was asked by some members about what we would do. After some discussion, it was an easy decision to make that we would go ahead with the plans and participate in honour of him. It was a remarkable event to be part of. It was well organised and executed. We had to prepare our costumes to be picked up by the organisers a few days before the event, then the transport was sent for us, as arranged, and we were taken to our costumes. I was mesmerised by the whole process and the space allocated to us. I never imagined there was so much space available in central London. We paraded down The Mall to Buckingham Palace and around the route back to our transport, where there was food waiting for us.

I was talking with a friend in the band after the jubilee celebrations about work. I had been off work for a month and was planning to return in the near future. She said to me, "Have you not cancelled your retirement next month? Surely there is no point in you retiring now!"

It was the first time this idea was suggested. I had not even considered any options. I thought about it for a minute and said, "No, I won't change my mind. I will leave the status quo." I said to her, "Vernon had a saying he always lived by, which is 'when you turn back, you lose." I wanted to acknowledge him by not changing my decision. Besides, I think I wanted a different life experience at that time; I was exhausted.

Sometimes I have thought about what life would have been like if I had continued working. I knew I had much more to give, but I felt burnt out. My plan was to keep my options open, in case retirement didn't come up to expectations. So I returned to work at the Enquiry, as my contract there had been extended for another year. I was in touch with all my friends at the unit and they remained supportive and kind.

CHAPTER THIRTY-ONE:
Retirement....A Time To Start Working At Living...

The Trust started making arrangements for a retirement party for me. It was a lovely affair with speeches, lots of midwives, and my children, and managers, lots of cake, food and wine. It was so nice, but something was missing. I think it would have been more cosy and personal at the unit, instead of the huge, beautiful ballroom of our neighbouring hospital. I got a large sum of money from the Trust and various other presents from friends. It did feel like the end of an era for me. I realised I would never progress any further there. I loved working in my management role, but I couldn't work and be effective under the current arrangements.

Vernon also set us up nicely with the preparation for the Notting Hill Carnival. He was always willing to mentor young designers, and that year was no exception. He was working with two designers and had approved some of their designs, so we were well ahead with our planning.

During his illness, he had spoken to me about the band, and if and how we would move forward. He said he wanted Symone to run the band, with her brother and me supporting her. He said, "She is a natural and would take the band to great heights. Kevin is a genius with technology and structure and artistry and is best suited for that role." My one regret was that I didn't make Symone and Kevin party to that conversation, because it took some convincing for Kevin to believe that he was not sidelined and we would both be working just as hard as Symone.

Symone was humbled by the confidence her dad had shown in her. She loved the culture and had become a good designer, so she embraced the role fully. The costumes we produced were exquisite and beautiful, with great attention to detail, just as Vernon had taught us. We continued our winning streak at the exquisite venue of the Covent Garden Opera House. It was a fitting place to make a tribute to Vernon. The master of ceremonies for the show read a tribute to him that brought tears to everyone's eyes, including mine. It was so moving and emotional and one of my proudest moments.

During August, my friends in Orlando called again. They were very apologetic that they were unable to attend Vernon's funeral, but they now had a good idea. They wanted to have a short holiday and had booked a cruise around the Bahamas and had included me with them. Was that something I would like to do? I was ecstatic and humbled by their thoughtfulness. I didn't hesitate to accept. So, at the end of September, I flew to Orlando and, a few days later, we drove to Cape Canaveral and joined the cruise ship. I was so blown away. It was a massive structure with thousands of people on board. It was my first experience of this kind of holiday. It was a lavish place that was like a floating city. The ship itself was luxurious, with every possible amenity you could wish for. There was food of all descriptions available 24/7. We got dressed to kill to have dinner at the captain's table.

One day my friend Jean and I met the ship's chef at a food workshop and, to our delight, he was a fellow Trinidadian. He promised us a surprise at dinner and we waited in great anticipation. We found he had cooked an amazing array of local Trinidadian dishes for our table alone. For example, he sent us rice, roti, curry chicken, curried spinach and pumpkin, aloo, pholourie balls. The food was exquisite and the whole dining room wanted to share what we were eating. The smell was intoxicating and we felt very special. It was all an amazing experience and very cathartic. I realised that I was beginning to relax and didn't cry quite as much.

After the cruise, we spent time roaming around Disneyland, visiting the areas I missed on my last visit.

Soon after my return home, I was yet again blown away by another astounding experience. One morning I took my mail off the postman as I was on my way to work. Once I settled in at the office, I opened one of the letters and screamed in disbelief, forgetting where I was. I had to reassure everyone that I was fine. To my absolute astonishment, the letter read:

"The Prime Minister has asked me to inform you that he has it in mind to submit your name to the Queen with a recommendation that her Majesty may be graciously pleased to approve that you be appointed a Member of the Order of the British Empire (MBE)"

I couldn't believe what I was reading. I tried to think who could have done this. I vaguely remembered that professional organisations had to be involved. I called the Royal College of Midwives and asked to speak to my friend, Carol. She exclaimed, "My goodness – at last! At last! I am so happy for you. I did this eighteen months ago."

Then I asked her why I was recommended for this accolade. She explained the process. She had been asked to join a special panel led by the president to select midwives worthy of accolades. My name was put forward by a member of the panel. All the panel members agreed, then they were allocated the nominees to process each application. She said, "It was not because you were a good midwife. The college has 38,000 midwives like you on their books. It was because you always used your initiative, and never said no to a challenge. You were creative and imaginative and innovative. You went the whole nine yards and then some. You worked outside the box as well and fought for the women and their families in your care."

Carol was asked to process my application. Secrecy was paramount, so she was forbidden from telling me anything about it. This accolade is particularly special because this was initiated and recommended by my peers, who had noticed and acknowledged my passion for my work over many years. On thinking about it, I realised how busy I was within the profession. I was an active member of the trade union and professional arm of the college. I attended all the annual general meetings around the country and regularly debated on those occasions. Many of the projects I led allowed the college to use our unit as a place of excellence and we were constantly showcasing our unit, nationally and internationally.

I continued to look at the paperwork and follow their instructions. As I checked the details, I had to complete some missing information, which was my nationality. I wrote that I was a Trinidadian and sent the papers off. Well, all hell broke loose! I received a phone call from the prime minister's office. The officer stated they have to manage my award differently because I was not British. The queen can only grant awards to people who are citizens of a country where she is the head of state. This was because Trinidad and Tobago became an independent nation in 1962, but remained in the Commonwealth. I then got a letter of confirmation, saying that the Foreign and Commonwealth Office would be asked to seek permission from the Trinidad government via the British High Commission in Port of Spain.

Well, talk about bursting your bubble! I was so disappointed, but I was reassured the award would not be removed. I had letters of apology from the prime minister's office and congratulations from the chief executive of the NHS and the president of the Royal College of Midwives. The worst thing was that all this was confidential and couldn't be discussed. I was told I could tell my children, as there would be no breach of protocol now. I just had to wait until the approval was granted. Symone and Kevin were fit to burst and ecstatic about the award.

Christmas was fast approaching and my daughter gave me the best news ever. She had been dating for the past year and she and her boyfriend were planning to get married in September 2003. I was so delighted for her, although her boyfriend would not have been my choice, but I wasn't marrying him.

I continued my work at the research organisation until my contract ended in March. I lunged into the costume production for the carnival and helping my daughter with her wedding preparations. Our friend, Sister Monica, remained very supportive to the family, and she felt that I needed to keep myself occupied. She introduced me to a Caribbean charity in Ladbroke Grove that needed new members on the board to help move them forward. It seemed like a worthwhile venture, so I became the chair of trustees for the charity. The systems and paperwork were in the dark ages. The members, though, were delightful men and women who had attended the club for many years, since their own retirement. The Pepper Pot Day Centre was started about forty years before as an African-Caribbean resource centre for the over sixties. It is intended to help members combat loneliness and isolation and help them take charge of their lives. The centre provides meals and activities that meet the needs of the members.

I got really involved in changing the face of the centre. There was a great deal of politics going on because the centre was on a prime site and there was always talk about it being closed down by the local authority. One of the first things I did was to clarify our status. I learnt that the centre had a 25-year lease on the site and its status was relatively safe. Symone was employed as a clerical officer, as she had not resumed her degree studies after her dad passed away. We worked long and hard and succeeded in making positive changes. After a few years as chair, I resigned from the charity, but remained available if they needed help.

In June 2003, a letter came from the Foreign and Commonwealth Office stating:

"On the advice of the Secretary of State for Foreign and Commonwealth Affairs, the Queen has been pleased to appoint you as an Honorary Member of the British Empire in recognition of the outstanding services you have rendered over many years to the development of midwifery services for women."

I was sad that I was unable to go to the palace, but I was honoured with a champagne reception arranged by staff at the Honours Section at the Department of Health. I was presented with the royal warrant and the insignia badge by the parliamentary undersecretary of state for community services at the Minister of Health. I was thrilled that I could invite many friends and family to the reception. I still feel like I'm being scraped off the ceiling. This award showed my work had been acknowledged and appreciated as a passionate professional who fought to make a difference in her profession. This award has yet to be topped as the greatest achievement of my professional life.

I decided to take on the role of wedding planner, and I started early to ensure that I addressed every detail. I was so happy to have been able to finance the whole event, as the bride's family is supposed to do, traditionally. Symone and I thoroughly enjoyed the process. Her friend Cati was a fashion designer student at college and agreed to make Symone's dress. Cati was my husband's protégée, and he encouraged her to get formally trained because she was so talented.

We made an event plan, outlining a timeline and all items to be sourced, like finding a venue, material and trimmings for the wedding dress. In fact, everything we possibly needed was obtained. My favourite part was planning and preparing the food.

My sister came over again and we had an amazing time. My goddaughter, who lived in America was also studying here for a year, so she was at the wedding too. We had 300 guests, and my daughter surprised us all by playing the steelpan for her guests. Her husband and all his friends and family were in awe, as they had never seen her play. I was the only person who knew she was practising with her friends for the event. All arrangements went according to plan. There were so many people having great fun and dancing and eating to their heart's content. I was happy that all our guests were so happy.

CHAPTER THIRTY-TWO:
New Blessings In My World

One highlight of the wedding was that my son and his girlfriend, Michelle, announced that she was pregnant. I felt so blessed and honoured, as I looked forward to working with her and guiding her through her pregnancy and the delivery of my first grandchild.

This was such an enjoyable experience, giving one-to-one antenatal care to someone. It took me back to the good old days as if I never left. I talked through a full range of classes, and I did full examinations alongside the ones she got in hospital. Michelle was a star pupil. At the hospital of her choice, I knew staff midwives I managed previously. Audrey, who was a sister there, asked me to call when Michelle was coming in, which I did. When we arrived, we were allocated the biggest delivery room I had ever seen. I was told I could share giving care with the midwife and I could do the delivery, but the midwife would be there and would sign all the paperwork. In the labour room, Michelle had fourteen members of friends and family supporting her in labour, including both sets of grandparents and her parents, which meant they would become great-grandparents and grandparents of the baby.

It was wonderful. It was my son's twenty-fifth birthday that day, the 20th. Michelle had laboured with me at home for a few hours, then we went in about 11 p.m. and she delivered about 2.30 a.m. the following morning, the 21st. We were hoping against hope that she would deliver that night, but it didn't happen. Michelle was the perfect patient in labour. She screamed and cussed, as she had minimal pain relief. This is perfectly normal, because it is more important she listened to me when I needed her. She delivered normally of a healthy, screaming baby girl with an intact perineum and no significant blood loss. It was a magical moment.

I was further blessed when Mum and Dad and baby stayed with me and I looked after them for about four weeks. The greatest honour of all is that Kevin and Michelle called the baby Layne, which is my maiden name. When Kevin was a small child, he discovered I was called Allyson Layne before I married his dad. He absolutely loved my surname and asked why he wasn't called Kevin Layne. I said it was because it was my name and he had to be called Williams, because it was his dad's name. I am just fit to burst that my name will live on through my granddaughter, my special angel. She has been a shining light in my life since then.

Life was settling, and I strongly felt some withdrawal from work and a deep sense of grief about my husband's passing. I was constantly thinking about whether I had made the right decision to retire, but they were usually just fleeting doubts. I was being kept very busy by the college, either lecturing at midwifery study days or editing articles for publication. I had a great idea to join the bank at the hospital and work out with them when I would be available to work. I had also decided I would travel a bit, so I needed this type of arrangement. I loved being able to do some kind of work, and I was lucky to have been sent to the community midwifery service.

In 2004, Layne's other grandmother was going to be on holiday in Barbados with her parents. We agreed I would join them in the new year for a short holiday, as I had to return for the carnival celebrations in Trinidad. Barbados is very beautiful. Parts of the island are full of rich people who have built lavish, expensive houses on the western side of the island. Every day, we would walk to the beach and spend some time in the sea.

On my return to London, I learnt that my application for a British passport was successful and I had become a naturalised British citizen. It seemed like such an anti-climax. My sister called to invite me over for my birthday and to accompany her to Texas to visit her best friend, who had moved back to her home. I was excited about the idea, so I went to New York, then we travelled to Houston first. My sister, Pene, had arranged with our cousins to visit them. Pene had spoken to them, but I had not seen them for many years. We spent several days with them, the highlight of which was visiting the NASA facility and a butterfly sanctuary. These were magical. Then we flew to Dallas, where Pauline lived. Texas was mind-blowing. It is so vast, with miles and miles of open space everywhere you look. One day we drove for miles and miles until we got into Oklahoma. We also picnicked at an open-air concert headlined by the famous group Maze, featuring Frankie Beverly. What a performance.

Later that year, my friend Bernice invited me on a weekend coach trip to the races in Paris. It was not on the scale of Ladies Day at Ascot, but it was lovely all the same. In 2005, I went home to

Trinidad with my friend, Bernice, who was going to visit her sister and mother. We enjoyed a busy time attending all the exciting shows and calypso tents that were on at the time. Bernice and I had been invited to Antigua to visit with the priest who conducted my husband's funeral and was a good friend of Bernice. He had recently been transferred out there. We travelled to Antigua after the carnival and stayed at the priest's residence. We were very lucky to have the help of his housekeeper to look after us. He was an excellent host and very popular with his parishioners. We toured the island with him to see all the important sites. We were wined and dined at several exclusive venues and at the residences of one of the oldest business families living there since the colonial days. We also met a pilot and his family who had lived there all their lives. The pilot had flown for more than thirty years all around the Caribbean and had some wonderful stories to tell.

Unfortunately, Bernice became very ill later that year. She had been having treatment for various conditions, and finally succumbed to the complications. She sadly passed away and I still miss her terribly.

On my return, I noticed my right knee was hurting occasionally. I had been diligently attending the gym with Bernice as well as our usual jaunts at socialising As you would imagine, I was trying hard to keep my weight down as part of the management of my high blood pressure. I saw my doctor, who referred me for an MRI, followed by a referral to an orthopaedic surgeon. I was diagnosed with tears in the meniscus in my knee, so I needed surgery, but we had no idea when this would happen. I just had to wait. In the meantime, I was banned from using the machines at the gym.

CHAPTER THIRTY-THREE:
Being Bitten By The Travel Bug

It was now 2006, and I had an invitation to my goddaughter's wedding in New York. My sister and I had agreed that, when I visited her in New York, we would visit somewhere else. She and my goddaughter's parents had a chat and agreed we should go to Las Vegas after the wedding. The wedding was a wonderful occasion. I met old friends and we had a wonderful time. It was wonderful seeing my goddaughter again after her study and time spent with us in London three years previously.

Two days later, we went to Las Vegas for a week's holiday. The city was colourful and wild and noisy. It was quite something. The waterfalls and casinos were beautiful. We attended several shows that were amazing. My sister and I took a two-hour coach journey to the Grand Canyon via the historic Hoover Dam. It is a stunning and ethereal place. It is so majestic and awe-inspiring. It is certainly a place that everyone should visit. It should really be one of the wonders of the world. The rock formation is extraordinary, with myriad colours of rock sitting on top of each other. It was a memorable site to behold.

My sixtieth birthday was approaching and I wanted to have a spectacular party. It was my daughter's turn now to manage this event, since she had studied event management at master's degree level. The party was held in the ballroom of a hotel near my home. Social media was undeveloped, so invitations had to be sent in the post, and responses came by post or telephone. Symone and her friends did a wonderful job with the decorations and setup of the ballroom. I was so lucky, as the staff from the charity I worked for came to help with managing the refreshments and drinks. I baked my own cakes, but my friend Alison decorated them for me. I booked a personal shopper at Debenhams to help me find a dress. I catered most of the food and I had 120 guests at the party. My family, especially, were so happy and fully involved. There were speeches from my son, daughter and a few friends. I was very bold and requested, very nicely in my invitation, that I would prefer cash gifts, as I already have too much stuff. Of course, I still got gifts, but I was eternally grateful to have received hundreds and hundreds of pounds. The package included a room in the hotel for my use until 2 p.m. the next day. After packing up, I went upstairs to bed and had the best night's sleep ever. This was yet another memorable milestone in my life.

Finally, a few months after my birthday, I received an appointment for surgery to my right knee. This was done in September and the event created a huge milestone in my life. The surgery itself was uneventful, but they couldn't wake me from the anaesthetic. After several hours of observation, I finally woke up. I now have to make doctors aware of my difficulty with anaesthesia.

I went home the next day and, with my daughter's help, hopped around from bedroom to bathroom in severe pain. Slowly, after a few days, the pain was more bearable. Suddenly I realised I had not smoked for some time. From going nil by mouth the night before surgery, to that point, added up to six days. I couldn't believe that, in that time, I never wanted to smoke. I had been smoking about ten cigarettes a day for the previous twenty years. So I stopped and spoke to myself. I said, "Allyson, if you did not remember that you were a smoker, and you haven't smoked for six days, then you don't need it. It's a sign. You must stop now."

I listened to myself, and I have not smoked another cigarette to this day. My children did not realise either, or believe me when they did realise. I had to prove it by showing them my stock. My children had politely refused to buy me cigarettes for many years, so I always kept well stocked with duty-free supplies I bought when travelling. I gave my son my supplies to donate to his friends. To this day, my children don't understand how I have managed to go cold turkey for so long. I think it's purely mind over matter, and this was a perfect example to prove that point. I still love the smell of a cigarette, but I find the smell of stale cigarette so disgusting. I was embarrassed to think I smelt like that for so many years.

*

So, it's official: I can now be called an old-age pensioner and/or senior citizen. Thankfully, I don't feel like either of those. I started enjoying this time of my life and completely loving my retirement and feeling relaxed about the flexibility of it. I don't know when I would have found time to do a full-time job with so much else going on. My children were so thrilled to see me enjoying myself and travelling so much. I never believed this would ever happen, either. I often thought about if life had gone according to plan, and my Vernon had not passed. I wondered if any of my travels would have happened. Would we have travelled together, or would I have gone off alone or with girlfriends, or maintain our plan of living six months of the year in Tobago and the other six months in London?

However, as the saying goes, life is what happens when you are busy making plans. I still missed the staff at the hospital, but I didn't miss the unit. I continued to do my part-time community midwifery job between travels and I was really enjoying it. I also continued to work as the midwifery advisor for Bounty. I was responsible for updating all the facts, policies and procedures in midwifery for their publication twice yearly. This was a paid consultancy that contributed handsomely to my travel nest egg.

Then, in 2007, I received an invitation to attend a wedding in Lagos, Nigeria. I have talked about reuniting with my old friend Evadne, who had returned to London after living in Africa for some years. Her daughter had graduated from university and was marrying a Nigerian she met there. I was so honoured to have been asked, because we had such a hiatus in our relationship. I became part of the family party who travelled there together and stayed together at the family home. The experience was awe-inspiring. First of all, I never imagined that I would ever travel to Africa. It seemed unreal, but I often listened to Evadne telling me of her experiences when she lived there. I often wished I had gone with her, but of course my life would not have been the same.

We arrived at Lagos Airport and it was an incredible culture shock. The poverty and slum housing was so close and fully visible from the airport for all the world to see. It seemed on a scale twenty times worse than I had seen back home in Trinidad. Our drive from the airport to home was a frightening nightmare too. Our host forgot about the government's directive that dictates there should be no travel on the roads on that day as this time was set aside for doing repairs and cleaning on the roads. So we were subject to verbal abuse and so many stops on the road by the police and the army. They were so frightening and intimidating, and were threatening our host all the time. It was almost as if we were on the set of a very bad movie. It was so surreal and they were really menacing. He had to keep negotiating and saying we were friends and family of a famous chief. They would walk around the cars staring at us with their guns on show all the time. Our host kept bribing them with large sums of money to allow us to move on. One of the ladies in the car was beginning to have a panic attack. We had to try to keep her as calm as possible in case it antagonised the soldiers. Our driver kept asking her to stay calm and quiet. I prayed quietly all the way that I would get out of that situation alive and be able to see my children again. Thankfully, we came through safely, breathing sighs of relief.

Lagos is like a city of two halves. Not far from those slum dwellings were gated communities, where the rich and famous lived in large, luxurious houses. All of the friends and family of our host lived in these areas.

I had the wonderful experience of having a traditional outfit made for me to attend the wedding. The dressmakers there are exceptionally skilled and work so quickly. I looked like a million dollars.

The wedding was a spectacular affair. The first surprise we had was that the groom's village from the north of the country came to Lagos and arrived in front of the house, dancing and playing music as a welcome to the bride. We stood on the balcony to acknowledge them performing this important tradition. The wedding was huge, with about 500 guests. There was a great amount of tasty and spicy traditional food and drink. The groom's mother and her village also came from the Cameroon for the wedding. It was quite an education being there. We also had a housekeeper from Benin who worked for our host and who did everything for us. It was a real reminder of my own childhood, as we had a housekeeper who looked after us because Mum and Dad worked full-time.

After the wedding, we were treated to several adventures, like house parties, shopping trips and visits to restaurants with various members of the family. This was my first trip to black Africa and I was in awe and feeling truly blessed to have achieved the milestone.

My adventures continued as I was delighted to receive an invitation for me and my sister, Pene, to attend the graduation of my godson from medical school in Minneapolis, in the state of Minnesota. I flew to New York and spent some time there before flying to Minneapolis with Penelope. I even made and iced a cake for the celebration party after. I was so proud of my godson and I knew his mum was even more so. The graduation ceremony was grand, with hundreds of graduates and their friends and family, then we went back to the hotel for the party. My godson is now a fully established obstetrician in California. His wife is a university professor, and together they have nine children. I relish the day when I can get out there to see them. My friend Pat, his mum is especially proud of him and his brothers. Her three sons have given her a total of fourteen grandchildren.

I regularly attend the meetings of the Mas Bands Association (NHMBA) to participate and share ideas with other band leaders and give feedback on any good or controversial issues raised about the management of the carnival. As you can imagine, I was usually very vocal, with lots of constructive criticism. After all, I had been involved for many decades. As luck would have it, my enthusiasm for all things carnival got me appointed to the board, as the mas band representative. This was a very difficult experience, mainly because of the gallons of testosterone flying around at each meeting. I was one of two females on the board, so it was hard work being heard, trying to get my points across. There were other representatives on the board representing the other genres in carnival, such as the steel bands, the music DJs, the sound systems and the Calypsonians and Soca artists. This meant that every representative had issues that never seemed to get resolved, year after year, so there was constant arguing and bad tempers flying about at meetings. I was not at all surprised that the event could not get the respect and recognition it deserves. One of the issues was that the carnival company was not registered as a company, so corporations would not take us seriously.

The chief executive at the time was an excellent professional with a lot of ideas and vision, but he too had to fight to make a difference. The most interesting highlight of my role was being asked to temporarily become the chair of the board. It was imperative that the board had someone in place for the carnival season. I accepted, as I knew this was important because there was an important event coming up. I was asked, as acting chair of Notting Hill Carnival, to receive the Olympic torch from Beijing at the end of the summer Olympics, in conjunction with then Mayor Boris Johnson, as well as the Olympic flag from the mayor of Beijing. It was a lovely event that firmly established the Notting Hill Carnival as a serious event.

During this tenure as acting chair of the board, I was invited to the launch of a ship called the Sunbourne Yacht Hotel that was built in London. It was commissioned by the Nigerian government to become a floating hotel, as part of the development of tourism in the port around Lagos. It was a lavish affair and it was interesting to meet ambitious businessmen, and represent the carnival at this corporate event. Unfortunately, this role finished by the end of the year, but not before I was exposed to the amazing and complex work done by the police and other strategic partners in preparation for the carnival event. I had no idea all this work happened on our behalf and I truly appreciated their roles. I also was blown away by my visit to the command centre set up to monitor all activities in the area over the carnival weekend. It was quite an eye-opener. I was also lucky to be given an access-all-areas pass that allowed me to travel through the footprint unchallenged. I had not done this before because I was always in our costume band. This was my first experience of walking around the footprint as a normal civilian.

Unfortunately, due to complications in the board, a few of us had to resign, including me.

Later on that year, because of my connections with the Nigerian tourist board, I was invited to join a group of celebrities going on a tour of Ghana, Nigeria and Morocco to learn about the unique history of those places. We were called the Freedom Pilgrims 2008. The tour was organised to reconnect Africans in the diaspora with the motherland. Wow, wow. This was so big for me, first of all because I never thought of myself as a celebrity. I was humbled to have been asked. It was a deep and lasting personal experience. The organiser wanted to provide us with a revealing and exhilarating experience of life in Africa and an insight into where we all originated from. To support the growing African economy, we stayed in African-owned hotels in each country.

In Ghana we visited the castles Elmina and Cape Coast, which were the centre of the transatlantic slave trade. This was very emotional for us all when we actually saw where the men and woman were taken out to sea on the slave ships. Elmina Castle is now listed as a UNESCO World Heritage Site. Cape Coast Castle is recognised as a testimony to European exploitation and abuse of Africans. Accra is Ghana's capital city and it is a very lovely place with several interesting buildings. We visited the famous Kakum National Park, which has the world's seventh tallest canopy walk, built 80 metres above the rainforest. This was a spectacular sight and I summoned up the courage to walk on this canopy that swayed in the wind as you walked across it. It was truly scary but also invigorating, and gave me an amazing buzz when I accomplished the feat. We also tried to see Rita Marley, Bob Marley's widow who lives in Ghana.

Unfortunately, she was not at home at the time, but we visited her home and talked to her staff.

In Nigeria, we saw the town Badagry, where more Africans were transported to America, Europe, South America and the Caribbean. We also spent some time at the Tropicana Beach Resort on the Atlantic coast.

We used Casablanca in Morocco as a transit stop, but when we were travelling back to London, we were able to spend time exploring the city and doing some shopping. The Moroccan architecture is truly stunning and very intricate.

Evadne invited me to join her on a holiday to Uganda and Kenya. I couldn't believe that I was again getting an opportunity to visit Africa. Her former partner was very keen on education and he educated most of the children in his brothers' and sisters' families. A young lady, Carmen, was studying in England and getting married at home in Kampala, so she invited us. We also planned to travel via Kenya, so we could meet our benefactor. He had offered us the accommodation in his home in Ginja, a village in the north of the country, and the services of his housekeeper and his driver. This was the perfect arrangement. We felt so special because having a driver at our disposal was comfortable and sheer heaven. He took us everywhere we wanted and, in turn, we shared food and drink with him.

The highlight of my trip was travelling to Lake Victoria to see the source of the Nile in the middle of the lake. I had no idea that the Nile started in Uganda. It is only ever mentioned in association with Egypt. There is also a bust of Gandhi at the side of the lake. Half his ashes were scattered there and the other half in the river

Ganges in India, because Gandhi wanted his legacy to be scattered in the world's great rivers. This was more history and geography that I didn't know.

Uganda is also famous for two other events. Idi Amin was president of Uganda and one of the most brutal dictators in history. He is reputed to have killed more than half a million of his own people. We visited the ravaged north-east of the country where most of the wars took place. The countryside there remained derelict and run-down, almost as a testament to the savagery and brutality that took place there.

We also visited the south of the capital city, Kampala, where the Equator passes through the country, one of only thirteen such countries in the world. It was a lovely family occasion for Evadne, as she was reunited with her daughter's Ugandan family. We were also lucky enough to attend a second wedding during our trip. We were treated to a luxury weekend at a five-star hotel, where we were wined and dined and pampered unashamedly. Our journey to Kenya was short, as it was just a stopover for the day to meet James and say thanks for his kindness and unstinting generosity. He too was bowled over by the gift we took him. I was staggered to hear him explain his surprise by saying, "I am not used to anyone giving me anything. People always want something from me." This holiday was so memorable, educational and totally relaxing.

I felt extremely blessed to learn that my son and his partner were having another baby. Yet again, I jumped into midwife mode and did my usual to support and guide Michelle as much as I could. I had already been keeping myself busy with my beautiful granddaughter, Layne. She was adorable, so smart and she was my little princess. Her mum and I devised a plan when she started her nursery school. She would attend for three days a week. Her mum was working as a nursery nurse and studying for her first degree, so I tried to give her as much space as possible. She was also plagued by bouts of sciatica during her pregnancy, so she had to rest. I used to keep Layne with me as much as possible. Sometimes her mum wouldn't see her until the end of the week. I was often the adult of choice to escort her on school trips. It was such a wonderful experience being involved with young children again.

Michelle delivered a beautiful baby boy in May. Unfortunately, I was not involved in her care, as I had no colleagues at that hospital. Thankfully, after a few weeks, her sciatica was beginning to resolve itself but, as usual, I went into midwife mode and remained constantly at her side.

Our next holiday jaunt was to Dubai, and included Evadne and a friend of ours who lived between Nigeria and London. Dubai was an interesting place, with a very luxurious perspective about it. Most of it was new and very artificial, but there were some parts of the city that looked and felt very Middle Eastern, with many souks and shopping markets. The city was still being modernised and the long term aim was to gain fame and notoriety with the building of luxurious mega structures as part of the development of tourism around

the world. There was an enormous building in the city centre that was built as a ski mountain with artificial ice and snow and ski lifts. The tallest building in the world is there and was still being built. Most of the city is completely man-made, because of course it sits in the middle of a desert. This includes the island in the lake where the famous Burj Al Arab hotel is built. It is a spectacular piece of engineering and dripping in gold decorations, and registered as a five-star hotel. My friends and I decided we had to have lunch there before returning home. It was quite something and the most expensive lunch I have had before or since. We had to book in advance and paid through the nose, and I mean hundreds of pounds. When we got there, we were first taken on a tour of the eight restaurants in the hotel, so that we could make an informed choice. We were even shown the helipad on the roof of the hotel. We chose to go to the Arabic restaurant, which was buffet-style. The food was different but truly wonderful. We were able to stay there for the entire lunch period from 12.30 to 3.30 p.m. There was no one waiting for your seat, which is such a civilised arrangement. Of course, we tried to sample every dish available, as we were determined to get our money's worth. We were not at all disappointed and lapped up the lavish surroundings.

We did all the tourist bits like quad biking and shopping at souks and in the jewellery quarter. It was an interesting place to visit and explore, but I felt that Dubai had no soul or personality about it. It was just expensive and lavish, with a lot of richness and megastructures all around. It was nice to be able to say that I was there when they were building the richest and tallest buildings in the world. Somehow, it's not somewhere I would want to visit again.

My friend Alice came to live with me. She had sold her home nearby after her divorce. In the blink of an eye, she was reunited with an old school friend who was her first love as a child. Immediately, she started preparing to emigrate to Jamaica with him to get married again and live there. We were both excited and nervous at the same time. I could fully understand the whirlwind effect this was having on her. The difference was she was just divorced and didn't give herself time to think or breathe. But who the hell cares what I think? This was moving into new and unknown territory for her. She invited me to attend her wedding and be the master of ceremonies on the day. I was truly honoured.

We shopped until we dropped for as much as possible for the wedding, and for the new home she was planning to build. We baked the cakes and took them with us. We were picked up by her fiancé when we arrived on a Tuesday, as the wedding was on the upcoming Friday. On Tuesday and Wednesday, we iced and decorated the cakes, then we packed everything and drove to the wedding venue, where I was booked to stay in a luxurious room in the same hotel. We were busy and excited and frustrated but, with the help of the hotel planners, everything was coming together. On the day before the wedding, we even managed to have pedicures and manicures in the town. On the day, it was so lovely to be beautifully dressed in the warm sunshine. My friend looked stunning, as did her bridesmaids. It was my first experience of attending a wedding outdoors and it was a lovely setting by the sea. The reception progressed well and I was so pleased to see the majestic display of the wedding cake that the bride and I produced. I also managed not to embarrass myself as the master of ceremonies before we danced the night away. The next night, we had even more fun dancing and drinking the night away, before the wedding party all dispersed to their various destinations.

I continued my vacation, but I gave the newlyweds some space, and went to stay with a friend in Maypen who had returned back home from London. We had a lovely few days, spent in a spa and local shopping. Then I stayed with another friend, Donna, in Kingston, who trained with me and relocated back home many years before. Donna also kept me busy. We went to salsa dance classes, a drinks event, a river cruise, a house party, Montego Bay and the seaside. It was just wonderful to reunite with Donna and catch up on each other's lives since she left London. Jamaica is such a beautiful place, my favourite being Bamboo Avenue, which is a long cool road, where huge bamboo trees grow to a great height and meet in the middle, forming an arch. It was an awesome sight.

On my return, my daughter was excited to find out that she had been selected to have in vitro fertilisation because of her history of infertility. I was so excited for her, but unfortunately, after all the preparation and a successful implantation of an embryo, Symone miscarried after six weeks. She had to be hospitalised for a few days, during which she had a blood transfusion. She was devastated and distraught, but I encouraged her to get better first, and not to stop trying.

CHAPTER THIRTY-FOUR:
"Don't Judge Me Until You Walk In My Shoes"

The next few years were mixed blessings that changed my life forever. I take full responsibility for my arrogance and determination that I could make a difference in other people's lives. My daughter invited me to join a strategic group at the Tudor Rose nightclub that was looking at becoming a charity to provide mentoring and guidance and training for young people experiencing economic deprivation and social exclusion. I was very interested in the idea, and I joined the group to develop the project. We were successful in securing funding to develop the project and move forward. We were making good progress and even started to have a workshop with a few youngsters.

At the same time, my beautiful daughter was headhunted as a costume designer online by some officials in the Cayman Islands, who were planning to restart the island's carnival celebrations, called Batabanu. She had the honour of being the first international invited to do so. After the formalities of approving designs, she made some prototypes and took them to the launch of the carnival in Grand Cayman about six months before the event. They were very happy so, on her return, we started production. I was thankful for her to have achieved this vote of confidence. I worked hard to make sure the costumes were produced to the highest standard. I was honoured to be invited by my daughter to accompany her to the carnival. It was a really special treat. Grand Cayman is very beautiful with a very luxurious feel to it. My son-in-law's sister worked there as a hospitality manager, so she was able to find us the most beautiful accommodation on the beach for a very reasonable cost. We had a few hiccups on the way, but were very happy to have finished all we were commissioned to do. Carnival on the roads was spectacular. The route was wide and generous with lots of security and help along the way. The band had a wonderful group of people, both locals and visitors, who wanted to have a lived experience.

After this wonderful experience, Symone's luck was happening again when she was contacted by a band leader from the band Dream Team in Trinidad, and was commissioned to produce costumes for a section in his band. We were fit to burst. This was amazing, as we never knew of designers invited to work in Trinidad, the home of the carnival. This opportunity was mega.

This event then led her to decide on getting married in Tobago after the carnival, at the luxurious Magdalena Grand Plantation hotel. She had been dating for a few years since her first marriage had broken down. So we got busy organising the two events. There were many ups and downs, especially with the costume band. Symone engaged the services of her cousin in Trinidad to tie up loose ends and make contacts and decisions on Symone's behalf. We almost had a disaster, because when we got there, the men's costumes that were ordered and paid for were not made. We were horrified, as we then had to make them ourselves, which caused us to miss a major social event, but we had no choice.

In the end, the band was a huge success, and Symone was congratulated by everyone for her beautiful designs and well-finished costumes. She was so blessed to have friends from London and their families to support her. It was the first time in my life that I wore a bikini costume on the road, and I looked really hot! It had been a while since I played mas at home, and I felt the thrill of crossing the big stage in the Savannah and the other stages in Woodbrook and down town. The freedom and space we had at our disposal was unsurpassed and nothing like the fight for space we experience in Notting Hill.

At the same time, Symone was also planning her wedding in Tobago after the carnival. Our family and friends in Trinidad were delighted about attending the wedding. Symone's friends from London all went there for carnival and came over to Tobago for the wedding. My sister Penelope, who lived in New York, surprised me by travelling down to the wedding and got our cousin to help her with the surprise. I was so happy to see her. It was really easy to plan the wedding, as the hotel was arranging everything. We just had to turn up. The wedding was also a stunning affair in very luxurious surroundings. I baked the wedding cake in Trinidad and iced it as well. It was very difficult, due to the heat.

Symone and Curtis left immediately after carnival for Tobago, but my friend and I travelled later on the boat over to Tobago with the cake. Pene arrived just in time to join us on the boat. One of the most famous locticians in London, Morris Roots, came especially to do Symone's hair for the wedding. I was so humbled by this selfless act. The wedding was outside on the grass, surrounded by the sea. The reception was equally pleasant. The menu was exquisite and really tasty. There were a few guests who didn't attend due to travel and other issues. The hotel was magnanimous and refunded the cost of those absent guests. I was very happy for my daughter, who had found love again.

I was delighted we had such a good time with my sister at and after the wedding. When she returned to New York, she informed me she had been diagnosed with breast cancer. This was a devastating blow to us all. She had suffered a series of illnesses throughout her life which she managed admirably. The worst of them was the lupus, which she had for many years. Her surgery was done immediately and she started chemotherapy. She found this toxic and difficult and the doctors stopped the treatment for about three months before changing it to radiotherapy. This was welcomed by Pene, as she had some respite from the nausea and vomiting. We had discussed that I would visit in November for thanksgiving, and we would possibly travel somewhere else if she was up to it. We were excited, as she slowly continued to recover, and even started back at work.

I was attending a line dance weekender near the coast, organised by my dance teachers. A call came to me at the hotel to say that Pene had collapsed and was in hospital. I knew that she was about to restart her treatment after three month's rest. My brother informed me that she was restarting her treatment that day, and the transport had arrived to take her to hospital. As she was going down the steps at the front of the building, she fell down the stairs. The driver stayed with her until the ambulance came to take her to hospital. I was devastated and sobbing uncontrollably. I returned to London and made arrangements to travel to New York immediately.

When I arrived two days later, Pene was semi-conscious and weakly squeezed my hand to acknowledge that she knew I was there. She never fully regained consciousness. I never left her side until she died the next day in the afternoon. She was my special baby sister and I loved her so much. Our cousins came from Trinidad almost immediately and were a source of a great deal of support for me. She was a very popular member of her church choir and was the greatest person that I knew to have a large and amazing number of friends. People seemed to gravitate towards her. She was affectionately called Grandma or Mommy Pene because of her old-school and mature attitudes. Every time I went to New York, she would take me on some adventure or the other. We always did exciting things like attend concerts in Central Park, or at Madison Square Gardens or jazz in Greenwich Village or the Lincoln Centre or attend plays on Broadway. Since my retirement, we agreed to go on holiday together and, for the last few years, we left New York and visited somewhere else, like Las Vegas, the Grand Canyon, Dallas and Houston in Texas and Minnesota.

She would always have a collection of drop-dead gorgeous clothes for me to try because of her lengthy career in retail. She too was yet another very creative and talented person in the family. She was a prolific piano player and steelpan player and excelled in knitting and crocheting, baking and cooking.

Her funeral was beautiful, and held at night with the full choir and a huge number of friends and families in attendance, followed by a lavish reception in the church hall in the basement. Her body was interned overnight at the church then, the next day, she was buried at a cemetery outside New York. I have been so sad and I miss my beautiful sister so much. She was the glue that held us all together. I realised that I have not returned to New York since her death, except at the end of the first year, when I went to hold a memorial service for her. I am still in touch with many of her friends by social media, but I haven't seen them. Pene's passing was certainly the end of an era.

During our work with the charity, my colleague and I were asked to look at becoming involved with the nightclub. The club was known to me and was one of my favourite places to socialise. I had been there many times, as had my children. It was a world-renowned place to showcase Caribbean calypso and reggae artists. I was excited and my friend in the group, Bella, decided we would take on the management of the club for five years. The owner and his lawyer gave us a lease, which we had scrutinised by our own lawyer, who said it was fine. Our lawyer said he would have liked more time, but nevertheless, it was fine. That should have been a red flag to us, but we believed him and proceeded. We embarked on this journey and soon realised that we had been seriously misled. There was so much information that was withheld from us, and the management of the building was exhaustingly physical and demanding. My own car became the transport vehicle for the club. We had some amazing events, but these were few and far between. There was no system in place about managing security, staffing and stocktaking. Within the first year, I began to regret my involvement in the place. My colleague, Bella, walked out on us and left me to carry the can. I was shocked and distraught, because she clearly didn't understand that, with her signature on the lease, she was still responsible. I carried on, but I began to get unwell. After investigations, I was found to have gallstones, and I needed surgery. My doctor recommended I must have three months to heal, so I was signed off work.

At last, my long-standing booking for a trip to Israel and the Holy Land with members of my church was due. It was an awe-inspiring experience, although it was quite an uncomfortable process being interrogated by airport staff with guns and rifles.

We had a very scary time when we got to Israel. One of our members was arrested and interrogated at length, and we had no idea why. After two hours, he came back to us, only to explain that they were suspicious of him because of his middle names, which were Mohammed Hussein. His deceased father was Muslim and his mother was black, both from Sierra Leone where he was born.

Israel to me was surreal. In my mind it put the Bible into full perspective and made it believable. I have always wondered if these places actually existed. The names of the places – Jerusalem, the Sea of Galilee, the Garden of Gethsemane, the Wailing Wall and the River Jordan – were all there. We sailed across the Sea of Galilee and walked in the River Jordan and bathed in the Dead Sea. We saw Jews and Arabs and Christians all living together, except that we were not allowed to travel to the war-torn areas in the West Bank. I truly enjoyed the prayers and sense of community. Our group bonded so well and I totally enjoyed the company of my friends, Carol and Mervyn, who had travelled from New York to join the group. There were other people from Trinidad and Grenada and other churches in London who also joined the group. It was a life-changing experience for me.

I noticed my daughter was using an inhaler towards the end of the carnival season. Symone had been diagnosed with asthma as a teenager, but she hadn't used one for some time. She said she was getting breathless at times and feeling tired, but I rationalised that she was working hard for the carnival season. She saw her doctor after the carnival, and he sent her to A & E, as he thought she was severely anaemic. To our surprise, her haemoglobin was 4.6g, with the normal being 14g. The staff marvelled about how she was functioning. She was immediately admitted to the ward and given four pints of blood. She was also referred to a gynaecologist, as they identified that she had fibroids. The gynaecologist recommended surgery, which was done the following February. I was terrified. She was three hours late out of the theatre and I was having kittens. The surgeon came to say that they had to abandon the keyhole surgery, as they couldn't keep her safely ventilated. They had to remove all the gas in her abdomen and start again with a GA. She also had to be transfused as her haemoglobin was 5.8. After a day, she had to be transferred to a major surgical centre in the larger hospital in the group, as she needed more intensive nursing care. I thanked God that he answered my prayers, and she was home within a week. We all assumed then that her asthma was affecting her again.

In June I was off again to participate in a pilgrimage to Rome with members of my church. Rome is a beautiful, exotic and regal place. The buildings are exquisitely beautiful and I thoroughly enjoyed exploring the sites, like inside the Vatican, the Sistine Chapel, the

Spanish steps, St Peter's Basilica, the Trevi Fountain and the Colosseum. I was like a kid in a candy store, staring wide-eyed at all the historical places, and especially indulging in the exquisitely authentic Italian food. Yet again, history had come to life.

Over the Christmas holiday, my cousin June came on holiday as usual from New York. She enjoyed spending the new year in Europe and meeting up with her friends. She had planned with them to spend the new year in Edinburgh but, due to unforeseen circumstances, the plans had changed. As my luck would have it, June asked me to join her. What a treat. I was wined and dined in a four-star hotel and we explored the city and its famous castle and the Royal Mile.

Despite all the problems going on in the nightclub, I was approached by a production company to take part in a documentary about the black nurses who saved the NHS. It was some wonderful light relief that I enjoyed very much. My interview was meant to form part of the pilot presented to the BBC. The BBC was very impressed with my contribution, and the documentary was commissioned. I understand the BBC requested that my interview be used in the finished film. That was so exciting to me. The film finally aired about a year later in 2016. My cousin Janice was here on vacation. She was returning home to Trinidad after a vacation in Botswana and South Africa and the producers invited us to his offices to view the finished film before it was shown on air the next day. It was such a privilege to be the first two people in the world to see the film. We cried with joy. I was so elated that he was able to capture the commitment and passion of these immigrant nurses who came to rebuild the motherland. I was very impressed by this excellent piece of work. It highlighted the awful levels of racism we endured, as well as our survival through all this adversity. I hoped that the nation was impressed and grateful and more informed of the huge contribution we all made to the development of the NHS. The film has become the flagship of the BBC's productions. The BBC have always thought it was an amazing piece of work. It is always a pleasure when it's repeated so much.

My cousin Janice was also responsible for one of the best experiences of my life. On her trip to Table Mountain in South Africa, she met an English woman called Carol. Janice was invited to her home when she returned to London, and I accompanied her. Over time, Carol and I became great friends. She is the most generous and kind person I have ever met. She invited me over regularly, and I eventually discussed my nightclub dilemma with her. She even invited a friend who was a lawyer to talk to me about my untenable situation. I was so grateful for this type of support.

CHAPTER THIRTY-FIVE:
Dealing With The Body Blows Coming Thick And Fast

Symone and I had lunch with our friend Ansel at my home in February. We wanted to brainstorm about what plans we could explore for the forthcoming carnival. We had a wonderful salmon lunch and parted late afternoon. Symone and I joked that we had a fish fest that day, as she had cooked fish for her husband as well. A few hours later, Symone called again and said to me, "Do I sound funny to you?"

I said, "Yes, why are you speaking with your mouth full of food?"

She said, "I am not eating. My face has dropped on one side and my arm is limp and I can't raise it. I can't hold anything." I froze and I think my heart stopped for a few seconds. I told her to call 111 immediately and have a drink of water, while I made my way to her. I knew what had happened to her, but I prayed furiously that I was wrong. I was near her exit when she called again and said the ambulance was there and taking her to hospital. She said to them, "Can you wait for my Mum?"

The paramedic said, "Hell no. She will have to find us."

I was so panicked, as Watford had a game at their stadium and I was stuck behind people and traffic. When I found her, I hugged her so hard. The doctor said she had had a stroke and they were so happy that she got there so promptly. She was eventually warded, because she had to have investigations into the cause of the stroke. I stayed the night with her. After a few days of tests, they discovered that Symone had a congenital heart abnormality. The science has proven that if a young adult has a stroke under the age of 40, they will have a congenital heart defect, usually a hole in the heart. Often this is diagnosed very early in the baby's life. We were all staggered by this diagnosis. Symone had enjoyed such an active life. She was on the school's football, track, netball and basketball teams. She danced ballet from age 5 to 13. She rode her own bike and had played the steelpan since she was 10. The doctor said she was a true statistic.

She was introduced to the stroke team, who gave information and advice, and exercises to strengthen her arm. These worked well, so she didn't have to be referred to physios. Her arm returned to full function after a few months, but she has remained with what is called residual brain impairment. This means that, occasionally, she loses her train of thought when talking to someone. She was also found to have a low positive result for an autoimmune disease, but it was never formally confirmed. She was regularly followed up by her local hospital, but they eventually transferred her to Hammersmith Hospital, as it was world-renowned as a cardiac specialist centre. It was inconceivable to me that my precious daughter could be so ill with such major issues in her life. I have been in such awe of her, as she has the most positive and uplifting attitude of anyone that I know.

We were invited to take part in the opening ceremony of the Shanghai tourist festival in September 2016. This was beyond my wildest dreams but it remained up in the air due to Symone's healing after the stroke. Nearer the time, the doctors gave her the all-clear to travel and we went with forty other people. It was the journey of a lifetime. China is vast and noisy and very dirty and smelly. We ate authentic Chinese food and performed at the ceremony with great success.

After some fun-filled days of sightseeing and socialising, we moved on to Kuala Lumpur for an extended tour. The group had been to Shanghai several times, but this was the second time they had extended the trip. The first time was the year before when the group went to India. Kuala Lumpur was a stunning place and reminded me completely of my home in the Caribbean. All the flowers, fruits and trees and the temperature were the same. The food was sensational and the city boasts the twin Petronas Towers and the Royal Selangor pewter factory. I am proud to have been a student of their School of Hard Knocks, where I made my own pewter bowl.

During my sick leave, I learnt that the club had been closed down because someone was stabbed outside. It was alleged that the man came from inside the club and this was against health and safety. We always had meetings with the licensing team, who kept up a lot of pressure about security. They must have been in seventh heaven when this incident happened. I had to go to court to contest the closure. We did this on five occasions, but we clearly didn't stand a chance. The licensing team presented every breach that occurred at the club for the previous twenty years. The disastrous consequence of this was that there was no business for money to be made. Our debts were mounting and the landlord was relentless with his demands. He refused to negotiate, because we pleaded that the lease was obsolete as the club was closed by the police. We went to court and my lawyer didn't turn up to fight my case. It is complex and painful to describe all the details, but in the end I have used up my savings, so I had to sell my home to stop the mounting charges and penalties.

I was distraught and terrified about my future prospects. My children were devastated for me, and have been by my side at all times. I felt embarrassed and dehumanised. I was ashamed that I had put their legacy in such jeopardy. However, I had a clear conscience that I went into this venture with a good, clean heart, trying to make a difference, but I was stupid and arrogant to have gone into a venture so blind, with no experience of the business. I also had no experience of dealing with such ugliness; the owner's behaviour was less than human.

My seventieth birthday was fast approaching, but I was not in the frame of mind to celebrate with a huge party. I decided to visit Trinidad for the carnival with my daughter Symone and her husband. We both needed some respite after all we had both been going through. Symone was transferred to Hammersmith Hospital as a referral to the cardiologist, because the doctors at Watford wanted a second opinion and believed she may need surgery. At the same time, I was working through the trauma of potentially losing my home.

On my return, I put my home on the market through a local estate agent, as I thought this was the only way to get rid of these awful vultures and try to get my life back. I was so frightened. A friend asked me if I ever wondered what my husband would think of this situation. I was so angry at the question and I said, "That is a stupid question, because if my husband was alive, these people would never have been in my life. We had our own plans, so this situation would never have arisen."

On our return, we had several visits to the cardiologist, and after investigations, he confirmed Symone did need surgery. She continued to be cared for, with several visits to the hospital. The doctors were puzzled about the cause of her low haemoglobin. She was transfused at her local hospital prior to her referral to Hammersmith Hospital for a consultation with a renowned cardiologist. Symone's surgery was booked for the end of July. I thought that was very timely, as I was planning a simple church celebration for my seventieth birthday, which was a few days before her surgery. I was really happy she would be able to celebrate with me. I had a special service, where Kevin and Symone gave a tribute to me and Natasha sang. I baked a cake and had refreshments for the congregation. I felt blessed and grateful that many of my family and friends were able to attend. I feel blessed and give thanks and praise for my life and service to my family and community.

A few days later, Symone had surgery to close the hole in her heart. She had to have several transfusions of a substance called Ferritin, which is a liquid iron compound, as her haemoglobin was low. She remained in hospital for a few days, after which she was discharged home.

Once I had agreed the sale for the price stated, I was introduced to a firm of conveyancing lawyers who would process the sale. To my horror, I found out from the lawyers that the nightclub owner had put a charge on my home for some time without my knowledge. A charge is also called a charging order. This means if you have a debt with someone, the charge ensures the payment of the debt is a priority when your assets are considered. In the end, God was good and I got the full asking price for my beautiful home. After paying the debt to the landlord, the end of my mortgage, the lawyers and estate agents, there was very little left, which I passed on to Symone and Kevin. I made sure the settlement was a full and final one, even though there was some outstanding money on the landlord's final bill. I didn't want any more interactions with these people. My lawyer did warn me that the landlord may possibly choose to go after my partner for the outstanding money.

So, after a busy and fulfilled life with an adoring husband and sensational children in our beautiful home we had for thirty-eight years, I was technically homeless one week before Christmas. It was a gut-wrenching experience clearing out my home under those circumstances. How much can you save from a fully furnished, three-bedroom house with a conservatory full of plants and a garage full of tools, with nowhere to go? As luck would have it, my neighbour came over and said a young girl in her church had just been allocated a new home and she had nothing. I said they should come with the biggest truck they could find. When they came, they were bowled over. They got wardrobes, a bed, tons of bed linen, kitchen equipment, pots and pans, cutlery and crockery, curtains, an IKEA sofa bed, leather chairs. The young girl and her partner were very happy and grateful for the haul. I left a garage full of tools for the new owners, and I offered my neighbours anything they wanted. I was able to store things of importance, as I had no idea what my future had in store. This was the start of my sofa surfing for about six months. I was truly down and depressed, but not out. I always told my children that I didn't have much sympathy for anyone who suffered from self-inflicted pain, so I really disliked myself at this point. I had no empathy for me and my stupidity.

CHAPTER THIRTY-SIX:
Redefining All Aspects of Life

You must have heard the saying that God does not give you any more than you can handle. Well, I believe I certainly put that belief to the test time and time again. I would not have believed that any one human being could experience all that I have been through and not have a mental breakdown or become seriously ill in the process. There were times when I did think I would go crazy, but I also remembered that my children and grandchildren had already lost their dad and granddad, so I had to be there for them to the best of my ability. I loved life and always gave thanks and praise for my health and strength and my positive attitude. I prayed constantly for recovery and renewed strength to come to Symone. I prayed that I was able to continue giving back and making a difference. My daughter has always said that she has agreed an inscription for my tombstone that says:

TELL ME SOMETHING I DON'T KNOW!

Mrs. Allyson Ingrid Layne Williams MBE;
Wife, Mother, Sister, Daughter, Cousin, Auntie, Grandmother,
Friend;
The woman who would never say no!

She was quite right, of course. I always found time to do anything I was asked to do. I sewed clothes and cushions and quilt covers in African materials for the family and everyone who asked. I baked and decorated many, many cakes for birthdays, anniversaries and funerals. I was asked to do interviews or write articles about the Windrush generation and Notting Hill Carnival. I became an active member of the London Diocese of the Mothers Union. I would do radio interviews as well. I loved every minute of all that I did, because the interviews and writing and presentations were an extension of all that I believed in and was passionate about. I also relished my ability to travel so frequently and truly explore aspects of the rest of the world, which was my original vision. Although it was part of my master plan, I had no idea that it would actually ever happen.

My first sofa surf was at my daughter's home in Bushey, near Watford. Just before I left my house, my friend Carol invited me over to hear of my progress. To my sheer delight, she said I could stay at her home until she and her husband Arnie returned from their annual holiday in Thailand. They are away from the 27th of December until the middle of April each year. I couldn't believe it. She said her three daughters thought she had lost her mind because she didn't know anything about me. She reassured them that she believed in her heart that I was a good person who would respect and look after her home. So I moved in immediately after New Year's Day and stayed until the middle of April.

Carol's flat was beautiful and felt like a safe haven after the last few years of painful drama. I felt so comfortable and relaxed that I was able to invite friends and family over for dinner on several occasions, especially in February, which has the most family birthdays for me. After Carol's return, I stayed in Acton at my old school friend Julie's home from the middle of April until I was rehoused by the council in Stonebridge Park in July.

I will always be eternally grateful to Carol and Julie for rescuing me. It felt like such an undignified and dishonourable time of my life. I was so embarrassed and ashamed. I felt the ground should open and swallow me up. One day a neighbour said to me "I can't believe that someone of your intelligence would let this happen to you."

I simply replied, "Well, I can't believe it either." What else could I say? That was my truth. It made me feel that maybe most people were thinking just that, but I couldn't accommodate such thoughts or I would go crazy. I have always believed in the saying, "Never judge anyone until you walk a mile in their shoes."

This experience of being homeless was another sharp learning curve for me. I had lived in my own home for thirty-nine years. Prior to that, I lived in a privately owned flat, and prior to that, in the nurses' home at the hospital where I trained. I visited the housing office to explain my plight and ask to be rehoused. The officer was pleasant but tried to tell me to go away and sort myself out. I said I preferred to get help because I was a vulnerable adult who had just suffered huge trauma. On his advice and instruction, I applied to a specific department through a locator system. Shortly after, I received a response from a manager who said the council couldn't help me because I didn't live in the borough. I had to be living in the borough in the immediate period prior to my application. I was incensed, as they didn't seem to appreciate or understand my situation. I was homeless and had to accept offers of accommodation as they came to me, regardless of which borough the offers came from.

I returned to the housing officer to ask why I had not been informed of this rule. Did my thirty-nine years in the borough count for nothing? He said it was not his responsibility to tell me anything! It was now several months of going backward and forward, with emails and phone calls, with no progress being made. I was asked to contact a manager to discuss my case and appeal against the decision, but I could not get hold of him. I remembered my mother's philosophy that, if you have a problem, you start at the top to resolve it and work your way down. So I wrote an email letter which I sent to the mayor, deputy mayor, the director of housing, the leader and deputy leader of the council and the four members of parliament in the borough. I stated that their staff were unhelpful and disrespectful to me as a vulnerable senior citizen. Their attitude of not providing information to clients amounted to entrapment. They did not understand their duty of care to me as a senior citizen and pensioner. I was elderly and vulnerable and scared, and that was the reason I would like the security of being a council tenant. I was a long-standing and loyal resident in the borough for thirty-nine years and I expected to be treated in a more dignified way. I also complained that I had not been able to contact the named manager I had been asked to speak to about my application. I immediately got responses from all of the above, acknowledging my case, and stating they had passed my letter to the relevant personnel.

At the same time, I attended a health seminar one Sunday afternoon at my barber's hair salon. At the end of an interesting session on important health issues, the barber thanked the people who helped him organise the event. To my great surprise, one of the people named was the manager I was trying to contact. I asked to be introduced to him and explained my frustration. He also apologised and stated he had to take annual leave or it would have been lost at the end of the financial year. He promised to follow up on my emails. In a few days, I received a lengthy email message from a manager, apologising profusely for the way I had been treated. She confirmed that they did have a duty of care to me and they would use my letter as part of their training for staff. She said I would be contacted by a senior manager who would help me.

I was delighted and relieved, because I was beginning to feel worthless. After a week, and to my delight, I heard from a manager who happened to be the gentleman I met at the health seminar. He informed me that he had found a suitable home for me. I was ecstatic and in disbelief. Of course, I cross-examined him extensively about what it was like. How old was the building? Was it clean and did the building have a lift, as I was old and had bad knees. He said it was a one-bedroom flat on the third floor in a building of four floors that was six years old. It was well managed and clean and there was a lift in place. It sounded perfect, and I accepted the invitation to see the flat. Symone and I made arrangements to meet the housing officer to view it. We were not disappointed. The walls were painted a mint green, which made it very warm and inviting. It was cosy yet spacious and also had a balcony which screamed flowers and plants and colour to me. My greatest thrill was that I no longer had to live with creaking wooden floors, as the flooring was concrete. I was delighted to accept the tenancy. Finally I could get organised and settled in my new home. It was quite an operation to move in after moving three times in the previous seven months. I also had to bring out all that I had in storage. It was quite a strange experience as well, as I had no experience of living in council housing with no greenery around you. I had to remind myself of my ideas to downsize from living on my own in a large rambling house to a flat. Although this was not the way I planned to do it, I was grateful and humbled by the experience.

Symone continued to heal well, but more trauma was to come. In January 2018, she had more iron by transfusion. At her follow-up procedure, it showed that the hole in her heart was only partially closed. The surgeon was not worried, which was strangely reassuring. He told her the hole would continue to close over the umbrella device. He told her to go away and enjoy her life to the fullest.

On reflection, I realised Symone had been ill for more than two years. I felt so useless and insecure as I was unable to help her, except by being there for her. I knew that I would never leave her to fight on her own. Since her surgery in 2015, she had not been the same, as the lethargy never seemed to go away. Her husband was having a difficult time with their situation, as he was frustrated he was unable to build his savings and look after her at the same time. Words fail me to rationalise that type of thinking, and my poor baby was truly devastated. Long story short: he agreed they should separate, and I became her principal carer and escort to all appointments. I was heartbroken for her, but we had to soldier on to get her fit and well again.

Symone began to experience heavy and continuous periods that were becoming unbearable and difficult to manage. Her gynaecologist confirmed she was developing a condition called adenomyosis of her uterus, which is an incurable disease. This chronic condition could cause many complications, including infertility, so this actually made sense and explained her many previous miscarriages. I was very scared for her, but I was by her side all the time.

On one occasion when I was visiting, she felt unwell. I called an ambulance because she was bleeding so much. I didn't think I could manage her if she passed out. When we got to A & E, they started their investigations. Symone asked to go to the ladies, and the nurse said yes and we would help her up. As she stood up, she had a massive blood loss, and she passed out on us. We screamed and staff rushed to her bedside. We got her back in bed, but she was lifeless. They tilted the bed up and I kept slapping her face gently and crying, "Symone, please wake up." The doctors gave her oxygen and put up a drip.

I kept screaming at her, and after what seemed like a lifetime, she shuddered and, after a few seconds, she simply said, "Yes Mummy, I can hear you."

She eventually opened her eyes and looked around. She asked why her bed was tilted up. The nurse said it was to get oxygen to her brain. She squeezed my hand and asked, "Mum, did I nearly die?" I said she scared us because we could not wake her up. She said she thought she had died. She described: "I felt myself floating in space, surrounded by stars and planets. The planets were themselves surrounded by rings of fire in beautiful, bright colours, like red and green and gold and yellow. I could see a light in the distance and I wanted to go towards it. Suddenly, I changed my mind and thought I don't want to stay here. I want to go back. So I turned around to go back." I think that must have been the point when I saw her shudder. She said she then heard my voice telling her to wake up.

She was eventually stabilised and warded, as she needed to have blood transfusions. I stayed with her overnight until I felt she was safe. When I left the building, I sobbed uncontrollably. It had been the most terrifying experience of my life, and I couldn't imagine what Symone must have felt. I couldn't imagine losing my precious daughter. She was too young and vibrant, with the whole world at her feet.

Early in the new year of 2019, I was awakened by a call from a friend in Trinidad at three in the morning. She apologised for getting the time wrong, but we chatted for a while. I tried to get back to sleep, but I started to feel strange. I was shivering and feeling nauseous and having slight chest pain and my temperature was just blowing up. I got frightened and called an ambulance. The operator was very casual and said I could wait between ten minutes and two hours. I got tearful and said "could you try hard for me. I am a pensioner and very scared, and I didn't want to die alone".

Within ten minutes, the paramedics arrived and, after examining me, they said I needed further medical care. When I got to hospital, they diagnosed pneumonia, after several X-rays and blood tests. I was given intravenous fluids and antibiotics.

The staff were wonderful. The paramedics called Symone for me so, after a few hours, I had an entourage of visitors: my son and his partner Natasha, Symone, Evadne, Julie and Rosa. They were such a comfort being there, but I was so weak and lacking in energy; I slept most of the time, so I couldn't chat. By six in the evening, my temperature was much lower and I was more alert. After a further few hours, they explained I was able to go home if I wished and continue my treatment. I prayed and prayed that my health would not fail and I become a burden to Symone and Kevin. They already had so much on their plates.

The last few years had not been easy for any of us when Kevin and Michelle separated. They had never been married but they had two beautiful children who are the apples of my eye. It was a very sad time for us all and I have deliberately said little about this situation. I am not in a position to judge their circumstances. My role was to love them both as I always had and to be there for them and the kids. I chose to be the solid and consistent one and soft place for them all to fall. I hate conflict of any kind, so I preferred to take this stance. The kids continued to spend as much time as they wanted with me. However, I did have a talk to both Michelle and Kevin about their idea of co-parenting. I demanded that they should not use the children as pawns or objects of their negative feelings for each other. Both of them were very bitter and angry, but I reminded them that they were both responsible for the situation they were in. There was no one person to blame. It is always a work in progress, but they have managed to work well together for the benefit of the children. Baby Kayden was very angry about whose fault it was that Daddy left, but after much talking and discussion with mum and dad and other family members, he was calmer. Both kids regularly spent time with dad and his new partner, and the immediate family on the whole is able to manage better than the rest of the extended family. The whole situation remains a work in progress.

I went home from hospital about ten o'clock that night and Symone stayed with me. Slowly and surely, I began to feel better. I had to go back to the hospital a few times, as they queried some of the bugs found in my results and wanted to confirm I was recovering. I prayed to be well enough to support Symone, as she still faced the impending surgery. I also prayed to be well, as I had a long-standing booking to go on a cruise with my friend Evadne and forty of her fellow churchgoers in May that year. I planned this trip because we had all hoped that Symone's surgery would be done and dusted by then.

Symone continued to have various procedures and follow-up appointments with the gynaecologist. At one of these meetings, he talked about the possibility of surgery. He said it would be determined by her decision, when she believed that her quality of life had deteriorated because of her pain and discomfort and heavy bleeding. She had already lost a job, because although her work was excellent, her frequent absences were not conducive to her job, and she was released after her six-month work probation period. It also meant that this final procedure of having her womb removed would mean she could never have any children. She did not take long to decide, because the condition was incurable and she was not prepared to live in that unpleasant and debilitating way with no control over her own life.

It took more than nine months to get this surgery organised. The gynaecologist was very cautious. It was cancelled twice, which was very frustrating for all of us. The gynaecologist was adamant he had to ensure that he had lined up a group of the best experts to assist him in surgery. This was because of Symone's previous heart surgery, surgery to remove fibroids, unconfirmed autoimmune disease, previous stroke and low haemoglobin. Finally, after careful planning, her surgery happened with a top team of surgical consultants. She spent three days in the intensive care unit and a further week on the surgical ward.

The surgeon came and explained everything that happened, and we were fully reassured the surgery was an absolute success. He said he felt justified to be so cautious because surgery was so difficult. Many of her organs were stuck together; her bladder, bowel, rectus muscle were adhered to each other. Her distended uterus weighed 2.4 kilograms instead of the usual 60 grams.

I was so very sad for Symone, but relieved her trauma was over and she could work at healing and getting her life back on track. I truly admired her spirit and resolve to not dwell on the sadness or pain of it all. The gynaecologist was an amazing professional and continued to follow up with her care, to ensure she was healing well.

At the same time, the Notting Hill Carnival was experiencing trauma and dissent, and the existing company had fallen apart. This was the culmination of years of neglect, lack of vision and foresight and no teamwork. I was part of this scenario previously and it was tedious and soul-destroying.

The local council – the Royal Borough of Kensington and Chelsea – decided to invite tenders for the management of the carnival. After a public tender and selection process, Carnival Village Trust won the tender with a very impressive presentation and set of proposals. I was invited to be part of the advisory group that first discussed any ideas and proposals which were then put forward to the board. After working with this group, I was invited to join the board, which I accepted readily. I am happy to be part of a group of people who are not screaming and having tantrums and missing the bigger picture altogether. Imagine, our biggest hurdle, after surviving more than fifty years, is still establishing ourselves as a bona fide concern and thus being taken seriously by corporate companies. Also, we still have a struggle in securing appropriate funding for all the genres within the carnival arts. We continue to make slow but steady progress in taking the carnival arts to a higher level. There is very little acknowledgement that the carnival already holds its own in terms of the local community.

A few months later, when Symone and I were both well and back to normal, I went on my Caribbean cruise. It was an amazing experience. I had enjoyed a short cruise before, but this was on a different level. There were forty-four of us travelling together. They were all very interesting individuals and Methodists, so they knew each other well.

The trip started when we flew to Fort Lauderdale, where we stayed overnight to pick up the cruise liner the next day. Then we visited several islands I didn't know. We went to the ABC islands, which are Aruba, Curacao and Bonaire, Antigua and St Thomas, before sailing back to New Jersey. Then we stayed in a wonderful hotel in New York from Friday to Monday, when we flew back to London. Throughout the trip, the lead minister had arranged visits with fellow parishioners, so we were well looked after, with tours of the islands and lunches.

Life on the ship was equally colourful. We dressed formally for dinner each night and were served a variety of amazing and exotic food. After dinner, we would go off to various forms of entertainment around the ship, most of which was very good and professionally done. We also had several days at sea, so we often met at lunch and had various activities during the course of the day as well.

My weekend in New York was a good one. I tried to catch up with as many friends and family as possible, so I invited them all to meet me in the hotel lobby area on the Sunday afternoon, as my brother had taken me to see a friend in hospital in Brooklyn. I was told that the lady at the bar came over to take drinks orders and said, "Is this a party?"

Almost everyone said, "We came to visit our friend from London."

She exclaimed, "Are you all here to see one person? This person must be really special." When I arrived five minutes later, they pointed me out to her. In the past, I would see my friends and family in New York on a yearly basis, but since my sister Pene died, I hadn't been to New York. I was very humbled and privileged to see my friends Carol and her husband, Mervyn, Abbe my niece and her fiancé Paul, Janiqua, daughter Jazzy and mother Alecia and my brother, Arthur. I was so happy but equally sad, as my precious baby sister, Pene, wasn't there.

When I returned to London from my Caribbean cruise, I was in for a treat. Plans were afoot for the wedding of my son Kevin and his partner Natasha. I was so delighted and happy for them. I was so excited to get involved and work towards the end result. As luck would have it, Natasha's friends were very organised, and with the help of the venue, all arrangements were made very smoothly and professionally. Layne and Symone were bridesmaids and Kayden was a page boy and they all looked so stunning. The bride and groom changed into spectacular African outfits and there was also a surprise in store for all of us especially the bride. Kevin had arranged for the world renowned singer Omar to sing to his bride. We were all bowled over and honoured to be part of this celebration. There was one major crisis that almost scuppered all the plans. Kevin had damaged his knee and was in total agony throughout the ceremony and for some time after. He had to get married using crutches, we could all feel his pain, but he managed it well with such dignity.

CHAPTER THIRTY-SEVEN:
My Continuing Journey

I had a very interesting experience when I was asked by the CEO for the Notting Hill Carnival to give an address at the opening ceremony of the carnival at 10 a.m. on Sunday. I asked what I should say and he suggested I talk about why the carnival started, and why in Ladbroke Grove. So on the day, I welcomed everyone and said I would give a brief history of why we were there. I talked about the culture and history of the emancipation of slavery, which we celebrate as carnival. I said our Windrush elders moved into the area and lived in the area, which was a slum, as they couldn't get housing elsewhere because of their race. The area was noted for its racist signs in the windows of houses that said, "NO BLACKS, NO IRISH, NO DOGS." They worked hard to improve their living conditions, and many were able to buy property and rent to their fellow Caribbean people. They began to express their cultures and traditions, which included the establishment of the carnival, which had evolved to what it is today. So the legacy of the carnival is firmly rooted in the area.

When the ceremony was over, I left and joined my children's band on the road. Along the route, some women came running to me, saying, "We want to thank you so much. We heard you this morning at the opening ceremony of the carnival. We had no idea of the rich culture and the meaning of the carnival. We thought it was just a big street party. I have lived in the area for thirty years and I never knew of the carnival's history or legacy. Thank you again. I now have a full appreciation of the carnival and will look at it in a different light." I was initially quite shocked, but I also felt so great to have enlightened a resident to that extent. I vowed that I would keep educating the public about our culture at every given opportunity. It was quite worrying that residents were so uneducated about the history and relevance of the carnival celebrations. As a member of the board, it is imperative that we continue to educate and inform the public of its relevance and legacy for generations to come.

Symone had learnt that one of our friends in our step dance class was arranging a trip to her home in St Kitts for her sixtieth birthday, and she invited her fellow dancers and family and friends. It sounded like a dream trip and we agreed to go, if the doctors gave Symone the all-clear. The trip was in October, which is Symone's birth month as well, and she was keen to relax and recuperate. When we first heard of the trip, there were twenty people going. By the start of the trip, there were eighty-four of us in the group. We did tours of the island, shopping trips and we went on a day trip to the sister island, Nevis, in a power boat.

The birthday party was an all-white affair. We stepped (line dance to R & B music) all night and had amazing food. It was magical. I reunited with one of my husband's friends, who just walked into the hotel and saw me there at the bar. He reminded me of the first time we met, when my husband came home with a group of friends including him, who were all tipsy from their night out. When I went to meet them, I found this gentleman sitting with his feet up on my coffee table. I was horrified and offended and told this stranger off vehemently and walked away. He was so ashamed, especially as no one had pointed it out to him. The next day, he sent me the largest bouquet of flowers I had ever seen, with a note of apology. Now there we were, sitting at a hotel bar in St Kitts having a good laugh about it. Since that incident, he completed his law qualifications and had successfully returned home and enjoyed a glorious career in law and politics.

Symone was beginning to talk about the loneliness and isolation she was feeling on her own. Her husband had left and she stayed in their flat, all the way in Bushey. I was gutted that I had lost our home and couldn't invite her to share it with me. I encouraged her to relocate in London nearer the family. She and her godmother were very close and they chatted about her dilemma. Her godmother suggested she should move in with her, as she was on her own in a four-bedroom house. I was relieved and happy that Symone had this option to consider.

Then, in early 2020, we had a narrow escape in that we cancelled our plans to visit Trinidad for carnival, otherwise we may have been unable to return to London. The world changed so dramatically in a frightening and negative way. It was so devastating to learn about how many people were dying all over the world, from Covid-19. I prayed that my family would be spared from any such danger. I was reminded, over and over, that I was a high-risk elderly senior citizen because of my history of having pneumonia, so my fear of contracting the disease was ever-present. The worst of it was being isolated from friends. As a family, we formed a bubble, so we still managed to see each other. Also, we all learnt about the magic of the virtual world. It was difficult at first to work from home and get set up on all the different social media platforms, but it soon became the norm. We mastered Zoom and Teams and our lives then revolved around the home.

Symone was the first person to make face masks for the whole family. We were all meeting for a family birthday dinner, and a passing stranger complimented us on the masks we were wearing made from African materials. Symone quickly saw the gap in the market and the need for masks and set up a business to make them. She had labels made and set up a service to produce them. She advertised on social media and the orders came rushing in. Customers asked for them with their country's flag, so we worked with our screen printer, Alan, to print these flags and any other requested designs. At the end of the first year, we had made over 600 masks and shipped out most of them around the country and abroad. It was hard work keeping up with demand, but thankfully Symone could sew well, so we made a great team. It is always such fun when you see and hear from satisfied customers who are complimentary about your work. After a while, shops then became flooded with masks, so demand for ours slowed down considerably.

CHAPTER THIRTY-EIGHT:
Consequences of The Pandemic

It was quite an experience being forced to isolate myself at home. It was so interesting because it was so different. I loved the idea of enjoying my own company, and I would often stay at home by choice. I did that quite a lot when the children were growing up. I would often stay at home when we were invited out, and I would say to Vernon he had to go and represent us. Now there was no choice in the matter. At one point, I stayed at home for three months in a row, except twice when I went shopping for food at the allotted times for the elderly at my local supermarket. I continued working, though, for the Mothers' Union and the carnival company because, by then, Zoom and Teams had become established and I continued to attend meetings through them.

Symone had moved to her godmother's home and was trying to settle down. It was some time after her move that we noticed Julie's behaviour was becoming different. She was forgetful and quarrelsome when challenged about missing events we had planned. Her friend Susan and I compared notes about what we noticed. She refused every offer of help, as her memory was becoming worse. Over time, we were able to convince her son, who lived in Nottingham, that he needed to be nearer his mother. Fast forward to several months later, and her son moved in to live with her and become her carer. This has been the most devastating and soul-destroying event that has happened to me regarding a dear and close friend. Julie was diagnosed with dementia, and the wheels were set in motion to give her all the help she needed. She has gradually lost touch with her family, except through her son, as she is unable to use the phone. I have known her since I was 12, and she sometimes would ask me who I was, and other times she would ask Symone about me or she would say, "Ask your mother to come and see me."

It has been a rough road for us all. We remain in the dark about her affairs, both financial and otherwise, but we are slowly working our way through. It is truly painful and unsettling watching a loved one decline in front of your eyes, knowing that it is totally out of your control. We have no idea how long it will be before caring for her at home will be impossible, but for now she is happy at home and I am still able to see her and talk with her.

It wasn't until Christmas came that my family was directly affected. My son and his wife caught COVID and had to isolate at home. They both concerned me, because they did not get vaccinated, so I was scared the virus would hit them head-on. Kevin was very ill for a short time, but slowly recovered fully. On Christmas day, I cooked up a storm, and Symone and I and the grandchildren took an abundance of food and drink and presents to them. We had to leave everything on the doorstep and speak to them from the garden.

The long-term consequence of my son's decision is that his acting career has suffered, as roles were withdrawn because he was not vaccinated. In my mind, this action has been a huge blow to his prospects and self-confidence since then. I continue to pray and manifest that he would get a chance to continue on his career journey.

Don't get me wrong. He has had the most fascinating journey so far. At the beginning of his career, he had roles in *Star Wars* and *Jurassic World*. This was truly phenomenal. The best accolade he achieved was to have a Lego figure in his image from his role in *Star Wars*. So, in effect, his face is immortalised in the history of film. I was fit to burst and I still am. This was achieved because his role in the film was as the number one bomber pilot, Finch Dallow, in Episode Eight – *The Last Jedi*.

As it is customary, Lego always created figures and sets based on the *Star Wars* films. So, in this eighth episode of the series, they produced their sets with figures of Finch Dallow, who had always been a white actor as the Number one bomber pilot. However in this film, Finch Dallow was played by a black British actor called Kevin Layne – my son. Well, he and his agent got into fight mode and created great waves in the industry with their formal complaint about this misrepresentation. Kevin spent months on the phone to the executives at Lego and even spoke to Steven Speilberg's office. Finally, the Lego figure in my son's image was created. They also created different sets to include the black Finch Dallow, which have become rare and expensive collector's items. I am such an admirer of his work and his achievements. He also started in *Jurassic World* and a film with Benedict Cumberbatch. He has also successfully completed two films in Africa without the need to be vaccinated. I was so honoured once, when he was filming in Africa, when he called me on WhatsApp and I got to speak to his co-star, Olga

Kurylenko, a former Bond girl. How special is that. She sent greetings to my brother in New York, as my son told her that he was her biggest fan.

As you may imagine, our band Genesis became very low-key due to Symone's illness, from five years previously, when she had her first surgery. Luckily, we were invited to collaborate with our friend Ansel Wong CBE, who ran Elimu Mas Academy. This was a good arrangement which allowed us to produce our own costumes and participate as a section within the larger mas band. We thoroughly enjoyed the freedom to create a smaller number of costumes without the pressure of managing the overall infrastructure, like finding a truck, generator, diesel, DJ, scaffolding and two drivers. We also had the privilege of helping some of the young designers who were part of the mas academy.

The pandemic resulted in me getting involved in different types of activities. Besides the hundreds of masks we were making, I was asked to sew reusable sanitary pads for young girls at home and abroad. This request came to the trustees of the Mothers' Union London Diocese, asking for help from any members who had sewing skills. I was delighted to help and successfully completed 120 pads. Symone came up with the idea of making quilt covers from African materials for herself, so we embarked on this quest. It all became so easy once we knew how, but we have one rule: no material that needed matching. It's a nightmare!

In the first year of the pandemic, I was asked to represent the Notting Hill Carnival on two very special occasions. First, we were asked to do a photo shoot with the *Metro* newspaper, as part of their exposé on the pioneers of the carnival, including the origins and development of the carnival from our perspective. This was heaven for us, as it coincided with Genesis' forty-year anniversary. We were so devastated that our plans for a memorable celebration of this anniversary were foiled by this universal pandemic. A journalist came to our mas camp to interview us, and it was a wonderful opportunity for us to explain the significance of the carnival and its everlasting legacy, as well as outlining the history of our band. We were also given an opportunity to explain how we embarked on our face mask business. It started with Symone making masks for the family, then I gifted masks to my local Mothers' Union members, then the orders started coming in and we made and sold hundreds online.

As if the newspaper article was not enough of an honour and privilege, we got another call, this time from *British Vogue*. We were fit to burst. They wanted to hear from carnival leaders about their history and involvement in the carnival and hear our thoughts on how we would facilitate the idea of a virtual carnival. The photographer met us in Ladbroke Grove and we walked around the area, with us taking pictures. These pictures and the interview are now part of a social media profile online. It is so exciting that our history and legacy are recorded for posterity. My son also had the honour of being interviewed by *GQ* magazine. We also had the privilege of doing an interview with *Time Out* magazine and an interview with Radio London.

CHAPTER THIRTY-NINE:
The Joyful Experience of Re-Imagining Carnival

As a member of the Notting Hill Carnival Board, we were tasked with finding a way to re-imagine the carnival and find a way to continue to celebrate the occasion virtually. I was very proud of our CEO and staff for all the amazing work that was produced. I have to admit that I had no idea how this was going to be achieved, but we were not disappointed. It was an amazing opportunity to see and admire the work of fellow band leaders and costume designers. We were able to accommodate all the genres of carnival in a totally different environment. We were some of the performers in costume who were filmed in well-known film studios around London. The presentations over the usual two days of carnival were really special and very professionally done. I found the music and being able to see other costume bands very refreshing, as this never happens under normal circumstances. We were especially proud of our management of the virtual carnival that we streamed online this first year because of the pandemic. It was a glorious exposé of so many talented artists working so well as a team. It was an extraordinary production that made me very happy to be part of such a talented and creative team. We secured the use of so many prestigious venues, like the Royal Albert Hall, Abbey Road Studios, Haymarket Theatre and other filming studios.

After the carnival, I had a decision to make about whether I would take the COVID vaccination. I did my research and decided that I would make an informed decision and have the vaccine. I had many reservations about this vaccine, especially from my perspective as a health professional. I remembered we were all used to receiving vaccines as children in the Caribbean for smallpox, polio, tetanus and tuberculosis, as adults when we were travelling. I gave them to my children and I have taken the flu vaccine every year. The speed of the manufacture was of great concern, but I learnt that the scientists didn't start from scratch. This virus has been studied for over fifty years, so there was a great deal of data to work with. International collaboration allowed the sharing of funds and supporting advanced technology, and allowed simultaneous trials around the world. There was no prolonged negotiation for funding and resources. The ingredients were suitable for vegans. I chose to take the vaccine, as I believed that it meant if I caught the virus the side effects would not be fatal and would be short-term.

I was asked again to take part in a television documentary about the history of immigration and the unsung heroes of the NHS. This documentary was narrated by the famous historian, David Olusoga, although I never had the pleasure of meeting him. I was fascinated, so honoured, to be involved. It confirmed that 13 per cent of the 1.2 million people working in the NHS were from overseas, representing 200 different nationalities. Once the health service became national, the demand became excessive, because people were relieved that they could access healthcare without the fear of huge doctor's bills. In fact, none of the public services could operate fully because of the shortage of labour due to both world wars. The British government had no choice but to appeal to their citizens from across the world. I think that the world needs to realise that, after the British had raped and pillaged the riches from lands all around the world, they in turn had to appeal to these citizens to help rebuild the motherland. We were like children coming home to mother, except our true motherland was always to be in Africa!

The documentary was excellent, as it showed that immigrants were coming to the motherland before and after the inception of the NHS. The NHS attracted nurses, doctors and other hospital staff from some of the British nationals from around the world. This was informative and important information for our children and grandchildren to understand, because we all represented the elders from the Windrush generation, who brought and passed on the legacy of their culture and traditions that their children and grandchildren still enjoy.

As the year progressed, I got involved in several projects for carnival and Black History Month. I might have said this before, but my daughter calls me the lady who will never say no. It is quite true, because I never do. I feel compelled to get involved and participate, because I have the knowledge and the information and the interest and I have an obligation to speak up and participate and somehow make a difference in other people's lives. I also think I have an obligation to target the young people in our community to teach and inform them of the legacy they have inherited. I strongly believe in the statement made by Maya Angelou when she said, "If you don't know where you have come from, then you don't know where you are going." I believe that I have a responsibility to share my knowledge and experiences of being black, being a member of the Windrush generation and being a pioneer of the Notting Hill Carnival.

We participated in carnival showcases sponsored by the Royal Borough of Kensington and Chelsea at World's End, and Portobello Green in Ladbroke Grove. Our CEO and I were interviewed by TikTok at the Rum Kitchen in central London. For Black History Month, I held a workshop at Oasis Academy in south-east London, where Symone and I gave an address to the whole school assembly about the Windrush generation, my experiences of coming to London and our history and our involvement in the carnival. Then we went to individual classrooms to answer questions and share some of our photographs and costume pieces.

One incident in the classroom will live on in my memory. A young black boy raised his hand and said, "Please Mrs Williams, can you tell me how you handle yourself being black, because I am having a hard time." I was gutted that I couldn't go and hug him, because it was against the pandemic rules.

I said to him, "I am very sorry you are struggling with your skin colour. I am afraid you will have to learn to embrace your colour, as it can't be changed. You have to learn to love yourself and be proud of who you are, rather than fret about how you look. Your teachers are here and I know they will help you as much as they can." I really felt his pain, as I recalled how I felt when I was called derogatory names during my training. It is also difficult now for young people and teenagers to escape the social media influences that are confusing and unrealistic.

The pandemic was affecting everyone in a very negative way. There were so many sad stories of health workers dying from this infection. The scandal was that a high percentage of these deaths were of the black and ethnic minority staff. One of my friends told me how the black staff were badly treated and pushed onto the frontline without adequate protection. She personally stood her ground and refused to comply, but many other staff could not stand up to the senior white authority.

We were now getting into the third year of the pandemic and, thankfully, the statistics regarding deaths, hospital admissions and the uptake of vaccines were changing. Then we had the added stress of dealing with a new variant called Omicron. I was so grateful to have not succumbed to the virus for the first two years, especially as I was labelled high-risk.

Early in the year, I had sad news from my dear friend Tom. He called me to say he had been diagnosed with stage four lung cancer. I visited him immediately and he asked me to give a tribute about his life with the midwives at the maternity hospital. I received many tributes from the midwives which I used in the service. My children and I paid tribute to him as well. He was a wonderful friend and he will be sorely missed.

Finally, I succumbed and I tested positive for the coronavirus, two years after the start of the pandemic. I was so shocked because I hoped and prayed I had missed it. I was nursing a head cold with lots of catarrh and a runny nose. I had no fever or pain and I didn't lose my smell or taste. It was my daughter who suggested that I test myself, as she felt my cold was lasting too long. I am convinced that having the vaccine and booster helped me to recover well.

As I began to feel well again, I realised time was fast approaching toward my seventy-fifth birthday. This was a milestone I longed to reach but never dreamt it would happen. I felt blessed and so special that I have this opportunity to be around to help and support my children and grandchildren. Never mind that a few months before my birthday I received the diagnosis that I had multi-layered degenerative disease of my spine. What the hell is that when it's at home? I just know that, in layman's terms, my whole body aches – my neck, back, hip and shoulder. I'm getting shorter and my neck is slowly collapsing. Just so you know, I'm not complaining, I'm just saying. I'm happy to continue to keep Panadol, Voltarol and Ibuprofen gel in business, as there is little that can be done to help me. My life is so full and enjoyable that I refuse to dwell on sickness or sadness.

And would you believe that my actual seventy fifth birthday was celebrated in great style. As a director of Notting Hill Carnival Limited, I shared the hosting of a very special royal visit, when Prince Charles, the now king and his wife, Camilla, visited us at the carnival offices. I had to look after the Tabernacle Seniors (a group of retired men and women who have tea there once a week) and arrange for her to sit and chat with them. They were very keen to have a presence and publicly show their support for the carnival returning to the streets. We showcased a huge variety of costumes and performers, and the royal couple was certainly very impressed. My daughter had the pleasure of speaking with them about her work and getting her picture in the papers. All in all, it was an interesting and enjoyable event. I felt that it was a magnanimous gesture to the carnival community that they, the royals, appreciate and acknowledge the important legacy of the carnival arts.

In true twenty-first century style, the invitations to my 75th birthday party went out online and Symone became the event planner. The party was a resounding success. I was banned from cooking, but I made and decorated the birthday cake and helped where I was allowed. There was a steel band player, Justin, who serenaded us, and the wonderful DJ Piper, who played amazing music. I was so grateful and honoured and happy to see more than 100 guests at the party. My guests even included one of the priests from my church. I continue to give thanks and praise always for life, love, laughter and joy, family and friends.

In complete contrast, on this year's birthday I was visiting a darling young costume designer called Onike, who was losing her four-year fight against breast cancer.

July was a very sad time for us all, and I experienced four unexpected tragedies. I was reminded of the saying, "Never complain about getting older. It's a privilege denied to so many." As time progressed and carnival approached, I was very pleased to have accepted the challenge of becoming a judge for the performing bands and also reviewing the judging process. I was thrilled to have succeeded in putting together a dream team who did an exceptional job. I got the bit between my teeth, as I used to do when I managed the hospital. I could picture the outcome I intended to achieve, and I worked towards that goal. It works every time. My heartfelt thanks and gratitude go to Rhonda, Elsa, Karla, Leroy and Michael.

CONCLUSION
(What Do You Think About It So Far??)

It is such a profound pleasure to have you join me on my long and winding life journey. I have loved my life experiences, even though I did not think so for some of the time. On reflection, I think I switched on very early to the benefits of hindsight. I realised that the perks gained when you behave well as a child far outweighed the punishment and the agony of getting "licks". I also think that being born under the Cancerian star sign was an added bonus. We tend to be intuitive and perceptive, home lovers who love to please others, hate confrontation and are peace lovers and negotiators. We also have a strange quality in that we appear to know things without knowing how we know. On the other hand, we are fundamentally laid-back, but can work hard when we have to do that we particularly enjoy or when we have a specific challenge ahead of us.

My husband was my slice of heaven. You have heard me talk about him with joy and passion. When I met him, I knew immediately that he was the one. I was mesmerised by him from day one until he died, except the few times when I wanted to beat him up! I have reflected so many times on my life with him. I often wondered why I was so convinced and adamant that I would only marry a fellow Trinidadian. Who says that? However, this was another example of knowing something but not knowing how you know! He didn't disappoint, which convinced me that he had to be Trinidadian as well. We were a terrific double act. He was laid-back and horizontal, and I was the cantankerous one asking how, why, where, when? I think that my strength and belief in everything Trinidadian was so strong and very clear that I firmly believed my dream would manifest itself.

My children have been a source of unending joy in my life. I secretly go around, "rubbing my badge" because I feel my husband, and I can be proud to have successfully guided them through life in this crazy world. They are amazing human beings, who are loving, kind, respectful, honest and well disciplined. Most amazing of all is that their lives are steeped in our culture and traditions. They are accomplished pannists and prolific costume designers and carnivalists. When my teenage daughter told her friends she was a Trinidadian, but she just happened to be born in London, I thought I had died and gone to heaven. It summed up all I wanted to achieve in life. I wanted my children to learn about our home and develop a strong sense of identity. I think it is imperative our children are knowledgeable about their roots and exposed to the culture and legacy of their parents. I am convinced this firm foundation has been the reason my children are so solid and streetwise and obsessed about everything Trinidadian. It has given them a strong sense of identity. I firmly believe also that a strong sense of identity gives our children so much self-confidence and self-esteem. I am well aware that on the other side of the coin, some parents had different experiences and never want to be reminded of their past.

I was just supposed to train as a nurse and midwife, give my services to the motherland and return home to serve my country and be with my family and have a rich and fulfilling life there. I never expected to have a life in London; I was only passing through. They say life is what happens when you're busy making plans. That is certainly true. At the end of my nursing training, my parents and brothers and sisters moved to New York, so the Big Apple became home. Then I met my husband, when I was making plans to join my family in New York. We married and had our children and got our own home, so life in London became a reality.

My first five years in London taught me how precious and special my life and upbringing in Trinidad had been. We were never well off, but we were rich in family life and the love our parents gave to us. My teenage life was filled with special energy and excitement, from my school days right through to the time of making plans again to travel abroad. My parents loved life and that was infectious and inspiring to me. We socialised regularly as individuals and as families. I was in awe of my mother and her talents and her attitude and her rationale for everything in life. She was a firm disciplinarian always but was unfazed by problems because she believed that no problem was insurmountable. I have lived by the many mantras she taught me in life:

"If you aim for the skies, you could fall on top of the trees, but if you aim for the top of the trees, you can fall flat on your face."

"You have to lick ass to kick ass."

"You have to play dead to catch them alive."

"Do so, don't like so."

"If you can't do something, well, don't do it at all."

Her many sayings and idioms seemed to stand me in good stead. She taught me self-respect and tolerance and the difference between right and wrong. These attributes collectively helped me to live life to a high moral standing. I was often told that I behaved like a snob, but a few friends who got over that obstacle learnt about the real me.

As I embarked on this journey, the publisher asked me why I wanted to write this book. I didn't hesitate to respond. I wanted to share my West Indian family values that I learnt and pass them on to my kids. I wanted to explain the value of receiving discipline at the same time as getting unconditional love from parents. I wanted to reiterate that no one should be put down or defeated by racism. I wanted to emphasise that being poor is only about not having much money. Respect, kindness, love, laughter and empathy are all free and full of riches. I wanted to stress the importance of choosing a career or vocation that you love and working hard at being the very best you can. This is the recipe for true happiness. I wanted to show that, despite my many heartaches, mistakes and disasters, I still managed to have fun and live my best life. I wanted to demonstrate that real love conquers all. I now believe my husband completely when he used to say the only discipline a child needs is lots of love, because when you then have to punish them, they will know they deserve it and it is not because you don't love them.

When I had to give up my home after nearly forty years, I felt like a failure and such a disappointment to my family and friends. The saying is that everything happens for a reason, but it is beyond me what that reason could be. I hated myself for being so arrogant and unable to recognise I was completely out of my depth. I felt I could rescue the place with my determination and hard work. I was so naive and simple-minded. I realised too late the landlord saw us coming and he used and abused us. But, you know, my husband used to say I must have led a very sheltered life. When we shared stories about life in Trinidad, there were certain things I didn't know or never experienced while growing up. I felt the hurt mainly for my children, but they made me feel human again with empathy, love and kindness. As important as money is in this world, it is not the highest priority for them either. I then had to turn it around in my head for it to make sense. I was able to furnish the flat of a single mother who had nothing ... My mistake was seen as just that among my friends and family. Many friends wanted to go and, "fix" the landlord on my behalf, but I convinced them we would not get down to that level.

The highlight of my life in retirement has been my ability to travel and experience some of the wonders of the world. It has been a magical journey and, God willing, I will be able to keep working my way through my travel bucket list.

You may have noticed I have not mentioned returning to Trinidad to settle in my old age. That's because I don't see it as a viable proposition at the moment, unless I meet this imaginary gorgeous man who wants to offer me a life to which I am not accustomed! My mind and my life are embroiled in my children and grandchildren, even if they don't realise it themselves. I still love Trinidad and its people, but without my husband it will not be the same. I will continue to visit for long periods of time and keep connected with friends and family, but for now, and as difficult as life has become since the pandemic, I will cherish the myriad facets of my life in London. I don't think I would want to move away and start at the bottom again. My work with the London Diocese of the Mothers' Union, All Saints Church in Notting Hill, the Notting Hill Carnival Board, and my endless work at baking cakes and sewing clothes and costumes, fill me with passion and great satisfaction.

I am also blessed to be a blood donor, having given nearly forty pints of my blood to the service over the last fifteen years. I learnt that I have a rare subtype in my blood that is specifically needed for the treatment of sickle cell anaemia patients. I will continue to do everything in my power to sustain this important contribution.

I would never profess to be famous, and certainly not rich, but I don't think you have to be either to share your experiences of life with others, because many of our experiences are similar and resonate with each other. I have read books where I feel relief that I'm not the only one with a certain experience. We all have participated in aspects of black history, simply by being descendants of the enslaved and victims of the brutal colonisation of our ancestors. I think we owe it to each other to share our life's journey with others. It will also form part of our legacy we can share with our children and their children, so they understand our history informs all we do today.

www.marciampublishing.com

BV - #0042 - 031024 - C10 - 216/140/15 - PB - 9781913905798 - Gloss Lamination